Iltudus T. Prichard

The Administration of India from 1859 to 1868

the first ten years of administration under the Crown - Vol. 2

Iltudus T. Prichard

The Administration of India from 1859 to 1868
the first ten years of administration under the Crown - Vol. 2

ISBN/EAN: 9783337272517

Printed in Europe, USA, Canada, Australia, Japan

Cover: Foto ©Suzi / pixelio.de

More available books at **www.hansebooks.com**

THE ADMINISTRATION

OF INDIA

FROM 1859 TO 1868:

*THE FIRST TEN YEARS OF ADMINISTRATION UNDER
THE CROWN.*

BY

ILTUDUS THOMAS PRICHARD,

GRAY'S INN, BARRISTER-AT-LAW.

IN TWO VOLUMES.

VOL. II.

London:

MACMILLAN AND CO.

1869.

LONDON :
R. CLAY, SONS, AND TAYLOR, PRINTERS,
BREAD STREET HILL.

TABLE OF CONTENTS.

CHAPTER XVII.

SOCIAL PROGRESS.

CHAPTER XVIII.

THE HISTORY OF LEGISLATION.

CHAPTER XIX.

THE HISTORY OF LEGISLATION (*continued*).

CHAPTER XX.

FINANCE.

DIRECTIONS TO THE BINDER.

The Map of " The Peshawur Valley and the adjacent Territory " to be placed before Chapter XV., page 45.

ADMINISTRATION OF INDIA

FROM 1859 *TO* 1868.

CHAPTER XIV.

THE BHOTAN WAR.

IT is always easy to be wise after the event ; and considering what a little there was to gain, and how much
might be lost, by hostilities with such a country as Bhotan,
it seems strange to us, now the affair is over, that the
Government of India were ever so infatuated as to embroil
themselves with the country at all.

It is hardly within the compass of this work to go back
and trace the history of our connexion with Bhotan from
the earliest time. But some acquaintance with the causes
of the rupture that eventuated in war is absolutely necessary to enable the reader to understand the story of the
campaign.

Bhotan is a mountainous country lying between Bengal Proper and Assam on the south and Thibet on the north. To the west is the territory of Nepal and Sikkim, to the east again Thibet. Indeed it may be regarded as a piece cut out of Thibet ; to which country it very possibly, as asserted by Dr. Rennie, originally belonged, having become separated owing to the difficulty experienced by the Thibet Government in keeping the people in subjection.

Our quarrels and disputes with mountain frontier tribes are almost always a repetition of each other. Our barbarous neighbours are almost—in fact, we shall be safe in saying always—the aggressors, and generally wanton aggressors. All along at the foot of the lofty ranges that skirt the boundary of Hindustan on the east, as well as the north and west, lie rich and fertile valleys, studded for the most part with villages, and peopled by a community often perhaps connected with the adjacent Hill tribes, but as a rule peacefully disposed, and inclined to agricultural pursuits. But their farms and houses, their cattle and grain, their sons, daughters, and wives, are an incessant source of temptation to the Hill people, who ever and anon descend and help themselves to slaves, women, cattle, or grain. Having harried the district, and swept off the inhabitants and cattle, they return with their booty to their fastnesses in the mountains, and the survivors come weeping to the nearest British authorities, and tell the sad tale of desolated hearths and ruined homesteads. Then follow measures of reprisal: a force has to be despatched into the mountains to chastise the robbers, and if possible recover the booty. Sometimes these expeditions are successful, very often not. Or, if success attend our efforts, it is very dearly purchased by the loss of valuable lives, and a profitless expenditure. Under the most favourable circumstances, our troops almost always get a very severe handling; and although practically the victors, having gained the object of the expedition, they are generally seen out of the country by the mountaineers, who, having retreated before our advance, now harass our rear, loot our baggage, and finally mount the heights commanding the road into the plains, whence they fire their last shot and throw their last stone at the retreating column.

A disciplined force always fights at a disadvantage with undisciplined barbarians, because it is unwilling to resort to the only method of coercion that can be practised with effect. The necessity, however, is unavoidable, and in these expeditions we generally leave behind traces of our visit, in the shape of blackened ruins of villages and the ashes of crops destroyed by fire; and if the force has been openly resisted, the loss of life inflicted is usually severe.

There is another method frequently adopted of bringing these people to reason. It generally happens that the inhabitants of bleak, rugged mountain regions are dependent in a great measure on the plain country for supplies of grain for themselves and cattle. In such cases, to blockade the passes leading from the mountains to the valleys is to deprive them of the necessaries of life. This system is almost always successful, and only fails in those exceptional cases where the mountaineers can depend on their own resources for the supply of grain.

Military expeditions are occasionally necessary, but to send envoys or representatives, with secretaries, and all the paraphernalia of an embassy, into the interior of a difficult mountainous country, among a semi-barbarous people, who know nothing of the law of nations, with whom treaties are little else than waste paper, who are accustomed to settle disputes only by the sword or knife, seems to be the height of political folly. No good results can possibly follow from such communications.

If a treaty is made, we may be sure it will only be observed as long as it suits the interest of the tribes to observe it. Promises are not binding on them; whereas, they are binding on us. It is, of course, desirable to

induce such men to enter into trade connexions, to inter-
change commodities, and encourage commerce, because
commerce is the only means of civilizing them. But until
they have made some progress in civilization, until they
have learnt that their interests are best subserved by
cultivating peaceful relations—that, in short, trade is more
profitable than war—it is never safe to trust them with
the lives and liberty of an envoy and his suite. To keep
a strong or an efficient force upon the frontier, to punish
promptly all aggression, and at the same time hold out
inducements to the Hill people to settle in the plain country
and engage in agricultural pursuits in their own ; to teach
them gradually to submit their internal disputes to other
arbitration than the sword, is the only policy that can be
pursued with safety and advantage. How much more
imprudent does it seem when the embassy is sent under
the circumstances that attended the Hon. Ashley Eden's
mission to Bhotan, where there was actually no Government to which the envoy could be accredited, when the
country was in such discord and confusion that even the
people themselves could not tell who were their rulers,
and when at almost every step the mission took it was
met with hints, remonstrances, and commands not to
proceed.

Bhotan formed no exception to the general rule, the
inhabitants of the highlands being mainly dependent upon
the lowlands for their support. To these lowlands, a tract
of fertile soil· running along the foot of the mountain
ranges, they laid claim. The breadth of this strip of fertile
valley land is from ten to thirty miles, and the extreme
length of it from west to east may be estimated at a
hundred and twenty. The portion of the land that lies
next to the hills is, as would naturally be the case, rugged
and irregular—forest land, tenanted by wild beasts.
Beyond this, we come upon a rich black soil, capable
of producing perhaps crops of any kind, but especially
adapted for cotton. This valley, or strip of level country,

at the foot of the Bhotan mountains, is called "The Dwars" or "Dooars." There is a good deal of uncertainty as to the origin and exact meaning of this word. It would seem that the lowlands are connected with the interior of the hills by a series of passes or roads, by which alone ingress and egress can be effected. These passes were, as Dr. Rennie says, looked upon as doors or gates leading from the highlands into the valley. The word "Dwar" in Hindee means a door or gate, and hence the term "Dooars" has come, by a figure of speech, to be applied to the valleys into which these passes lead. The "Dooars," however, are eighteen in number. There are eleven which are called the Bengal Dooars, because they border on Bengal, and seven called the Assam Dooars, because they lie contiguous to the Assam frontier. But it does not seem that there are anything like so many as eighteen passes or Dooars proper. There appear to be only five passes from the Bengal Dooars, each of which is presided over by a Bhotanese officer, called a Jungpen, who has also control over the land adjoining his pass, and to which in some instances only the same name is given as that which belongs to the pass itself. Altogether, the derivation of the word "Dooars," as applied to the valley district, is scarcely satisfactory. The five passes from the Bengal Dooars which formed the points of attack of the different columns of the invading British force are called, commencing from the west end, Dhalimkote, Chamoorcha, Balla, Buxa or Pusakha, and Bishensing, and they were nominally defended by forts bearing the same name. To the eastward of Bishensing is the Dewangiri pass and fort, a locality which acquired the greatest notoriety during the war from the circumstances attending the capture of it by our troops, their expulsion, and its final recapture and destruction.

To trace the causes of the dispute it will not be necessary to go back further than the annexation of Assam, together with which province the Government assumed the relations existing at the time of annexation between it and the Bhotanese. These were rather of a complicated character, and just of such a nature as to embroil us with our semi-barbarous neighbours. The former rulers of Assam had made over to the Bhotanese the seven Dooars, on condition of receiving a tribute annually of yaks' tails, musk, gold dust, ponies, blankets, and knives. These articles, which were supposed to represent a stated sum of money, used to be sold by auction, and, as might have been expected, did not always, and came at last very seldom, to realize the necessary amount. When the British Government demanded arrears, the Bhotanese rejected the claim, because, as they said, the articles given in kind were sold for less than they were worth. At the same time, the Hill tribes took to indulging their predatory habits, made raids into British territory, kidnapping men and women, and carrying off cattle. This was the state of things in 1837, when the Government sent Captain Pemberton on a mission to the Bhotan capital. This mission failed in effecting any real good, as such missions to such states must, and Government, then the East India Company, determined to annex the Assam Dooars. They agreed, however, to pay the Bhotanese Government ten thousand rupees annually, as compensation for the loss of territory. This arrangement was carried out in 1841, and appears to have been successful so far as putting a stop to raids in the Assam Dooars.

About 150 miles to the west of the Assam Dooars, between the river Teesta and Mahanuddee on the frontier of Bengal Proper, is a tract of country called Ambaree Fallacottah.

Many years ago, as far back as 1784, this district was taken from the then possessor of it by the East India Company, and made over to the Bhotanese. In consequence, however, of its lying twenty miles within our frontier, the possession of it by Bhotan was a source of constant trouble; and after the arrangement alluded to with regard to the Assam Dooars had been carried out, the Bhotanese desired the Government of India to effect a similar arrangement with regard to Ambaree Fallacottah, —that is, to take possession of it and pay them a certain sum in money annually in lieu of its revenue. This was accordingly done in 1842.

But no political measures, however skilfully conducted, no treaties or agreements, however equitable and just, can secure tranquillity upon such a frontier. And the more prosperous the agricultural communities inhabiting the plain country at the foot of the hills became, in consequence of the security afforded by British rule, the more they accumulated wealth in the shape of cattle and grain and crops, the greater was the temptation to their lawless neighbours to come down and help themselves. There is very seldom any controlling power in the shape of a central government strong enough to prevent such outrages, and the result is a constant state of petty warfare. It would be tedious to trace in detail the series of successive outrages that were committed from 1828 to 1861. Suffice it to say, they were a source of incessant annoyance to the British Government, the more so from the fact that the climate of that district was so unhealthy that it was impossible to keep regular troops stationed there. And although a force might be marched up into the hills to make reprisal or to exact compensation, or to recover captives, the moment the soldiers' backs were turned, down would come these robbers from their fastnesses, and recommence their deeds of violence. In the Assam Dooars the state of things was better, but throughout the Bengal Dooars the outrages continued, till it was resolved to see whether the withholding the revenue paid for the district of Ambaree would have the effect of putting a stop to them. At the same time it was intimated to the Bhotanese, that the payment would be resumed upon their complying with the demands made upon them, and restoring certain British subjects who had been kidnapped and carried away. No good result followed.   The aggressions still continued, and instead of at once employing force, it was in an evil hour resolved to send a mission into the country to confer with the head of the government, under an idea that the cause of failure in the negotiations was the fact that the resolutions and orders of the British Government never reached the Bhotan Court.   The aggressive spirit of the Bhotanese was further manifested by an intention to attack the district of Darjeeling, information of which reached the authorities from four distinct sources, and was borne out by the appearance of a considerable force of armed men on the frontier who were making preparations to cross the boundary, viz. the river Teesta.   At the same time the chief or jungpen of Dhalimkote pressed his demands in an insolent manner for the arrears of the Ambaree rents due since its attachment in 1860.   The threatening movements were checked by troops being advanced to the frontier, two companies of H.M.'s 30th regiment and a company of the 10th Native Infantry being moved up in support.

The Government of Bhotan, like that of Japan, as far as we understand its constitution, consists of two nominal heads ; one called the Dhurma Raja, or spiritual head, and the other the Deb Raja, or temporal ruler.   In effect, there appears to be this difference between the constitution of the government in Bhotan and Japan, that while in the latter the Tycoon, or temporal ruler, is supposed to have the chief power, in Bhotan his authority is merely nominal. But, in truth, it seems very little was really known about the actual condition of the country, for it is not easy to understand how, if it had been known, the project of deputing an envoy to the capital could have been entertained.   On the other hand, it is equally difficult to comprehend the policy of deputing an envoy to the sovereign ruler of a country which, as regards its internal political state, was a *terra incognita*.   This much was clear, that whether the power of the central government was vested in the spiritual or temporal head of the kingdom, it was little more than nominal, the different jungpens, or chiefs, acting pretty much on their own independent authority, and acknowledging in a very slight degree, if at all, the authority of their nominal rulers.

The Dhurma and Deb Rajas, according to the theory of the constitution, are supposed to be assisted in the affairs of state by a council composed of the chief secretary to the Dhurma Raja, the prime minister, the chiefs or governors or jungpens of three of the principal forts, the chief secretary to the Deb Raja, and the chief justice. In addition to these there were three extraordinary members of council, who were liable to be called on to assist in its deliberations in any emergency, and who regularly attended when they happened to be at the seat of government. They were the governors respectively of Western, Eastern, and Central Bhotan, called Penlows, their distinctive names being the Paro, the Tongso, and the Daka Penlows.

The first step taken to open negotiations with these intractable people was the despatch of a native messenger to the court of the Deb Raja in 1862, from Assam, with letters announcing the intention of the Governor-General to depute an envoy to confer on such matters as required explanation between the two governments. The Bhotan authorities were also requested to indicate the route by which the envoy should enter the country. This messenger did not get back to Assam till December, having been delayed by obstructions caused by the frontier officers. His reception was not a very friendly one, and the letter he brought back from the Deb Raja not such as to encourage further diplomatic measures. In the letter he admitted having received complaints from the British officers of the misbehaviour of his own subjects on the frontier, but gave it as his opinion that they were not of sufficient importance to be referred to the Dhurma Raja, and thought the British Government should not listen to them either. He threw cold water on the project of the mission, saying it would be attended with much trouble, owing to the state of the

roads; and, moreover,.the Dhurma Raja did not want an
interview, but he promised to send certain officers, called
Zinkaffs, to settle all disputes. These officers never came,
however, and the Government determined to start off the
mission without waiting for further reference to the court.

In November 1863 the envoy, the Hon. Ashley Eden,
reached Darjeeling on his way to the Bhotan capital. The
escort consisted of ·100 men, half Sikhs and half Sappers
of the Sebundy corps, a corps raised expressly for service
in the Darjeeling district. Captain Goodwin Austin,
Bengal Staff Corps, was appointed Assistant Envoy and
Surveyor; Captain Lance commanded the escort; Dr.
Simpson was medical attendant; and Cheboo Lama, the
most important personage perhaps next to the envoy
himself, the Thibetan interpreter. This man is a native of
Sikkim, a priest by profession, and resided at Darjeeling,
as the political representative of the Sikkim Raja.

On the 10th September previously the Bengal Government had addressed another letter to the Bhotan authorities,
informing them of the preparation for the departure of the
mission, and requesting that an officer might be sent as far
as the river Teesta to meet it, and conduct it to Poonakha,
the capital. No reply was received to this, and on the
10th November Mr. Eden himself addressed the Bhotan
Government again, requesting that the chief or jungpen
of Dhalimkote, the principal fort on the westernmost of
the Dooars, and the nearest to the British frontier, might
be sent to meet him; and he added that if this was not
done he should report that no arrangement had been made,
which would be considered as indicating the absence of
friendly feeling.

The impolicy of sending a mission into the heart of such
a country was still further shown by information which
reached the Government after the despatch of this last
letter of Mr. Eden. It appeared that a rebellion had
taken place, the Deb Raja had been expelled from the
throne, and after withstanding a siege in his summer

residence, and being forced to surrender by want of water, had been permitted to retire into a monastery. The rebel, or rather the revolutionary party—for they seem to have been successful—was headed by the governor of Eastern Bhotan, called the Tongso Penlow, and consisted of all the members of the council except one, the governor of Western Bhotan, called the Paro Penlow, and the chief of the capital—at least, what formed the capital during the winter months—a place called Poonakha. For it seems that the Bhotan Court, like that of Cyrus in former days, and of British India in more modern times, had two seats of government, one for the winter and one for the summer months. This rebellion led to further political complications nearer to the British frontier, for the chief or jungpen of Dhalimkote, the officer whom Mr. Eden desired might be sent to meet and convoy him to the capital, was a follower of one of the members of council who had taken part in the revolution. But he was immediately subordinate to the governor of Western Bhotan, who had remained loyal. The chief of Dhalimkote was accordingly called on by the loyal governor of Western Bhotan to surrender his fort to a successor, who was sent to take it over. As a matter of course, he refused to do anything of the kind, and a force was despatched against him, which only raised the siege on hearing that Mr. Eden's mission had started.

The imprudence of opening diplomatic relations with a government in the condition of that of Bhotan will become more apparent, if we suppose the case transferred from Asia to Europe. Would any cabinet or any sovereign in Europe select the time when a political crisis of so grave a nature had just occurred, when the whole internal organization of the country was in disorder, to send a diplomatic mission for the first time to the head of the disturbed state? With such a race of semi-barbarians as the Bhotanese, what result could have been anticipated from the step now taken, but discomfiture and further political complications?

It looks as if the chief of Dhalimkote thought the present a favourable opportunity for doing something for himself. We have seen that the report of the departure of Mr. Eden's mission, which exaggerated the strength of the party enormously, had such an effect on the country as to cause the siege of Dhalimkote to be raised. What more likely under the circumstances, than that the chief of Dhalimkote should take advantage of his propinquity to the British frontier to secure the good-will of his powerful neighbours, with the view of making political capital out of it, which might enable him to secure something good for himself in the general scramble that seemed impending? Accordingly, we find him suddenly animated by the warmest feelings of friendship for Mr. Eden. He sent message after message, assuring him that the delay which had taken place in answering the letter, and making preparations for the reception of the mission, was the result solely of the disorganized state of the country. He begged the mission to wait, and promised every assistance in his power, and requested that Cheboo Lama might be sent over to have an interview with him. Cheboo Lama accordingly went, and had an interview which lasted several days. The chief renewed his offers of friendship, and hinted that if a reply to Mr. Eden's last letter, of the 10th November, did not arrive soon, he would for a consideration give every aid himself to the mission to enter the country, even if he incurred the displeasure of his Government by so doing.

The office of Governor-General was then held temporarily by Sir William Denison, to whom Mr. Eden referred in this crisis for orders, and the intimation was to proceed with the assistance of the chief of Dhalimkote, because, it was argued, the rebellion having been successful, it was probable that the new Deb Raja would be glad to strengthen his position by an alliance with the British Government.

It is, as I have said, easy to be wise after the event, but it does seem a most extraordinary line of policy to adopt, to send an envoy with his suite accredited to the head of a

Government which had but just passed—if it had passed—through the throes of revolution, into a most difficult and dangerous country, inhabited by predatory tribes at war with one another, when the permission to the envoy to enter the country at all had been accorded only by a petty chief, himself at war with the governor of his own province. Nevertheless, on the receipt of Sir W. Denison's instructions, Mr. Eden prepared to advance, and wrote to the chief of Dhalimkote that he was on the point of starting, and requested that a party might be sent to meet him at the river Teesta.

Mr. Eden's difficulties commenced at the very outset. The route which had been selected for the mission lay through such a difficult country that the only means of conveying baggage was by coolies or porters. Had they taken another route—the route subsequently adopted by the troops—the baggage might have been carried easily upon mules. As it was, the coolies collected at Darjeeling were afraid to enter the Bhotan territory at all, and actually abandoned the camp on the British side of the frontier, refusing to cross the river. The baggage and camp equipage of the mission were despatched from Darjeeling on the 1st of June. On the 4th, the members of the mission followed, and overtook the camp at the river, twenty-two miles only from Darjeeling, and 6,000 feet below it. Here the party had to halt three days before coolies could be procured to advance, and these were only got through the influence of Cheboo Lama, the interpreter, who summoned his own tenants from the fields to carry loads. One march up the mountain on the other side of the river brought the mission to a spot 3,733 feet above the level of the sea, and here it was forced to halt again in consequence of the fresh desertion of the coolies. The head official of the place where they halted—and here, says Mr. Eden, as everywhere else, there were two officers, one in power and the other not—requested them to proceed no further, but eventually gave them guides to show them the way to Dhalimkote.

On the 12th the camp reached the valley of Ambiok, immediately below the fort of Dhalimkote. But its progress had been marked by the continued desertion of the coolies and an insult offered to the envoy by the chief of a place called Dhurmsong, who shut the gate of the fort in his face and insolently refused admission.

The day before the camp reached the neighbourhood of Dhalimkote, the chief of that place had ventured upon the first open reception of the mission. He sent out musicians, ponies, and mules, the former of which preceded the retinue, performing a noisy and monotonous national air on silver flageolets and brass cymbals, and during the day of their arrival at Ambiok a fire of matchlocks was kept up from the fort walls in their honour. The friendship, however, of this chief resulted in little beside these empty compliments, for when Mr. Eden sent to him for supplies which he had promised, he refused to furnish any till he had been paid in advance at the exorbitant rate of seven rupees, or fourteen shillings, for a maund of eighty pounds ; while the market price of the commodity—rice—was only ten annas, or fifteen pence, for a similar quantity.

The next day, the 14th June, the chief visited the envoy in state. The principal topic of discussion, says Mr. Eden, was the quantity of spirits he could drink. He had as much given him in the envoy's tent as he called for, but finding that he was difficult to be satisfied and was repeatedly calling for more, Mr. Eden gave him permission to depart. He refused to do so, however, and after his visit had been prolonged for four or five hours he was at last forcibly carried off by his own servants. He, however, did not even then leave the camp, but repaired to the tent of the Thibetan interpreter, Cheboo Lama, where he sat drinking till late in the day. As he was leaving the camp he saw some of the coolies, who after having received large advances had deserted and were caught again, being flogged, whereupon he insisted on their release ; and when the officer in charge refused to acquiesce in his wishes, he drew his knife and rushed into the ring with his followers, threatening to cut down the commissariat-sergeant who was in attendance. The men of the escort ran to their arms, and the bullying and violence of the Jungpen and his followers was immediately changed to abject fear. "Seeing me approaching," says Mr. Eden, "he ran to meet me, trembling with fear, and begged for forgiveness. I ordered him out of camp, and the whole party ran off to the fort in a most undignified manner. I declined to receive any further visits from him until he sent me a written apology for his conduct, and this he did next day."

The whole of this scene, ludicrous as it is, indicates in the most striking manner the false nature of the position into which Mr. Eden had been forced. A British envoy, accredited from the Governor-General of India, has to flog his coolies for desertion, is forced to entertain a drunken savage for four or five hours, plying him with brandy, and then insists upon and receives a written apology for his conduct, as if he had been a member of a civilized community, and had misbehaved himself in a club or a mess-room.

The occurrence itself perhaps was not sufficient to induce the return of the mission after it had once set out, but it was quite sufficient to show that the mission had no business where it was.

The camp halted some days at this place, for it was found necessary to send Captain Austin back to the British station of Julpigoree to purchase supplies. Meantime Mr. Eden received a letter from the Deb Raja, who had been set up by the revolutionary party, desiring him to let the chief of Dhalimkote know what was the object of the mission, and he would arrange about the interview. The chief seems to have behaved with duplicity, lending colour to the opinion I have hazarded that his object all along was merely to make political capital to serve his own purposes out of his alliance with Mr. Eden. For, as that gentleman says, he evinced considerable interest in the success of the mission, leading the envoy to believe that he was inclined to assist it, and yet being unwilling that it should proceed without further specific instructions from the court. This shuffling and double-dealing is so exactly the policy we should expect a semi-barbarous chief to adopt under the view suggested that it seems strange it did not show itself to the envoy in this light. Mr. Eden, however, appears to have suspected nothing, but wrote an answer explaining to the Deb Raja that his business was of such a nature that it could not be settled by the chief of Dhalimkote, but must be referred to the head of the State.

Again the envoy was placed in an undignified position by the desertion of the coolies. There were not enough left to carry on that portion of the baggage which was absolutely required, and in addition to this it had become necessary now to take on provisions for the camp followers. Application was made to the chief, who pleaded all sorts of excuses, and on the 29th, Captain Austin having returned with fresh supplies, Mr. Eden arranged to leave behind nearly all his tents and most of his baggage and stores, together with half the escort. It is quite certain, from what we know of the resources of the country, that the conveyance of Mr. Eden's moderate suite was not too great a tax upon them. The mere fact of his having consented to reduce his escort by one-half, and to leave behind so large a portion of his tents and equipage, was quite sufficient to encourage the accumulation of obstacles of all kinds in his path. Knowing how much the natives of a country like Bhotan are influenced by the mere externals of office and dignity, we cease to wonder that the British envoy was subjected to the insults and outrages which have made the Bhotan mission unique in the history of British India and its relations with foreign States.

It is true that previous missions which had been sent into Bhotan had adopted a similar course, in so far as to diminish their camp equipage and baggage as they advanced into the heart of the country. But Mr. Eden's mission was proceeding under different circumstances altogether from the former ones.

The coolies that had been with so much difficulty procured at Dhalimkote had agreed to go as far as a place called Sipchoo, which Mr. Eden was led to believe was in a populous district, where there would be no difficulty in obtaining fresh men. When he arrived there, on the 1st February, he found it was just the contrary ; there were only five houses in the place, and not a man to be had. The official in command at the spot declined to give any assistance, saying he had received no orders, but if the camp would halt there for a few weeks instructions might arrive. Whereupon Mr. Eden committed another mistake, the inevitable result of the first, and left behind all the remainder of the heavy baggage, all the escort except fifteen Sikhs and ten sappers, Mr. Power, the uncovenanted assistant, the commissariat sergeant, the moonshees, the native doctor, and every camp-follower that could be spared.

On the morning of the 3d, they reached a pass in the mountains where the snow lay from one and a half to two feet, through which they had to push their way, spending the night at an elevation of 8,000 feet, and on the following day continuing their arduous journey. Many desertions of coolies had already taken place, but after crossing the pass, Mr. Eden adds, nothing but the fear of recrossing it prevented the great majority of the remainder from deserting too.

On the 7th, the mission halted at a place called Tsangbee, where the official, a jungpen, told the envoy that it was not the custom to allow persons to pass the fort without orders; but as the mission, even in its then reduced state, was too strong for him, he could not interfere, but would give no assistance in the shape of coolies. Many of those which had accompanied the camp were frost-bitten, particularly all the Nepalese, and Mr. Eden took a precaution which, with Dr. Rennie, we cannot help wondering had not been taken before, seeing it would have been one of the first

things any private traveller would have thought about—
viz. of providing the men with boots.

Finding that there was no prospect of being able to bring
on any part of his supplies, camp equipage, or retinue which
had been left with Mr. Power at Sipchoo, Mr. Eden sent
instructions to him to return to Darjeeling, taking with
him all the extra stores and baggage, and all the detachment left at Dhalimkote, with the exception of five sappers.
But he was to leave with the official at Sipchoo a store of
rice and all the presents from the Governor-General for the
Bhotan court.

On the following day an event of a novel kind altogether
befel the mission, for the people of a village through which
it passed, under the impression that Mr. Eden was come
to take possession of their country, assembled to pay him
their respects, which consisted, as we are told, after the
custom of the country, in setting fire to little heaps of
wormwood.

Up to this time, the indications of the existence of any
central government at all in the country had been so slight,
that Mr. Eden may well have doubted whether after all he
was not wending his way in pursuit of an *ignis fatuus.*
But at last he was destined to be furnished with some
tangible proof of the existence of a person claiming the
authority of a ruling power, in the shape of two letters
which some messengers were taking to the chief of Dhalimkote. As they gave out that these letters contained orders
to the chief to turn the mission back, they considered themselves justified in giving them to Mr. Eden to read. They
consisted of two contradictory orders, as Mr. Eden remarks,
" according to the Bhotan custom." One of these letters
from the Deb Raja to the Dhalimkote chief was full of
professions of friendship to the British Government, and
instructed him to do everything he could to satisfy the
envoy and settle any dispute there might be about the
frontier, but it contained not a word about turning the
mission back. The other letter, intended for the chief's

private eye, and containing the real indication of the Deb Raja's wishes, threatened the chief with death for allowing the mission to cross the frontier, scolding him frightfully for his remissness, ordering him to pay a fine of seventy rupees to each of the messengers, and telling him not to let the envoy go away angry, but to try and entice him across the frontier again ; and that if it was impossible to get rid of him, to send him round by another road, and to take care that supplies were furnished.

It is difficult to understand how Mr. Eden could have so far compromised his dignity as an envoy from the Governor-General, as to have allowed the question of his action to come in any shape before petty officials like these messengers. But this was not the only time he did so. Once or twice, if not oftener, during his progress, when beset by obstacles, he put the matter before some petty chiefs or officials in such a way as to lay on them the responsibility of his going on, saying if they liked to take upon themselves to refuse him permission to advance he would return, but they must answer to their own government for the consequences. Of course these men would not take the responsibility of interfering with the progress of the mission. Why should they ? But their refusing to do so did not place Mr. Eden in a better position ; on the contrary, the sacrifice of dignity he submitted to by laying the question at all before such men was a compromise nothing short of the most urgent necessity could have justified, and may very well account for the refusal of the council, when the envoy did reach the capital, to believe that in reality he was accredited by the Governor-General. On the present occasion, to these messengers (zinkaffs, they call them, probably answering to our Indian chiprassees) Mr. Eden put the question about his going or returning. To begin with, he had not improved his position by reading letters that were not intended for his eye. Then he says : " The zinkaff, after reading the letter, said it was clear that I should go back and enter the country by the

Samchee road." (This was the name of the road indicated in the letter.) Then an altercation seems to have ensued between the envoy and the messengers, who assuredly must have rather exceeded their instructions in reading letters entrusted to them to carry, and offering their comments thereon. At last the messengers wound up the conference by saying that the council had shown such folly in not giving proper orders for the reception of the mission, that Mr. Eden might go which way he liked.

On the 11th February, the mission reached a steep pass obstructed by snow; but though the elevation where the camp halted to spend the night was 11,800 feet, and the thermometer marked 13°, no individual out of the two hundred persons composing the retinue suffered seriously from the cold. Captain Austin remained behind in this pass for a day or two to complete some observations, but being caught in a snow-storm he had some difficulty in overtaking his chief, and lost several men and some property.

A little further in advance, the camp was forced to halt on account of the snow, but an effort was made to push on in consequence of intelligence that some more messengers were on their way to meet the mission and turn it back. Half the camp was accordingly sent on, under Captain Austin. This was on the 19th February. And on the other half preparing to start some hours after, the chief or jungpen of the place came down, and with a show of violence endeavoured to prevent them from moving, saying he had orders from the Government to stop them. Upon being requested to produce his orders, he declined to do so; affording a fair presumption that he had not any, and that all he wanted was to get a little money out of Mr. Eden ; which he did under the guise of a present for furnishing guides and sepoys.

The party had a difficult and, as it appeared at one time likely to turn out, a very disastrous march after leaving this place ; for, misled by information on the road, they did not reach shelter till 1 A.M. of the day following, perfectly exhausted, having been marching through the snow continuously for fifteen hours, and not having tasted food since nine o'clock the previous morning. At this place the deputation or messengers of whose approach Mr. Eden had heard, met him, and presented a letter from the Deb Raja of an evasive character, suggesting at one place that he should not go back, as the Raja had never declined to receive the envoy, and in another, that the complaints had better be investigated on the frontier, and demanding payment of the arrears of rents for the Ambaree district. The messengers, moreover, verbally told Mr. Eden that their instructions were to return with him to the frontier for the purpose of re-arranging the boundary and receiving over charge of the Assam Dooars. Mr. Eden very properly at this time declined to discuss the subject with these men, but he did tell them, as if it was for them to decide, that he would either return to Darjeeling or go on to the capital. They begged him not to go back, but promised to go to the capital and make arrangements for his reception.

The mission now drew near Paro, the place of residence of that governor of Western Bhotan called the Paro Penlow, who had taken the part of the Deb Raja in the recent rebellion, and under whose orders was the chief of Dhalimkote. There was every reason to expect a more favourable reception at this place than elsewhere; for although the chief who had taken the part of the Deb Raja and, it will be recollected, had sent a force to subdue Dhalimkote, had been ejected from his government by the successful revolutionary party, he still resided in the fort, and retained all the real power in his hands, the nominal power and dignity of office being vested in his stepson. But although Mr. Eden, at the desire of the chief, halted a day, in order that suitable preparations might be made to receive the envoy's party with due honours, when they arrived they were kept standing on an open plain for two

hours, without shelter, and without being allowed to pitch
their tents. Several efforts were made to get them pitched,
and a spot was selected, but the Bhotanese officials objected
to each in turn for some trifling reason, and when after a
long delay permission was granted to encamp, it was upon
one of those very sites which they had before been refused
permission to occupy. There seems to have been a determination or a settled design, from the very first, to subject
the mission on every possible occasion to studied insult.
Whether its advance under such circumstances is to be attributed to a mistaken sense of duty, or to sheer fatuity,
or to high-souled contempt for danger, may be disputed ;
but history, I believe, records no other instance of an envoy
from a mighty power like the Government of British India
submitting to such treatment from the hands of officials of
a court to whom he was accredited as ambassador, and
yet persisting in exposing himself to a continuance of it.

The indignities and insults to which the envoy was subjected at Paro, did not cease with the obstacles thrown in
his way in the selection of an encamping ground. The
officers and men were directed to remain in their tents till
further orders, and treated with insolence if they disobeyed.
Bhotan soldiers crowded the camp, stealing everything
they could, jeering the coolies and camp-followers, calling
them slaves, and drawing their knives upon them if they
attempted to reply. The servants were fined for going
about with their heads covered, and it was attempted to
make Mr. Eden and the chief officers of the mission dis-
mount from their horses, as a token of humiliation, on
approaching the residence of the police-officers. Bhotanese
were punished who were detected selling provisions, or
holding any communication with the camp. The chief, at
an interview with Cheboo Lama, the interpreter, had
declared that he had orders to prevent the envoy from
going on, but that if he would halt four days there would
be time to get an answer from the capital, whither he
would send at once, and meantime every effort should be

made to contribute to the comfort of the officers and men, and the mission generally should be treated with respect. When the series of petty insults—petty as taken separately, but in the aggregate, and as directed towards the person and following of an ambassador, most serious—had been continued for some days, and as the chief had not sent to the capital at all, Mr. Eden threatened to go back or to go on unbidden to the seat of government. After this the conduct of the chief changed ; he sent a message to the council asking for orders, and in an interview with Mr. Eden endeavoured to persuade that officer that the insults and annoyances he had met with proceeded from the malignant disposition of the ex-chief. He promised, however, that if any violence was attempted on the mission at the capital, he would assist it.

An answer could have been received from the capital in two days, nevertheless Mr. Eden was kept waiting sixteen, and then none came. It transpired afterwards that verbal instructions had been sent to this chief to seize Cheboo Lama, the interpreter, and to send the rest of the party back. He refused, however, to act without written instructions, and these the council were afraid to give. And the chief then advised Mr. Eden to go on without waiting any longer, alleging as a reason for the gross neglect in not replying at all to his reference, the unsettled state of affairs at the seat of government. Accordingly the mission set out, but before it had reached the capital some more Government messengers arrived with orders, as they said, from the Deb Raja to return to the last place (Paro); and if they thought it necessary after hearing what Mr. Eden had to say, they might send higher officials to treat with him. The same altercation ensued that had so often been repeated during this strange journey, Mr. Eden offering to go back to Darjeeling if they said he was not to go on, and they, declining to take that responsibility on themselves, telling him he had better go on or wait. Mr. Eden resolved on going on, but the messengers refused to return with him, having been, they said, despatched to Paro, where they were instructed to levy a fine on the chief for allowing the envoy to enter his territory.

At last, on the 15th of March, the wanderings of the mission came to an end for the present by its arrival at the capital, Poonakha, where every possible petty insult that could be devised by barbarian cunning was heaped upon it. On arrival the party were directed by a sepoy to move off the high road and descend a precipitous hill, so as to make their approach by a back way. This was the only notice taken of the envoy, till, after some delay, a demand was put forward for the surrender of two British subjects who had been kidnapped by the Bhotanese, and who had taken refuge in the envoy's camp. Mr. Eden gave up these men on a promise that they should be allowed to return after inquiry and investigation had taken place. As might have been expected, the instant they left the British camp they were sent off to slavery again, and Mr. Eden in reply to his demand for their restitution was told they should not be given up.

Two days after the camp reached the capital, the envoy was summoned to attend the council; and he did so, insulted by the crowd through which he passed, some of whom pelted him and his attendants. On reaching the council-house the British officers were kept standing outside, exposed to the gaze of the crowd, because the council were not ready to receive them. At last they were admitted, and as a favour allowed to sit on their own chairs, but no customary formalities were observed. Neither of the Rajas were present at this interview, and nothing in the shape of business was done beyond this,—that as neither party could understand a word the other said, it was proposed that the negotiations should be left entirely to Cheboo Lama, the interpreter, a proposition which came from the council, and certainly does no discredit to their intelligence. It is to be regretted that the same idea had not suggested itself to the Viceroy's council long before, when Cheboo Lama might have been sent alone on the mission, the prestige of the British name would have escaped insult, and an expensive war and the loss of a vast number of very valuable lives would have been avoided.

It was not till Mr. Eden had been at the capital five days that he was accorded an interview with the Rajas. On the 20th he was summoned to attend them, and the insulting and aggressive conduct of the Bhotanese officers culminated to a point on this occasion. Exposed to the sun, to the insults of the crowd, the envoy and his attendants were hustled first into one tent, then into another where the council were sitting. There they were refused permission to avail themselves of their own chairs, and were forced to seat themselves on mats in the burning sun while the interior of the tent was occupied by the Bhotan grandees. After this they were hustled through a crowd to another little tent, or canopy, where the Deb Raja was sitting, and where Mr. Eden and his officers were forced to stand uncovered in the sun while the Viceroy's letter was brought in by a common coolie and given to the prince. He shortly after rose abruptly and left the tent, the envoy and his suite being pushed rudely aside to let him pass. They remained for a short time in the same place, when they were summoned into another tent to the presence of the Dhurma Raja, where a similar scene was enacted.

Mr. Eden now complained of the heat, and desired permission to depart, but was ordered to wait till the council had seen him. The two Rajas then returned to the city, and the officers of the mission were kept waiting for an hour longer, hustled and insulted by the sepoys. After a tedious delay they were taken again to the council, where the unreasonable demands already put forward by the Bhotanese were renewed, such as the cession of the Assam Dooars, the payment of the arrears of rent, &c. ; the council assuring them that the injuries and matters of complaint were altogether on the side of Bhotan, and not

on that of the British Government. The interview ended
by the chief Tongso Penlow crumpling up the draft treaty
in his hand, and crying out, "Then we will have war! You
are nobody: you have no authority from the Governor-
General;" adding that they did not want Ambaree, and
that a chiprassee might have been sent to settle the dispute. He ended by saying, "I will have nothing more
to do with you—go."

On his return to camp, Mr. Eden indicated his intention
of taking his departure. But the cup of humiliation for
the British envoy was not yet full. Messengers came
from the other members of council, begging that he would
not take his departure, and endeavouring to excuse the
treatment to which he had been subjected, on the ground
that it was all owing to the Tongso Penlow, who was
endeavouring to usurp the whole government. To this
solicitation Mr. Eden yielded, and after a useless attempt
at negotiation by letters, which only resulted in fresh insult,
he consented to attend council again, on condition he was
not hustled by the mob, and that Tongso Penlow was not
present. Neither of the conditions was observed, the
envoy being hustled as usual, and stones thrown, and
Tongso Penlow being present in council, and as over-
bearing as before. A draft treaty was, however, agreed
upon, Mr. Eden having consented to omit two of the
articles which had been a great obstacle in the way of a
settlement, as the Bhotanese had from the first insisted on
their omission. These articles had reference to the residence of a British representative and of British traders in
the Bhotan territory. Having consented to get the draft
treaty as agreed upon copied as soon as possible, Mr. Eden
and his officers were allowed to return to camp.

On the 24th March, the treaty being ready for signature,
the envoy was summoned to the council. All this time
the custom usually observed in like cases, of a ceremonious
return visit paid by an officer of equal rank with the
Viceroy's envoy, seems to have been scrupulously omitted,

and that without attracting attention or eliciting remon-
strance. The fact of the envoy being repeatedly summoned to attend the council was in itself highly derogatory
to his dignity, and he ought not, except under compulsion, to have submitted to it.

The matter of the cession of the Assam Dooars had
not been mooted at the last meeting between the envoy
and the council, under the express understanding that
Mr. Eden would not attend the council at all if it was,
and, strange to say, the council on that occasion kept their
word. But at the next interview the Tongso Penlow
renewed his demands for the cession of these provinces,
and an altercation ensued between the envoy and the
chief, the other members of council showing that they
were quite in accord with the latter, and that their expression of regret at his former behaviour was altogether
feigned, for they continued laughing and talking, and not
attending to the business in hand. After a while the
council adjourned, taking the mission with them to another
tent in a more open space, surrounded by an immense
crowd. This was no doubt with the view of making as
public as possible the treatment to which it is evident
these Bhotanese officials had resolved to subject the
British envoy and his party. The personal outrage began
by the chief Tongso Penlow taking a piece of wet dough,
and rubbing Mr. Eden's face with it, pulling his hair, and
slapping him on the back, immediately afterwards pre-
tending it was all done in a friendly way, showing the
terms of intimacy that existed between them. The amusement of the lookers-on, however, at this gross breach of
propriety, showed how the matter was regarded. Another
chief next selected Dr. Simpson as an object of insult,
and, taking some pan leaf which he had chewed out of his
mouth, tried to make Dr. Simpson take it into his, which
he refused, and then threw it in his face. Cheboo Lama,
the interpreter, next came in for his share, and a watch
which he wore suspended by a ribbon round his neck, the

gift of the Viceroy, was rudely torn from him, and made over to one of the members of council, who secreted it in his clothes.

That the members of the mission, who were separated from their slender escort all this time, ever reached their camp alive after this treatment, is the most wonderful part of the whole story. In most semi-barbarous countries, insults such as these inflicted on an envoy from a powerful nation would naturally be followed by his assassination, and that of all his retinue. No such tragic result followed. After snatching away Cheboo Lama's watch, they seemed to think that they had perhaps exceeded the limits of official courtesy, and returned it to him ; and they also went so far, not a very great way certainly, towards the *amende,* as to request Dr. Simpson to wipe his own face, which he refused. After this the party were permitted to leave the tent, and reached their own camp without further molestation.

When they returned it was too late to commence the march back that night, and had they done so it is more than probable, from what afterwards happened, that open violence would have been resorted to, and that they would all have been seized and imprisoned.

Negotiations, or rather a process of intimidation, was next day commenced through Cheboo Lama, the interpreter, who was sent for by Tongso Penlow, and through him the whole mission was threatened with seizure and imprisonment unless Mr. Eden consented to sign a paper ceding the Assam Dooars. In vain Mr. Eden protested that he had no power to cede them, that even if he signed the paper his signature would be of no avail, that the British Government would not ratify it nor consider it binding ; all of which was communicated to the Bhotanese, of course, through Cheboo Lama, upon whose trustworthiness in translating correctly, and upon nothing else, Mr. Eden depended for the expression of his sentiments to Tongso Penlow.

Meantime the mission camp was straitened for supplies; sentries having been posted all round to prevent
communication. In this crisis, Mr. Eden summoned a
council of the officers of his camp, to decide what action
to adopt. Three courses seemed open to them; either
to leave Mr. Eden and Cheboo Lama on condition that
the rest were allowed to withdraw, or to make an attempt
to escape by night, or to sign the paper. The latter
course was determined on. When this resolution had
been communicated to the council, the envoy was summoned to attend them again on two occasions, on both
of which, however, he was treated with decent courtesy.
On the second (the 29th March) the treaty was signed
by Mr. Eden and Cheboo Lama, the former having written
above his signature, on the two copies that were made out,
the words "Under compulsion." Whether any of the
council knew what these words meant does not appear.
The presents, that had meantime been sent for from the
spot where they had been left, were distributed. A Bhotan
demon, or large wooden image, was brought in and carried
round the tent in state, notice having been given that
if any injury was done to the Bhotanese the demon would
resent it; and finally Mr. Eden received permission to
depart. As soon as he had left council, the chief Tongso
Penlow departed for his own territory, and the tents
being struck an immediate march was ordered. Even then
they did not get away without obstruction, a number of
Bhotanese sepoys having placed themselves on the road
and insolently demanded why the mission left without
permission from the official who took up the reins of
government on the departure of Tongso Penlow. Cheboo
Lama then went back to the fort to represent matters and
complain of the violence offered; the baggage and tents
were sent on, and Mr. Eden, with the Sikh escort, remained
behind to wait for Cheboo Lama.

He waited till it got dark, but the interpreter did not
come. He, however, sent a message to Mr. Eden, telling

him to go on and he would follow next day. Mr. Eden accordingly acted on this advice, and he was afterwards joined by Cheboo Lama, who had not, however, escaped without difficulty.

Next day, further attempts were made to detain the mission and to seize Cheboo Lama, but Mr. Eden having shown a disposition to resent any such attempt by force they were eventually allowed to go on, and reached the comparatively friendly neighbourhood of the Paro fort on the 31st.

Their difficulties here terminated, and in thirteen stages the ill-fated mission reached British territory in safety.

The announcement that the British envoy had signed a paper ceding to the Bhotanese the Assam Dooars was received by the English community in India with a yell of indignation. And before the circumstances were thoroughly known, it was assumed that Mr. Eden, acting under the orders of the Bengal Government, had made light of the sacrifice of a tract of country by the cession of which the class who would chiefly suffer were the European settlers and tea planters of Assam. How the insult to the British nation and Government, in the person of the envoy, was to be wiped out, and the treaty cancelled with a due regard to our national honour, was debated in every circle. If war was the remedy adopted,—war against whom, or what? and was it justifiable or prudent to sacrifice the prestige attaching hitherto to the word of a British envoy, by immediately repudiating the terms of a treaty entered into by him after full deliberation and in a formal manner? Much casuistry was thrown away in discussion as to whether Mr. Eden ought, from motives of personal safety of himself and his attendants, to have so compromised the Government; and a great deal of stress was laid upon the fact of the treaty having been signed under compulsion. It seems to me idle to adduce the introduction of those qualifying words as an element in the argument at all, because it does not appear that the Bhotanese had any

knowledge of their meaning and force, and they would
in that case be of no further avail than a mental reservation, which a man makes when he says "Yes," and means
" No." Had they known the full force of the phrase, it is
hardly likely, from what we have seen of their proceedings,
that they would have been satisfied with so transparent a
formality, or consented to receive a document in the face
of it null and void. The translation of the document, of
course, rested with Cheboo Lama, the interpreter, and it is
not very likely that he was so scrupulously exact in his
rendering of the whole paper as to have explained very
clearly the meaning of the two words which made the
whole treaty waste paper. The question resolves itself
into one of general principle, whether any circumstances
can justify fraud. It is clear that if they can, then was Mr.
Eden fully justified in purchasing the safety of himself and
the mission by the pretended cession of the Assam Dooars.
It would have been lamentable indeed had his life and the
lives of his companions been sacrificed in this silly attempt
to treat barbarians with the forms and usages observed
among civilized nations. And if the safety of the whole
party was purchased at the expense of Cheboo Lama's
conscience, perhaps the bargain may on the whole not
be considered a very bad one. I am not aware that the
Indian Government have ever adopted as their motto, "Fiat
justitia ruat cœlum :" if so, it has been adopted very
recently ; at any rate, it is clear they did not act upon it
in their relations with Bhotan, for the treaty ceding the
Assam Dooars was at once repudiated.

The British Government, however, did not at once
resolve on war; at first it was determined only to annex
permanently the Ambaree district, and to withhold for the
future the rent for the Assam Dooars. At the same time a
demand was made for the immediate restitution of all
British subjects held in captivity, the alternative being
the annexation of the Bengal Dooars. These terms were,
it is hardly necessary to add, not complied with, and in

November 1864 a proclamation of war was issued, and active preparations set on foot.

It will be recollected that the Bengal Dooars were protected or supervised by the chiefs of five forts, Dhalimkote the westernmost, then Chamoorcha, next Balla, Buxa, and lastly Bishensing.

The plan of the campaign was, therefore, to send a column against each of these forts, and the command of the whole force was given to Brigadier-General Mulcaster, with immediate control over the three right columns, the other columns to operate on the left being under the command of Brigadier-General Dunsford, C.B. A small reserve of Europeans was stationed at Darjeeling, the troops composing the force in the field being, with the exception of the artillerymen, entirely natives.

The first operation, the reduction of Dhalimkote, was attended with a sad disaster. The column sent against this fort consisted of three Armstrong Mountain Train guns, and two 8-inch mortars, a wing of the 18th Native Infantry, and the 30th Punjab Infantry. After one or two stockades had been captured without any actual resistance by a detachment under Major Gough, the column reached Ambiok, which it will be recollected was the halting-place of the mission camp just under the Dhalimkote fort, on the 5th December. Some communication passed between Lieut.-Colonel Haughton, the political officer with the column, and the commandant of the fort, which was attended with no practical result, and the guns and mortars were put in position. Owing to the nature of the country, it was found impossible to select a site for guns where the magazine could be deposited at a safe distance. The mortars were accordingly placed on a pathway where there was only just room for them, and the magazine on one side immediately below the ridge. On the column approaching the fort a fire of stones and arrows, and a few matchlocks, was directed against it. The infantry, after capturing a barricade, advanced to the foot of the ascent leading to the fort, where they were exposed to another volley of stones, arrows, and matchlock balls; Captain Macgregor, the Brigade Major, and Major Longmore of the 18th Native Infantry, being wounded, the former by a matchlock ball, the latter by an arrow. The two five and a half inch mortars were throwing their shell into the fort, when suddenly a terrible explosion occurred, and three officers— Major Griffin and Lieutenants Anderson and Waller—of the Artillery, with four gunners, were killed on the spot, some of them being so disfigured that their forms could scarcely be recognised; an officer of the Royal Engineers and several artillerymen were at the same time very severely wounded. All accounts coincide in stating that the accident originated from a premature bursting of a shell. The shock, with its terrible results, was so instantaneous that it is difficult for the survivors who were nearest the spot when the catastrophe occurred, to recollect exactly the position which the unfortunate sufferers occupied at the moment they were blown up. Dr. Rennie states that Major Griffin was engaged in weighing out the charges. No doubt that was his particular duty at the time, but I am assured on the authority of an officer who was present, that the moment before the explosion took place he was leisurely sitting on a barrel of gunpowder, smoking a pipe with that contempt for danger which is the invariable result of familiarity with it.

The fort of Dhalimkote fell into our possession on the evening of that day, the Punjabees having effected an entry by a breach made with an Armstrong gun, which had been brought up after the explosion. The Bhotanese retired from an opening in the opposite wall as our own soldiers entered, and several buildings in the place, including a monastery, were destroyed by fire.

The occupation of the country around, and the villages and forts dependent on Dhalimkote, which was accomplished without opposition, kept the column employed till the 19th December, after which Brigadier-General

Dunsford descended from the hills, and directed his march
towards the next fort, Chamoorcha. This was captured
almost without opposition. The Bhotanese, indeed, exhibited a good deal of courage in attacking the advance
party under Major Mayne, with arrows, stones, and matchlocks, but they appear to have offered no resistance at all
in defence of the fort itself, which was captured by a
party under Major Garsten, the garrison escaping and
flying over the hills as our troops entered. A detachment
of 100 men, under Captain Perkins of the Engineers, had
been sent to the rear of the village to intercept and destroy
the fugitives; an object in which, it is to be hoped, for the
sake of humanity, they were unsuccessful. There were
two men killed and three wounded on our side. The
Bhotanese had thirteen killed, and were said to have
carried off their wounded. The adjacent strongholds of
Buxa and Balla were occupied by Captain Watson without
opposition.

Meantime, operations had been conducted against
Dewangiri, the easternmost of the forts commanding
the Dooars, from the Assam side. The column under
Colonel Campbell, and accompanied by Brigadier-General
Mulcaster, advanced with all the pomp and circumstance
of war from a place called Koomree Katta, about twelve
miles from Dewangiri, in fighting order. On the 9th
December they made six miles, and halted near a pass
in the hills. Meantime Captain Macdonald, with fifty of
the Bengal police, had been sent on to reconnoitre. Early
in the morning of the 10th the column continued its march
in fighting order up the pass. About half-way through they
came to a fortified position or stockade, from behind which
they were assaulted by a shower of stones, and one man
was wounded. The advanced guard, consisting of a company of the 43d Assam Light Infantry, returned fire, when
it was ascertained that the position was exposed on both
flanks, and that there were fifty Bhotanese in it. Upon this
the advance guard was recalled, and the column halted for

the night.   Next morning, while the Brigadier-General was
reconnoitring, information was received that the fort of
Dewangiri had fallen into the hands of Captain Macdonald
and his police constables.   The stockade in front of which
the column had halted during the night was then examined,
and found to be evacuated.   Captain Macdonald's success
had been gained with the trifling loss of one man killed
and five wounded, for the garrison had offered scarcely
any resistance beyond hurling a few volleys of stones and
arrows, and one rude cannon shot, which occasioned the
only fatal casualty.

Somewhat similar were the operations against the now
only surviving fort, Bishensing.   Against this the Brigadier-
General marched with three hundred men of the 12th and
44th regiments of Native Infantry, and on arrival found
nothing but a solitary house, inhabited by an old Lama
priest.   " Thus was the capture of the Bhotan hill fort of
Bishensing effected," says Dr. Rennie, " for which duty a
fully-equipped column, about 2,000 strong, accompanied by
150 elephants, had been detached."

The capture of all the forts and Dooars having thus
been accomplished, the military force engaged was broken
up.   It soon appeared, however, that the Bhotanese were
not going to let so valuable a portion of their country
slip out of their hands without an effort to recover it.
Sundry warnings were given that they were making
preparations to recover the whole line of forts, but no one
paid any attention to them, though the peasantry in the
neighbourhood, who seem from the first to have welcomed
the advent of the British, on several occasions gave information that ought to have put our people on the alert.

Besides this, it appears a letter was received at Dewangiri from Tongso Penlow, the chief who had taken such an
active part in the ill-treatment of Mr. Eden; but as no one
could read the letter it had to be sent to Darjeeling, a
distance of 200 miles, to be translated by Cheboo Lama !
What a comment is this upon the way in which our rela-

tions with Bhotan were conducted! Even after we had taken possession and declared ourselves masters of the richest part of the country, and established our garrisons and our civil officers for the administration of justice, a letter written in a language commonly used in the country has to be sent two hundred miles to be translated! This missive afterwards turned out to be a timely caution to the officer in command at Dewangiri, that the mighty Tongso Penlow was coming to attack him if he did not evacuate the fort within seven days.

The garrison of Dewangiri consisted of a detachment of the 43d Native Light Infantry, a company of Sikh Sappers, some Bengal police, and some guns manned by Eurasian artillerymen. Early on the morning of the 29th January, 1865, the troops were surprised by a Bhotanese force under Tongso Penlow, who had kept his word. The utmost confusion prevailed, as it always does in attacks of this kind just before dawn. The noise which at first disturbed the garrison, who seem to have been content to do without the usual precaution of posting sentries, was like that made by loose cattle running over the fortified enclosure. The soldiers fell in as well as they could in the dark ; the artillery kept to their guns, and the infantry opened fire in the direction where the assailants were supposed to be. As soon as there was light enough to see the enemy, Colonel Campbell charged with the 43d and Sappers, and drove them out of the place. The only casualties were, Lieutenant Urquhart of the Royal Engineers, killed, and Lieutenant Storey, of the 43d, wounded ; four men killed, and thirty-one wounded. The loss of the enemy was put down at about sixty men.

The Bhotanese, however, were by no means disheartened; they only changed their tactics. Finding out that the only supply of water for the garrison came from a spring about a mile and a half distant, the water being conveyed by means of a bamboo aqueduct, they easily succeeded in cutting it off, at the same time occupying in force the pass which lay between the fort and the reserve of the British forces in the plain country. Colonel Campbell then applied to Brigadier-General Mulcaster for reinforcements, as he was not strong enough to dislodge the Bhotanese and recover possession of the springs of water so indispensably necessary for his troops. Brigadier-General Mulcaster, however, turned a deaf ear to Colonel Campbell's urgent solicitations, but consented at last to send him some ammunition; next to water, perhaps, the commodity of which the beleaguered garrison stood most in need. The ammunition, however, never reached its destination; for when the officer escorting it arrived at the foot of the pass he found it in possession of the enemy, and his detachment only consisting of thirty-six sepoys, he did not feel justified in attacking.

Thus the genius of contraries seemed to guide all our relations and operations with Bhotan from the first. The mission under Mr. Eden, which never ought to have been sent, when it started did almost everything it ought not to have done, and omitted to do almost everything it should have done. When war was declared, an expensive and elaborately equipped military force was despatched, under the usual organization of generals and brigadiers, to seize a number of empty forts, which might have been taken possession of by a few police. When the Bhotanese had mustered in force, and sent notice of their intention to attack us, the letter had to be forwarded two hundred miles before it could be read; and finally, when the garrison of the principal place wrested from the enemy was straitened, the supply of water being cut off, the general sent them ammunition, which never arrived because the pass was held by a strong force of the enemy, and the escort consisted of thirty-six sepoys only; and this is the same pass which, when it was occupied by a stockade garrisoned by fifty men who ran away in the night, it was thought necessary to employ a whole British column under the Brigadier-General himself to force.

Human beings, let them be ever so brave, cannot live without water; and in consequence of the refusal to send Colonel Campbell reinforcements, that officer was compelled to take the disastrous step of evacuating Dewangiri. This was done at one o'clock on the morning of the 5th February, the pickets keeping up a fire to divert the enemy's attention. 250 men of the 43d were told off to carry and escort the sick and wounded; 50 more to drag the guns, two twelve-pound howitzers; and the remainder of the force, about 200 men, were available for duty on the front and rear of the retreating column. Colonel Campbell, however, realized the truth of the old saying, that a retreat is the most difficult manœuvre to manage in the whole range of military operations, and above all a retreat in the night.

The main column lost its way, the usual result of movements in the dark; then a panic seized the men, the guns were abandoned, and, I am sorry to add, some of the sick and wounded—how many is not known; and, in short, the retreat turned to a flight; the gunners, unable to drag the guns when the sepoys of the 43d refused any longer to assist, acting under the orders of their officer, Captain Cockburn, threw them over the precipice with the view of preventing them from falling into the hands of the Bhotanese. The latter, however, managed to get them up, and retained them for a long while as trophies of their victory.

The ill-fated garrison at last reached the camp at Koomree Katta, the men and officers saving nothing but the things they wore or carried with them. The Bhotanese did not perceive the evacuation of the fort till about two hours after the troops had left, and then were too busily engaged in looting what had been left behind to think of pursuing the fugitives. The chief, Tongso Penlow, behaved exceedingly well, having treated with kindness and consideration the wounded who fell into his hands. Indeed, he sent a letter down to Koomree Katta, inquiring after the health of the Bhotanese prisoners in the British camp;

adding that the British prisoners in his possession were going on well.

About the same time that this assault was made on Dewangiri, all the other forts as far as Chamoorcha were assailed in a. similar manner. It would be tedious to relate the story of each attack in detail. Suffice it to say that in every instance except that of Dewangiri the attempt failed, either from greater precaution having been used by the defenders, or from reinforcements being promptly sent up.

The Government were resolved to take immediate steps to recover their lost prestige in Bhotan, and accordingly two batteries of Artillery, one from Meerut and the other from Calcutta, the 55th Regiment from Lucknow, and the head-quarters of the 80th from Dum Dum, the 19th, 29th, and 31st regiments of Native Infantry, were ordered at once to the frontier. At the same time Brigadier-General Tombs, C.B., V.C., was sent to supersede Brigadier-General Mulcaster, and Brigadier-General Tytler, C.B., to succeed Brigadier-General Dunsford, C.B., who resigned from ill-health. Of the force above detailed, the 3d Battery, 25th Brigade, R.A., the head-quarters of the 55th Regiment, and 29th Punjab Infantry were ordered to operate against Dewangiri, while the remainder of the force was attached to the left brigade.

It will easily be understood that the re-conquest of Dewangiri, and the work of driving the Bhotanese from the stockades which they had erected in the neighbourhood of some of the other forts, were very easily effected by the overwhelming British army now in the field.

Dewangiri was captured almost without any casualties on our side at all; an officer of the police, Mr. Weldon, having been shot in the groin, and three officers struck in the head with stones. There were about four-and-twenty of the sepoys also wounded.

While the British column was assembling for the final

operations against Dewangiri, two messengers were sent to Tongso Penlow to inquire after the prisoners. It was found he had treated them well ; the messengers, too, he did not despatch on their return errand till he had given them a good dinner. He sent his compliments to the officers in camp, saying that he was quite well, and hoped they were so too. The amiable sentiments and really good behaviour of the chivalrous Bhotan barbarian were, however, but poorly returned by our own people, who on the capture of the place indiscriminately slaughtered 120 Bhotanese they found there, many of whom were lying on the ground wounded.

Thus ended the Bhotan war, which was nothing but a series of mistakes from the first. It was born in ignorance, bred in mismanagement, and concluded by a bloody and cruel butchery. The casualties among our officers and men in the field, however, are far from representing the total loss which the war entailed. With the most exquisite scenery, abounding in undulating hills clothed with verdure and forest trees, here and there presenting a grand panorama of lofty mountain-ranges, with all their diversities of hill and dale, Bhotan possesses a most deadly climate. Of all the various kinds of malarious fever known in India, presenting some type peculiar to each locality, the fever of Bhotan is the most dangerous. Once in the system, it seems incapable of being eradicated for years. And numbers of those who served in the country during the war carried with them to other scenes of duty seeds of a disease that too often proved fatal. The habits of the Bhotanese are excessively filthy. Strangers, as all semi-barbarous tribes are, to sanitary precautions of any kind, these people seem to have vied with Nature herself in making their picturesque country a very charnel-house. Some of the forts, which were permanently occupied by our troops after the termination of hostilities, which had been for years before used as places of residence by the people attached to the locality, were found to contain a foot and more in depth of accumulated filth over their whole area. This was especially the case at Dhalimkote, where an effort was made to clear the place, and render it in some degree fit for human habitation, by removing the filth which covered the space surrounded by the walls to the extent of 7,000 feet, and a foot and a half in thickness. But the disturbance or removal of the dried surface of the mass of accumulated horrors seemed to let loose the foul miasma which had been, like an evil genius, imprisoned in the dirt that generated it. The consequences were most disastrous ;· men and officers alike fell beneath its baneful influence. Kept on rations insufficient to enable their system to rally against the effects of such a pestilential atmosphere, the native troops succumbed in a most pitiable manner. Even in a country remarkable for verdure vegetable food is scarce, and the men, in addition to fever and ague, began to suffer from scurvy. Again and again the officer commanding the detachment addressed his superiors, urging on them the necessity of supplying the men with more generous diet, and above all vegetables. But the senior medical officer would not support the application with a recommendation of his own. At last the frightful mortality among the men attracted the attention of the military authorities ; and when too late to save life, the long-solicited vegetables were sent up, at a season of the year which ensured their arriving in a half-rotten state, and additional rations were sanctioned.

In reviewing the whole story of our relations with Bhotan, from the starting of the embassy to the butchering of the wounded in the fort of Dewangiri—which it is but just to state the European officers endeavoured, but in vain, to prevent—the impartial historian cannot but see that, with the advantages of civilization and the teaching of Christianity on our side, even as regards those qualities which civilization and Christianity are supposed to foster, if not to beget, the balance is in favour of the despised, semi-barbarous Bhotanese. With the exception of the un-

gentlemanly (if such a word can be applied to a Bhotan
at all) conduct of Tongso Penlow in spitting in the face of
Dr. Simpson, and besmearing the features of the envoy
with filth, their conduct throughout was marked by at least
as much (shall we not say more?) good sense, straight-
forwardness, forbearance, and military skill as ours.   If
Mr. Eden obstinately persisted in pushing his way into the
heart of the country, they firmly and consistently from the
first did all they possibly could to prevent him from putting
himself in a false position.   No man could have had
broader hints that he was not wanted.   While their conduct, though occasionally vacillating, was for the most
part frank and honest, even to the extent of Tongo Penlow's declining to take advantage of the laxity of discipline
and want of alertness of the Dewangiri garrison without
giving notice beforehand of his determination to make a
struggle for the freedom of his country, a British envoy is
driven to a disgraceful expedient to secure his own liberty
and that of his suite.   A British officer in command
of an important outpost in a newly-conquered country
allows his garrison to be surprised, fails to take measures
to secure his men a constant supply of water, the most
necessary of all the necessaries of life, and is driven pell-
mell, with the loss of his guns and all public and private
stores, down the hills.   A brigadier-general, with a considerable force at his command, fails to keep open his communications with his own outpost ; while the Bhotan chief,
self-taught in the art of strategy, surprises a garrison, cuts
off its water, and secures its inevitable defeat.   When our
wounded, cast away in the hurry of disgraceful flight from
the abandoned fort, fall into the hands of Tongso, he treats
them kindly, and rewards our messengers, sent to his
camp, with good dinners, and sends them back with polite
messages.   When our men attack a scarce-defended fort,
we send a party to the rear on purpose to shoot down
helpless fugitives ; and when Dewangiri falls finally before
a British force, the garrison, including the wounded, are

butchered. Even the original cause of dispute, the alleged aggression of the Bhotanese upon British subjects, was by no means all on one side of the account, for the Bhotan authorities from the very first declared they had more reason than we to complain of frontier outrages, and the truth or falsehood of the allegation cannot be determined, for it was never investigated.

The termination of active hostilities resulted in leaving us victors in the field. The Dooars had been seized, and the hill fortresses attached to them were in our possession; but so long as the country remained hostile, it was obvious that we should have to retain our possession of those places which had fallen into our hands at an enormous sacrifice of life; for it would be necessary to maintain large garrisons at the principal strongholds. It was therefore resolved, at the conclusion of 1865 and commencement of 1866, to organize a strong force of 7,000 men to complete the conquest and subjugation of the entire country. Happily, the necessity of resorting to this extreme measure was avoided by the conclusion of a treaty with the Deb Raja and Tongso Penlow, by which, on condition of the two guns deserted by Colonel Campbell's detachment being restored, and stipulations for the future to put an end to all aggression or annoyance on the British frontier, our Government bound itself to abandon the idea of further hostilities, and to pay yearly, as rent for the Bengal Dooars, a sum of 25,000 rupees, to be doubled in the event of the terms of the treaty being faithfully observed by the Bhotanese.

It only remains to add, that the writers who have laid the blame of this miserable chapter of British Indian history on the shoulders of the Bengal Government have done so unreasonably. The policy, whether good or bad, was Imperial policy from the first ; and from Mr. Eden's mission down to the treaty of 1866, the Supreme Government is solely responsible. It is equally unjust to regard Sir John Lawrence as the author of the mischief.

It was begun before he arrived in the country; and although it would have been much better if he had at once taken the responsibility of ordering Mr. Eden back, and declining to sanction any further attempt at a hopeless task, we can easily understand how unwilling he felt to cancel and upset at one stroke the policy of his predecessor.

MAP
OF THE
PESHAWUR VALLEY
and the
ADJACENT TERRITORY.

CHAPTER XV.

THE outrages of the Sittana fanatics upon British subjects, their interference with traffic, and their threatening attitude generally, induced the Government in 1863 to send a force under Sir Neville Chamberlain to reduce them to order.

About forty miles north of the Attok Fort, where the route to Peshawur crosses the Indus, and on the west bank of that river, is a large mountain called Mahabun, about thirty miles in length from east to west, and 8,000 feet high. The summit is mostly covered with forests of fir-trees, and in the winter months wrapped in snow, but the sides of the mountain are bare and rocky, and in places very steep, and only to be ascended by spurs which run out at intervals into the valleys below, separated by deep rocky gorges, so that in passing from one spur to the other it is almost always necessary either to ascend to the summit and descend from the point where the spurs commence, or go down to the valley, cross the gorge, and ascend from the foot of the other projection. Interspersed among the gorges and spurs, the rocks and forests, that alternate over the surface of this splendid mountain, are plots of cultivation and small villages inhabited by the hardy races who have made their homes almost on a level with the eagle's eyrie. The tribe against which military operations were now directed were the Hindustanee fanatics, the descendants of a band of desperate men who formed a colony in the trans-

Indus district in the days of Runjeet Singh. Their principal stronghold and head-quarters of late years had been at a place called Mulka, hidden in a cleft on the northern side of the Mahabun mountain, which, as it runs from south-east to north-west, turns its southern flank towards the Peshawur valley, and its northern towards the hilly districts of Bonair, and other territories as yet practically unexplored. The Indus at this part of its course has a direction pretty nearly due north and south. At a small bend the river makes just where it approaches the north-western corner of Mahabun is the city of Umb, and at the foot of the south-west corner is the town of Sittana, another settlement of these fanatics, whither they resorted always when intent upon hostile designs against their neighbours, and by which name they are known to us.

The stronghold of Mulka was therefore most securely situated. To reach it there were only two routes, either right over the mountain crest and down the other side, or round by the foot of the mountain to the north-west corner, where lies the sheltered valley of Chumla. This valley is bounded on the whole of the south side by the spurs of Mahabun, on the north by the rugged country of the Bonairs. The entrance to it is effected on the west by a pass called the Umbeyla pass, from a village of that name at its mouth, just where it debouches into the valley. The other, or the western end of the pass, enters the hills from the south, connecting a tract of plain country, called the Eusofzie part of the Peshawur valley, and within the British frontier line, with the Chumla valley. The mountain heights (for where the country is all one mass of mountain ridges, the principal heights can only be distinguished in a general description) overhanging the Umbeyla pass on the north flank are called the Gooroo mountain, and are in the Bonair territory, as also is the village of Umbeyla and the adjacent tract. Away to the north and west of Bonair, across another high range, is the Swat valley, and beyond that again the eye rests on range after range, till the snow-capped summits of the Hindoo Koosh bound the distant horizon.

From this brief description of the localities, it will be sufficiently clear that, in directing its operations against the stronghold of Mulka, the British force could more easily penetrate to the mountain fastness by pushing through the Umbeyla pass, making its way along the Chumla valley, and then, by turning sharply to the right, take the enemy's position, as it were, in the flank. When Sir Neville Chamberlain took the field, there was, as far as we were aware, no combination between the Mulka or Sittana fanatics and their neighbours, the Bonairs or the Swatees. Our relations with the Bonairs, so far as any communication had taken place, were not unfriendly. We had no quarrel with them, and did not wish to seek one. But these fanatical Mahommedan mountain tribes are easily excited and very suspicious, and, above all, extremely jealous of having their territories explored by British officers or British troops : and although the route of the force on its way *viâ* the Chumla valley to Mulka would necessarily have to pass through the Bonairs' territory, yet as they only laid claim to the tract at the Chumla end of the pass, where stood the village of Umbeyla ; and as all the information which our civil officers on the frontier had been able to obtain about the pass led them to believe there were no physical obstacles to prevent a small force marching right through it in one day ; and as the next day would see the column out of the Bonairs' territory again, and fairly on its way to Mulka, it was hoped that no opposition would be offered to the passage of our troops. Moreover, the object was to surprise, and there were grounds for apprehension that if we made a formal demand to the Bonairs for permission to pass through their territory, or rather intimated our intention of doing so, although it was added that we had no wish to molest or annoy them, they might, from a feeling of sympathy, though there was no real clanship between them and the Hindustanee fanatics, apprise them of the approach of a body of infidels bent on their destruction. So it was resolved to let them know nothing of our movement till the force was at the mouth of the pass ready to push its way through, and then it was hoped it would be possible for it to march along the valley the same day, and by nightfall reach a place called Kooria, at the easternmost extremity, where the route would turn off to the right towards Mulka. In fact, it was as if we would commit a little trespass first, and when we had reached the boundary of our neighbour's grounds, and were on the point of quitting them, we might ask permission, regardless whether it was acceded or refused, and a proclamation was to be issued to the Bonair chiefs, acquainting them with our peaceable intentions so far as they were concerned.

Accordingly, on the morning of the 20th October, the force—which consisted of half a battery of Royal Artillery, the three guns being carried along on elephants, the 71st Highlanders, the 101st Royal Bengal Fusiliers, two companies of native Sappers, the 20th and 32d Native Infantry the 11th Native Cavalry, two native mountain batteries, with eight small guns carried on mules, the Guides (infantry and cavalry), the 1st, 3d, 5th, and 26th regiments of Native Infantry of the Punjab Irregular Force, and the 5th Goorkhas—entered the Umbeyla pass; the proclamation having been issued the day before to the neighbouring tribes, informing them that the object of the force was to enter the Mahabun tract and punish the fanatics, and that there was no intention of interfering with other tribes.

Colonel Wylde, an experienced officer in this mountain warfare, led the way with his corps of Guides and 1st Punjab Infantry, under Major Keyes. After halting about an hour at the village of Soorkhawai, at the mouth of the pass, Colonel Wylde, accompanied by the Deputy-Commissioner, went on to feel the way. The prospect was not encouraging, for the road lay up a watercourse, in which were huge masses of rock and clear running water, the hills

high, towering on either side, and covered with brushwood
and trees. The advance column had not proceeded far
before it was greeted by a couple of shots, which neces-
sitated crowning the heights on either side with flanking
parties of Guide infantry, whilst the 1st, or Coke's Regiment, advanced up the watercourse. The way being thus
led, the main body of the force, under Colonel Hope, of
H.M. 71st, followed. The road is a gentle ascent the entire
distance, without a single village. About seven miles from
Soorkhawai brought the column to the crest of the pass of
Umbeyla, where a halt was ordered, for none of the baggage had come up, and the men spent a most uncomfort-
able night. But a reconnoitring party, consisting of Col.
Probyn with his regiment (cavalry), Captain Hawes with the
Guides (cavalry), and a party of Sappers, were pushed forward under the command of Colonel Taylor of the Engineers
as far as Kooria, some ten miles further on. The people
everywhere were civil and obliging, offering their services,
and tendering submission ; but the Bonairs were assembled
in considerable force, part of them being visible from the
camp at the mouth of the pass collecting on the hillside
and occupying Umbeyla, the principal features of which
were flat-roofed houses and a mosque, with corn-stacks and
fields of tall-stalked Indian corn adjoining. It was evening,
and night was drawing on. It was impossible to attack the
enemy, for such no doubt they were, in a position of which
our officers knew nothing beyond what they could see at
a distance, and as yet no overt act of hostility had been
made. The mountaineers, however, came out of their fastnesses, yelling and shouting defiance as our reconnoitring
party returned, and the men of Probyn's regiment could
not be restrained. They charged all who had been rash
enough to leave the cover of the village. Hand-to-hand
conflicts ensued ; several of the enemy fell. Unfortunately
a dry nullah had to be passed in the charge, at which two
of the horses fell, and went over to the enemy ; of these
one belonged to the adjutant of the Sikh regiment. Several

of the Sikhs had their horses wounded, and one of the men received a smart sabre-cut on his head.

This affair occurring just below the camp, the 20th Punjab Infantry and a regiment of Muzbee Sikhs came down, and kept the enemy at bay until all our force had again re-entered the pass. It was by this time dark, excepting the moon's dim light, and the Bonairs pluckily followed our troops up to the crest, and continued to fight until three o'clock the morning following. The hills on both sides of the camp were lined with infantry pickets about half-way up the heights; nobody slept, and few got anything in the way of food or clothes, as the baggage could not be brought up; and for some days following provisions fetched exorbitant prices, flour selling at a rupee per two pounds, and bread at several rupees per loaf. The night was cold, but there was no want of excitement. A breastwork of commissariat stores was thrown across the narrow part of the mountain road in front, and defended by guns and infantry. Here the staff assembled; and here they witnessed the daring courage of the Bonairs, with which the whole force was destined to become more familiar. They advanced up to the breastwork—one man even leapt over it and cut down an officer of the Engineers, Lieut. Brown—while several of them crept stealthily into our camp, where they attacked any one they met. The night was too dark to allow of our men taking aim, but whenever a matchlock flashed through the gloom a shower of bullets from our soldiers' rifles sped in the direction thus indicated. But the enemy likewise availed themselves of this guide for their fire, and whilst the general and his staff were standing by the guns, a ball, which the lighted portfire had doubtless attracted, mortally wounded Captain Gillies of the Artillery, who fell shot through the heart. Meantime the pickets on the height were similarly occupied, and thus was spent the first night in the Umbeyla pass, in a hot though desultory engagement with an enemy with whom we had literally as yet had no quarrel. About three o'clock the firing ceased, and our jaded soldiers were enabled to snatch a little repose.

The difficulty of the situation now began to dawn fairly upon Sir Neville Chamberlain. It was certain he would have to fight every inch of the way; and, as far as mere fighting went, this he could have done; but his little army had to be fed, and where were his supplies to come from? He could not venture to advance without at least a fortnight's provisions, and how was his small but well-appointed force to fight their way, protect the baggage and supplies, and keep open their communications? For it was now clear that the very first device the Bonairs adopted, when the British force moved on, would be to close the pass. Thus circumstanced, he determined to stay where he was, and to send back for reinforcements and supplies, holding the position meanwhile. Stronger pickets were thrown out on both sides of the little camp, which was in the bed of the pass, flanked on the left by the heights of the Gooroo mountain, on the right by a high craggy peak to which our troops gave the name of the Craig picket, while the site selected for the picket on the left was called the Eagle's nest. The hardy and now excited mountaineers gave our troops no rest. Every day had its own story of little battles fought and won, vigorous attacks resisted, and the enemy again and again driven back, again and again advancing under the influence of their leaders, and hurling themselves upon the small compact force of British troops, who held their difficult position with the tenacity which British soldiers know so well how to evince. On the 26th the ranks of the enemy were swelled by the arrival of a number of the Swatees, who, assisted by a body of the fanatics from Mulka, against whom originally our efforts had been solely directed, made a desperate and combined attack upon the camp. The 20th Punjabees and Frontier Infantry Corps were hotly engaged, and their casualties heavy. A lieutenant of the former corps—Richmond, a man beloved by all who knew him—was shot

through the head, and died the day following; Major
Brownlow lost his senior native officer and several men in
addition to poor Richmond. Clifford, an excellent soldier,
the adjutant of the 1st Punjab Cavalry, and a volunteer
with the 3d Punjab Infantry, was killed, together with some
native officers and men. In all, our casualties were eighty
killed and wounded ; among the latter being Drake of the
Sappers and Barrow of the Artillery. The enemy suffered
much, but were nowise daunted or discouraged. The hill
fighting involved physical exertions to which many of
our officers and men may well have been strangers. To
mount the rocky paths which led to our pickets in some
cases occupied three hours, and it was necessary for every
party upon reaching a halting-place to protect itself by
erecting a breastwork of large stones and fragments of
rock, an art the enemy themselves taught us in their
sungas or stone breastworks, with which we first became
fatally familiar in the Affghan war.

On the 31st, Sir Neville Chamberlain wrote that there
was a general combination of almost all the tribes, from
the Indus to the boundary of Cabul, against us. Old
animosities were in abeyance, and, under the influence of
fanaticism, tribes usually hostile to each other were
hastening to join the standard of the Akhoond of Swat.
Meantime reinforcements were being pushed up, and by
the end of October the force had been increased by the
arrival of the 14th (Ferozepore) Native Infantry, the 4th
Goorkhas, and two field-guns of a native Punjab battery,
with additional supplies of food, ammunition, and medical
stores.

The Bonairs, or Bonairwal as they were called, are a fine
race of men. Clad in loose flowing garments, and turbans
of blue, they are as formidable an enemy as one might
wish to encounter. To watch any single one among them
coming to the attack might remind the spectator of some
tragic character fretting on the stage, as, with a huge
shield on his left arm, and sword brandished in the air, he

starts towards his antagonist, and inspirited by the shrill
music of the hill-pipe—which differs little from the Scot-
tish bagpipe—he shouts his war-cry. This is taken up by
a thousand of the wild band ; their drums beat and banners
are waved frantically, and one and all charge down upon
the breastworks.

With their swords and shields and matchlocks, and
carrying six days' provisions on their backs, these hardy
mountaineers rallied to the call that was ringing from
every mountain crest and in every cavern over the northern
frontier. The Akhoond of Swat and another famous
leader, the Molvie Abdoolla, from their wild homes spread
the fire of fanaticism far and wide, till the half-savage
tribes assembled in thousands to fight for their fertile
valleys, their hearths and homes, and above all their
faith.

General Chamberlain, finding that his sojourn in the
Umbeyla pass was likely to be rather prolonged, moved
his position to the right, so as to occupy higher ground
than that he held before, overlooking the pass below. But
another step was necessary to render his position secure,
and that was to provide safer communication with his
supports than the roadway through the pass itself afforded,
which might at any time be closed by the enemy, who,
occupying the heights on each side, could oppose very
serious obstacles in the way of an advancing party, and cut
off supplies. With this object in view, a road was marked
out by the engineers from our right defence to the rear
over the slopes of the Mahabun, and at the same time
another rough roadway was sketched out to facilitate the
advance from the comparatively elevated position the
force now held, when the time should come to push on.
Working parties of the 71st and 101st had been employed
upon the road protected by covering parties, but their defence was difficult; for the spurs of the Mahabun mountain,
as before mentioned, projected into the valley in parallel
ridges, "part covered with firs, and encumbered with

enormous rocks, and the intervening rocks are so precipitous that, to protect the workmen on one ridge, it was
necessary to detach armed parties to the next. The result
of this was, that the covering parties, although their actual
distance from camp was not great, were very isolated, as
owing to the ravines it was impossible to communicate
with or reinforce them except by first ascending the mountain and then passing down the particular ridge on which
they were posted."[1]

Friday, the sacred day among the Mahommedans, was
a day of prayer with the Bonairs ; and it was also the day
for their most desperate and determined sallies. On the
6th November (Friday) our pioneers had nearly completed
their work, and felt secure under the protection of their
covering parties ; but as the enemy was observed collecting
in great force at the bottom of the pass, about the hour of
midday, it was deemed necessary to withdraw the unarmed
workmen, which was done in good time ; but some mis-
conception of orders appears to have taken place regarding
the covering parties, the most advanced of which consisted
of fifty Europeans of H.M. 71st, under Ensign Murray of
that corps, and about the same number of natives of the
20th Regiment, under Captain Rogers, who being senior
commanded this unlucky body of a hundred men, now
becoming gradually surrounded by the enemy. Behind
Captain Rogers' party was a second under Major Harding,
to whom the previous day the general command of the
working and covering parties had been entrusted. About
eight hundred or a thousand yards still further to the rear
was a picket of the 1st Punjab Infantry and the 20th Native
Infantry under Major Keyes. The ground was a mountain
crest and side, thickly covered with fir and jungle, so steep,
precipitous, and rugged, that of the three parties posted
there no one knew the exact position of the other, and all
were a mile distant from the support of Keyes' picket. The
enemy collecting in force, the working party, according

[1] "The Sittana Campaign," by Col. Adye, C.B., Royal Artillery; 1867.

to instructions previously given, began to withdraw, and Murray's party, also being much pushed, retired towards its support. On its way it fell in with the 5th Goorkhas. Captain Rogers' party, a little further down the slope, was actively engaged, and Murray and Oliphant, hearing the sharp firing, joined him. By this time he was so encumbered with his wounded that he dared not attempt to retire, fearing no less than the enemy the displeasure of the general, without permission from whom no officer dared relinquish a post to which he had been appointed. The firing increased, and the difficulty of retreat became momentarily greater, because of the increasing number of casualties. The three detachments then took up a position under cover of an elevated ridge of rock, which acted as a breastwork, but served the double purpose, also, of a screen under whose shelter the determined Bonairs advanced, making excellent practice with their matchlocks. To raise the head above the ridge was certain death, and a cap or a piece of cloth held up as a decoy was riddled in a moment by the enemy's shot. Murray was the first to fall, wounded in the neck whilst peering over the breastwork to reconnoitre the enemy's movements. He fell back dead. Oliphant was also wounded in the shoulder. Major Harding, perceiving the importance of extricating the party from their perilous position, wrote urgently for assistance, and the note was carried by a gallant little Goorkha soldier, who ran the gauntlet through a perfect hailstorm of bullets. For a long time—for minutes in such circumstances seem hours—no answer came, and when it arrived it was in the shape of an order to retire, but without reinforcements. The mountain train guns, however, from Keyes' picket opened an effective fire, dropping shells in among the enemy's position. After trying several devices to deceive the enemy, sounding bugle calls to induce them to suppose that reinforcements were coming down the gorge, Harding ordered Oliphant and all the wounded who could walk to retire with Captain

Rogers and the detachment of the 20th, while he remained to hold the enemy at bay a little longer. The picket was about a mile and a quarter distant, and to this spot the party now under Captain Rogers made good their retreat. Harding and his party, after holding the enemy at bay a little while, followed as well as they could, but their gallant commander fell with a bullet wound in the neck. The Goorkhas tried to convey him away, but the enemy rushed on, cutting and slashing at them, killing poor Major Harding on the back of a gallant little Goorkha soldier, who was trying to carry him off.[1] One of the men of the 71st, who had been unable to keep up with his comrades, remained all night concealed beneath a bush among the dead and dying, watching the savage mountaineers stripping and mutilating the dead, and killing the wounded who were unable to escape.

This temporary success gave great encouragement to the enemy, and during the next few days they received reinforcements of 3,000 men from the distant territory of Bajour.

The Craig picket on our right had been more than any other point of our position the object of the enemy's attack. The movement of a portion of the force on to the elevated ground on the right of the pass, which preceded the transfer of the whole camp to that spot, as well as the construction of the road from the right rear towards the plain, led the enemy to believe that some intention of retreating from his position was in the mind of the British general. Buoyed up with this hope, excited by the repeated appeals to their patriotism and religious zeal, and encouraged by the accession of large reinforcements, they prepared for a combined and desperate attack on the Craig picket, on the night of the 12th November. About dusk the horde of men who had been seen collecting during the day, advanced, yelling and screaming, beating drums and blowing shrill pipes, towards the right of our

---

[1] Colonel Adye.

position and the Craig picket, which was held by Lieut. Davidson of the 1st Punjab Infantry, fifteen sharpshooters of the 101st, and some sepoys of the 14th Native Infantry. The nearer they came the more invisible they were ; for breaking up into single file they crept stealthily, like beasts of prey, shielded by rocks and trees, while the whole night they kept up an incessant and galling fire. At dawn they made a rush upon the picket, and the garrison, surrounded by hundreds of desperate combatants, were forced to retire. But Davidson and a small band of sepoys, who would not desert their commandant, as he would not desert his post, were cut to pieces. The loss of this outwork was a most serious disaster. It completely overlooked the other defences, so much so that the ground below was scarcely tenable while that was occupied by a determined enemy ; and, to add to the gravity of the crisis, many of the camp-followers, mule and camel drivers, becoming now fairly disheartened, began to fly. Sir Neville Chamberlain, who was in the camp below when the picket fell into the hands of the enemy, had his attention drawn to the noise and dust and confusion caused by the rush of the camp-followers and animals down the hill, and, feeling certain some reverse must have happened, immediately ordered forward the 101st under Colonel Salusbury, which gallant regiment was fortunately under arms at the moment. The Craig picket must be recaptured, and at any risk, and Colonel Salusbury was directed to do it. Immediately the order was given six companies of the 101st, like antelopes, sped up the gorge, then over the level ground from which arose the ridge held by the enemy, and, with a cheer, the soldiers bounded over the breastwork and drove the Bonairs helter-skelter down the hill the other side. Colonel Salusbury and his gallant regiment was well supported by Major Ross and part of the Ferozepore Regiment, and an officer named Inglis, of the 14th Native Infantry, was one of the first who were inside the sunga.

For the next few days there was a lull, the enemy making no fresh attack, and General Chamberlain took advantage of it to complete the movement already described, throwing back his left flank, and concentrating his whole force upon the right. On the 19th, Major James, the Commissioner of Peshawur, arrived in camp, having just returned from England. This officer's presence was worth a division; he had been for years in Civil employ upon this frontier, he knew more about the country and the neighbouring tribes than any officer in India, and had the most extraordinary influence among them. His return from England had been anxiously expected; but by the time he reached the camp matters had progressed far beyond the point where the influence of a diplomatic officer could be of much avail, except to keep those who were wavering true to their allegiance to the British Government.

No sooner had the new disposition of our camp been completed, and the ground so long held on the left of the gorge under the " Eagle's nest " deserted, than the enemy made a demonstration in force, headed by a mounted chief. Their advance was greeted by a fire from our artillery, and the chieftain's horse was seen to falter and fall; the gallant rider, however, undaunted, pursued his way on foot, and directed the attack upon a picket held by Lieutenant Mosely, who defended the post with a party of sepoys till all the ammunition he had was exhausted, when, with his men following him, he bravely leaped over the stone parapet, and charged the enemy with the bayonet. He was overpowered and cut to pieces with several of his detachment. He had not fallen, however, without an attempt having been made to render him assistance. Major Ross and Lieutenant Inglis, supported by a company of the 71st Highlanders, under command of Captain Smith, advanced to his support, but were driven back; Captain Smith and another officer, Lieutenant Jones, being killed, Major Ross slightly wounded, and Lieutenant Inglis dangerously so with a bayonet. Lieutenant Chapman attempted to bring away Captain Smith's body, but was shot in the shoulder while raising it; he endeavoured to speak a few words to Major Ross, but died ere he could articulate his last wishes. None of our killed or wounded could be brought away, neither on that day nor on the next, the 19th, when a party went out for the purpose but returned unsuccessful. The next day a chance shot killed Lieutenant Aldridge of the 71st, and two men in the picket, and wounded Lieutenant Stockley, of the 101st, in both arms.

On the 20th, which was Friday, another desperate attack was made on the Craig picket, and was again successful. It was held then by Major Delafosse, one of the few survivors of the horrors of Cawnpore, Captain Goad, Lieutenant Sanderson, and Dr. Pile, with two companies of the 101st. The sudden assault of the enemy, accompanied with a tremendous matchlock fire and the usual yelling and beating of drums, for a moment startled from his propriety one of the few officers and a company of the 101st, but Delafosse bravely held on with Sanderson and Dr. Pile and the other company till further resistance was hopeless. Pile and Sanderson lay dead, together with twenty-six out of a company of fifty men.

Great was the rejoicing of the enemy at thus wresting for the third time this important post from the hands of British soldiers. But they were not allowed to retain it. Then, as before, it must be retaken at any cost, and the 71st Highlanders, under their gallant leader Colonel Hope, the 5th Goorkhas, and some of the 5th Punjab Infantry under Captain Beckett, with Sir Neville Chamberlain and his staff, and Major Keyes and several other officers, advanced to the assault. Under a perfect storm of matchlock balls and showers of stones hurled from the summit, Colonel Hope deliberately formed his men at the foot of the Craig, and sending the Goorkhas to turn the enemy's flank, he placed himself at the head of his corps, and, with a cool determination which excited the admiration not only of his own men but of every soldier in the force, proceeded to scale the height. Shot and shell were poured upon the brave garrison of the picket by Major Salt's battery, which throughout the whole war did excellent service, and the hearts of the Bonairs failed them as Colonel Hope and his Highlanders mounted the crest of the hill, and they evacuated the post ere the bayonets were upon them. The picket was thus retaken for the third time and the last, but at a great sacrifice. General Chamberlain was badly wounded, Colonel Hope also ; Colonel Wylde and Colonel Vaughan, Colonel Tyler and Major Campbell slightly, and Lieutenant Anderson shot through the arm, and one of the officers of the 101st disabled for the time by being struck repeatedly with the stones which the enemy hurled on the advancing force.

This attack of the 20th November proved to be the last attempt on the part of the enemy to drive us from our position. A change now came over the spirit of the scene. What war could not effect, diplomacy and personal influence, combined with the persistent bravery of our troops, began to accomplish, and Major James induced several of the tribes of lesser note to abandon the enemy's cause and return to their homes. They were, however, still strong ; 6,000 men from the province of Dher, under their leader Ghuzzim Khan, having joined the Akhoond. Meantime, every day brought large reinforcements nearer and nearer General Chamberlain's position. That officer was indeed unable to take any further active part in the operations, owing to the very severe wound he had received, and Major-General Garvock, who had earned distinction and gained experience in the frontier operations at the Cape, arrived to take the command. At one time it was proposed to retire. It has been related in a previous chapter how the suggestion of abandoning our position in the confusion and disheartenment that followed on Lord Elgin's death came to be entertained, how it was scouted by Sir Hugh Rose, acquiesced in by the Council at Calcutta, but finally rejected by Sir William Denison.

A war policy having been determined upon, the only safe and prudent policy under the circumstances, no effort was spared nor time lost in carrying it out effectually. A brigade was assembled at a place called Hoti Murdan, about half-way between the Umbeyla pass and Peshawur, under Colonel Shipley of the 7th Fusiliers, to threaten Swat by another entrance called the Loond Khwar pass, composed of one troop of the 7th Hussars, 100 sabres of the Guide cavalry, Bunney's battery, some of the 7th Royal Fusiliers, and three companies of the 3d Sikhs; but by Major James's advice a move on Swat was not attempted. The troops in camp at Umbeyla, reinforced and under command of General Garvock, were divided into two brigades.[1]

On the 10th December negotiations had so far advanced that the chiefs of Bonair came into camp and had an interview with the Commissioner. They left again the next day, having agreed that they would now aid the British troops in accomplishing the destruction of the Hindustanee fanatic settlement at Mulka, and promising to accompany them. The negotiation, however, came to nothing, public feeling in the enemy's camp being too strong for the Bonair chiefs, and further hostilities were inevitable. Still, no move was made till the 14th, when messengers arrived with the intelligence that the Akhoond and the other leaders, as well as the tribes themselves, refused compliance with our terms. The next day, the 15th, General Garvock moved out to the attack.

---

[1] First Brigade, under the command of Colonel Turner :—Peshawur Mountain Train ; 71st Highland Light Infantry ; 7th Royal Fusiliers ; 5th Goorkha Regiment ; 1st Punjab Infantry ; 3d Punjab Infantry ; 5th Punjab Infantry ; 20th Regiment Native Infantry ; 32d Regiment Native Infantry.

Second Brigade under Colonel Wylde :—H.M. 101st Foot ; Guides ; Heavy Guns ; Huzara Mountain Train ; 6th Regiment Punjab Infantry ; 14th Regiment Punjab Infantry ; 23d Regiment Punjab Infantry.

About two miles beyond the Craig picket stood the village
of Laloo, and a few hundred yards in front of it one of the
great spurs running up from the Chumla valley terminated
in a lofty peak dominating the whole ridge.[1] Here the
enemy had established themselves in great force, and,
judging by the number of banners they kept flying, seemed
determined to make a stand. It was a conical hill, more
precipitous and considerably higher than the Craig picket ;
measuring its elevation by the eye, it appeared about 500
feet from the base to the summit. This position, strong
naturally, had been further strengthened by a long breastwork, running completely across its summit, and down the
steep towards Laloo. The scenery amid which the troops
marched to the attack was strikingly beautiful. The road
or rugged pathway led along the summit of the mountains,
covered with large fir-trees, interspersed with patches of
level land adapted for cultivation. Here and there small
stone breastworks had been thrown up, but these were
undefended.

As the several regiments approached the formidable
position they were destined to assault, they were formed
up under shelter of the higher ground, Colonel Turner's
brigade being on the right. When all was reported ready,
General Garvock gave the order to advance. It was a
grand and imposing sight ; for what might be wanting in
the number of those engaged, to lend it the interest which
attaches to great battles, and military movements on a large
scale, was supplied by the romantic nature of the surrounding scenery ; the grey rocks alternating with the green
foliage of the trees, and in pretty contrast with the many-
coloured uniforms of the different troops engaged, the picturesque costumes of the enemy, the rocky heights whereon
they had entrenched themselves, and the rough crags behind
which their sharpshooters lay concealed. Conspicuous in
front of the advancing force were the scarlet uniforms of
the 101st Fusiliers, a regiment which has been in the

[1] Colonel Adye.

thickest of the fight in almost every action that has been fought since Plassey, and always distinguished itself; but the natives, the Goorkhas, Sikhs, and Pathans, vied with their European comrades in the struggle to be the first upon the foe. From behind every rock and shrub at the foot of the conical hill, small parties of the enemy jumped up and fled as the advancing columns approached. To cross the level ground was the work of but a few seconds, then the foot of the hill was reached and the ascent began. From stone to stone, from rock to rock, from shrub to shrub, rifle in hand, the soldiers steadily breasted the hill-side, and when the summit was gained, with a terrific yell, leapt over the breastworks and plied the bayonet upon the now disheartened enemy. Ere many minutes had elapsed, the peak from top to bottom was in the possession of British soldiers. The *dénouement* of the affair was so sudden when the advance had once commenced, that a good many weapons were recovered, coats, blankets, &c., and some banners with Arabic devices. The 101st and Guides remained to hold the place till the destruction of Laloo had been completed by Colonel Turner's brigade, which had been sent round to the right against the town, while the direct assault was being made by the brigade under Colonel Wylde.

The next morning at daylight the force moved against Umbeyla, Colonel Wylde's brigade marching down direct upon it, accompanied by a regiment of Light Cavalry and Probyn's Horse, Colonel Turner's brigade meantime making a *détour* by Laloo. The enemy were at first driven up on a height in front of the village, but they abandoned that position directly the 101st Fusiliers, 3d Sikhs, 3d Punjab Native Infantry, and Guides approached, and fell back skirting the edge of the hills under cover of the broken ground. The heights leading up to the Gooroo mountain and the Bonair pass were crowded by armed men, who swarmed there in thousands; but they were disheartened, and afraid to venture from their fastnesses, whence they looked on while the cavalry scoured the plain and set fire to the village of Umbeyla.

Driven at last to the utmost state of exasperation, a party of them descended and attacked with the most sudden and desperate ferocity a line formed of the 23d and 32d Pioneers. So furiously did the mountaineers dash upon the 23d, which was commanded by Captain Chamberlain, that it wavered for a minute or two, and the commandant only preserved his own life by cutting down two of his opponents and wounding a third, he himself receiving a bad wound in the face. Lieutenant Alexander, another officer of that regiment, was killed, Lieutenant Nott badly hurt, and some thirty men *hors de combat.* Two companies of the 7th Fusiliers coming up to the support, the 23d rallied, and, supported by the 32d, charged the enemy and speedily drove them back. Meantime three field-guns under Captain Griffin (the officer who, as has been related in another chapter, was killed subsequently at the siege of Dhalimkote in Bhotan, by the bursting of a gun) had been shelling the heights, and the mountaineers, driven from the plains and unable to find shelter even in the rocks and crags of their native hills, abandoned the contest in despair.

The enemy had been driven back, the village of Umbeyla destroyed, and the Chumla valley was in possession of our troops, but the original object of the campaign, the destruction of the settlement of the fanatics at Mulka, was as far from completion as ever. To evacuate our position without penetrating to Mulka would have been tantamount to a defeat ; but the chiefs of the Bonair, now deserted by their allies the Swatees and their Akhoond, the men of Bajour and Dher, and the other tribes who had come to their assistance, bethought themselves of making terms with the British Government, so they re-opened the negotiations that had been on foot before the last operations which terminated in their defeat, and consented to send a large party, with a few British officers, to destroy the stronghold of Mulka. The chance was too good to be thrown away.

In addition to the great risk which would be encountered by detaching a body of British troops through a most difficult tract of country, and the risk of further embroilment with the excitable people who had given us so much trouble, the moral effect of the destruction of Mulka by the hands of the Bonairs themselves would be as great as if the work was accomplished by our own men. It would show that the coalition between the tribes lately in arms against us, founded as it was on the sympathy of religious belief and patriotism, was yet not strong enough to resist the pressure which the British Government could bring to bear. So it was agreed that a large party of Bonairs, accompanied by a few English officers and a small detachment of the Guides, should proceed against Mulka and destroy it. This famous stronghold proved to be a large, well-built village, recently constructed of pinewood, standing high on a northern slope of the Mahabun, whose snowy crest rose precipitously behind it, whilst in its front a vast panorama of mountains stretched away as far as eye could reach. The village contained numerous workshops and a rude powder factory, but was found deserted. It was fired in the presence of the English officers on the 22d December, and the great column of smoke, as it rose over the mountain-top, proclaimed that the object of the expedition had been at length accomplished. This, the final act of the war, was witnessed by a crowd of mountaineers belonging to the minor tribes of the Mahabun, who gradually collected near the spot and angrily watched the conflagration. There was sorrow as well as anger expressed by their sullen looks, for in the village were many fresh graves of relatives who had fallen during the campaign ; and what also deeply moved them was the hated presence of Englishmen in a part of the country hitherto sacred from intrusion. As there seemed a probability of their proceeding to acts of violence, they were addressed by Colonel Taylor, the late commissioner, and by an influential chief of Bonair ; and at length they went away silently to their homes, and the English officers with their escort marched back to the Chumla valley. On Christmas Day the troops left the mountains, and stood once more in the plains of Eusofzye, the mountaineers destroyed the entrenchment, breaking up the road as they marched away, and the war was at an end.[1]

If the political advantages secured by the Umbeyla campaign were not very great, the Indian Government at any rate learned experience. The whole of the delay, expense, and the risk encountered by Sir Neville Chamberlain was occasioned chiefly from the fault to which British officers are so prone, of underrating the enemy. It was perhaps all for the best, as matters turned out, that the route through the Umbeyla pass was so much more difficult than had been anticipated, as to force a halt. For, looking at the matter in the light which the experience of subsequent events throws upon it, there can be little doubt that had the force, as originally intended, pushed through the pass and penetrated to Mulka, it would have found it extremely difficult to get back again, and it might have been forced to halt further on in a position where communication with its own supports was a great deal more difficult than it was at Umbeyla. However, in the Black Mountain campaign, which was undertaken towards the latter end of 1868, the lesson learnt at Umbeyla was not forgotten, and no onward move was made till a sufficient force had been collected to overpower all opposition.

The Black Mountain is a high oblong range running nearly due north and south. It is on the left bank of the Indus, and on the opposite side of the river to Mahabun and Sittana, and thus, of course, nearer our own territory. It is flanked on the west by Cashmere and on the south by Huzara, the principal settlement in which is called Abbottabad. Between this place and the Black Mountain is a tract of country called the Agror valley, in which is situated the village of Oghee, where we have a police

[1] Colonel Adye.

station. The immediate cause of the offensive operations undertaken in 1868 was an attack on the police station at Oghee in the Agror valley by a party of the Hussunzai tribe. This was the culminating point of the offences of the Hussunzaies, and although the police behaved so well that the assailants were driven away with loss, yet it was deemed necessary to send a force into their country and exact reparation of some kind for the insult offered to the British Government. General Wylde, whose name has been so often mentioned in connexion with the Umbeyla affair, had succeeded to the command of the frontier, and directed the operations of the campaign.

It was in the height of the hot season that the attack had been made, and, in spite of the risk attending the movement of troops at that time of the year, active measures were taken to collect an overwhelming force upon the frontier, so as to be ready to meet any combination of the tribes should the excitement spread, as it had done previously in the Umbeyla campaign. The troops were massed under the orders of the Commander-in-chief without in any way weakening the frontier garrisons, regiments and detachments being moved up from stations as far distant as Allyghur, south of Delhi. All these preparatory measures took time, and it was not till the 26th September that the advanced part of the expedition moved from Abbottabad into the valley. The whole force was divided into two brigades, the first being under command of Brigadier-General Bright, and the second under Brigadier-General Vaughan. Three pretty and pleasant marches along a good road brought the General and his staff, with the last, or nearly the last, regiments of the force, to Oghee; and all the arrangements, military and commissariat, &c., having been completed by the morning of the 3d October, the two brigades, leaving all their sick and weakly men at Oghee, commenced their march against the tribes of the Black Mountain.

The entrance to the Agror valley is by a long and

sloping and tolerably easy pass, known by the name of the
Soosul pass. This position, as well as that of two other
passes and the camp at Oghee, was held by a contingent
which the Maharaja of Cashmere had sent down to our
assistance. On one of the spurs of the Black Mountain at
the northern end of the Agror valley, near the base, was
the village of Koòn Gullee, and at the summit of the spur,
one of the most elevated peaks of the mountain, was a
height called the Muchaie Peak. It soon became apparent
that this Muchaie Peak should be the main object of
attack. The 1st and 2d Brigades, under the command
respectively of Brigadiers-General Bright and Vaughan,
were to operate in different lines. The enemy had during
our stay at Oghee, and almost up to the moment of our
advance, shown in considerable numbers at the village of
Koon Gullee ; and whilst a portion of the 1st Brigade, led
by the 20th Punjab Native Infantry, closely followed by
H.M. 19th Regiment, assaulted this village by the direct
road through Dilbooree, a village at the most northerly
point of the Agror valley, a flank attack was to be made by
the 2d Goorkhas, and other regiments of the 2d Brigade,
upon the heights of Koon Gullee, by an approach from
the east. For this purpose a portion of the 2d Brigade
during the morning's advance had been deflected to the
right, and it was expected that this column of attack
would reach the Koon Gullee height about the same time
as the troops advancing in front.

While the 1st Brigade, with the head-quarters following,
were thus manœuvring, the main portion of the 2d Brigade
had been directed to advance toward the Black Mountain
range by a spur near to Oghee, known as the Sumbhul
Bhoot spur. Alternately the whole of the 2d Brigade,
on the completion of the flank attack on the east side of
Koon Gullee, was to proceed along the same spur of
Sumbhul Bhoot. The point they were told to make good
in the first instance was the fort of Killaghyc, held by a
friendly chief ; and had this movement been carried out

according to the original idea, the 2d Brigade would have reached the crest of the Black Mountain range by a spur known as the Akhoon Baba-ka-Choora, at a point considerably to the south of the Chutterbul Peak, where the 1st Brigade was ultimately to make good its position on the ridge. On the morning of the advance from Oghee it was not thought probable that the 1st Brigade would by that evening secure any position in advance of Koon Gullee, at the bottom of the spur, by which the crest of the Black Mountain was ultimately to be reached. Owing, however, to the vigour of the advance, more especially of the 20th Punjab Native Infantry under their gallant chief Colonel Brownlow, the direct line of attack having caused the enemy to evacuate hastily the village of Koon Gullee, the force was pushed some four miles further up the hill the same evening (Saturday); and ultimately the 20th, made good their position at Munna-ka-Dunna. An abattis of boughs and earth was thrown up, behind which the 20th entrenched themselves for the night.

There is no doubt whatever that Colonel Brownlow, or General Bright, or whoever the officer to whom the praise is due, acted with consummate judgment in pushing on to Munna-ka-Dunna; for had our troops rested content with their success at Koon Gullee, and halted there for the night, the enemy, firing at them from the exceedingly steep heights above Koon Gullee, would have terribly galled their pickets. At Munna-ka-Dunna the spur of the Black Mountain along which the 1st Brigade was advancing takes a little dip. The ground then becomes almost level for a few yards, after which it gradually ascends to a position where the enemy had assembled in some force at about 7,200 yards in advance of the foremost picket of the 20th Native Infantry. The 20th, by occupying this position, and throwing out an advance entrenched picket half-way down the slope, obtained for themselves against an attacking enemy exactly the advantage which the latter would have enjoyed had our troops remained at Koon

Gullee ; that is to say, the enemy could now only advance
up the slope to attack them.   They did advance once and
again ; and indeed this was the only occasion on which the
enemy showed any real pluck at all.   It is needless to say
their attacks made but little impression on the gallant
20th, whose men jeered and taunted the enemy, daring
them to come on.   It was not to be expected, of course,
that this success could' be achieved without casualties on
our side.   As the brunt of the attack fell upon the 20th
Native Infantry, so upon them fell all the loss.   Three men
were killed and four wounded up to Sunday morning.
General Wylde's head-quarters were at Dilbooree, but on
Saturday evening, when the advance column had driven
the enemy out of Koon Gullee, which is about a mile or
more above Dilbooree, the head-quarters were established
at Koon Gullee, where they bivouacked for the night.

As the day dawned, the enemy were obliged to draw
off from Brigadier-General Bright's position.   Our list of
casualties was small, but it was clear to the General commanding that unless an immediate advance was made the
harassing night attacks would be incessantly renewed in
constantly increasing strength.   Accordingly, on the morning of the 4th October, the 1st Brigade attacked the enemy's
position, upon which a well-directed fire of artillery had
long been maintained.   The force engaged consisted of
the 1st and 5th Goorkhas, the Huzara and Peshawur
mountain batteries, the 2d and the 20th Punjab Infantry,
and H.M. 19th Foot, 1st battalion.   The enemy made but
little stand against this overwhelming array, and Brigadier-
General Bright, after a rapid march and a short but sharp
contest, was in possession of the Chutterbul Peak on the
crest of the Black Mountain.   In the meantime the 2d
Brigade had reached Munna-ka-Dunna, and the 2d Goorkhas and 3d Sikh regiment were thrown forward to occupy
the breastwork from which the enemy had been driven in
the morning.   On the next morning, the 5th, the Muchai
Peak, a stronghold 10,200 feet above the level of the sea,

deemed inaccessible by the natives, was carried. The 6th was passed in completing a road which had been commenced up to the crest of the hill ; plenty of good water was found, and the troops had abundant supplies. Indeed, both public despatches and private accounts of this campaign are unanimous in speaking in the highest terms of the commissariat arrangements under Colonel Dickens. On the morning of the 7th the enemy had made no sign of submission, and a party was detached to destroy the village of the Pararee Syads, some of the most determined tribes arrayed against us. The 8th and 9th were passed in negotiations with the heads of the offending clans, who came into camp soliciting terms ; and the negotiations, which were somewhat accelerated by the burning of some more villages, resulted in a patched-up peace being concluded on the 10th with the chief Pathan clans. The 11th and 12th were occupied in withdrawing troops and stores to the camp of Munna-ka-Dunna, and after a kind of triumphant march through the adjacent villages, intended to impress the mountaineers with an idea of the imposing force that could be brought against them, even into fastnesses deemed inaccessible, the troops moved back to their camp at Oghee.

A great deal of dissatisfaction was expressed in India at the sudden termination of a campaign from which greater results were anticipated by those who were unacquainted with the views and policy of the Government. And none were so loud in denouncing what was called the pusillanimity of the Government as the officers of the force engaged.

It is one of the misfortunes of Indian administration that there is no machinery at hand for laying before the public the line of policy which the Government has marked out, and indicating the object and purpose of a military expedition. In Europe a declaration of war precedes active operations, and whether the object is to recover prisoners from captivity, to amend a line of frontier, or to

realize an idea, the public have some notion beforehand of
what it is intended to accomplish. In India the favourite
official theory is that there is no public. But it is a fatal
mistake; for every action of the Government is narrowly
watched by a public which, if it is wanting in individual
character in its component parts, numbers a good many
millions of people. The elaborate preparations which preceded the Black Mountain campaign gave rise to the belief
that operations were intended on a scale commensurate
with the expense incurred. Just at the time the army was
assembled, there was a good deal of excitement in the
native mind owing to exaggerated reports of Russian
advance, and the affairs of Affghanistan were, even for that
turbulent country, in a disorganized condition. Throughout
India, and from the Peshawur frontier right up to Cabul,
and no doubt far beyond, the report spread far and wide
that the British Government was massing troops upon the
Indus, with the intention of developing at last some decisive
policy in Central Asia. The next rumour spread abroad
was that after a few skirmishes this grand army had been
taken back to quarters and dispersed; and there is no doubt
it was generally said and believed that the British troops
had retreated in consequence of the attitude assumed by
the frontier tribes. Had a proclamation been issued in the
Government *Gazette* before the operations commenced,
setting forth the object of the campaign, and intimating
the line of policy to be pursued, the loss of prestige which
has undoubtedly followed upon one of the most successful
and best-conducted military expeditions which has been
undertaken on that frontier, ever since the annexation of the
Punjab, would have been avoided. In many respects the
history of the Black Mountain campaign resembles that of
the Abyssinian expedition, of which England is so justly
proud. The force advanced far into a difficult country, the
troops marched so lightly equipped that shelter and food
were as scarce as they were in Abyssinia, though the
deprivation did not last for so long a period. Formidable

heights were taken by the sword and bayonet, and mountain fastnesses stormed in defiance of an enemy who, though unfitted for fighting in plain country, was no despicable antagonist—as he proved at Umbeyla and on the Black Mountain—when fighting on his own ground and in his own fashion.

Still there can be no doubt that the policy which the Government carried out was sound and prudent, for these frontier tribes may be made far more useful to us as friends than they are dangerous as enemies. We have seen what they can effect in the latter capacity. It is troublesome to have our frontier posts attacked, the districts harried, the villagers molested and robbed, and "kafilas" interfered with. But after all these are matters of minor importance. It is not likely such practices will ever be wholly put down. Suppressed they should be, of course, and retribution exacted, but they cannot become matters of national or imperial interest. As for an invasion of the plain country by these tribes in force, we know that alone they would never attempt it. They might in the wake of an invading host sweep down upon a prey already deprived of the power of resistance; but of themselves, or backed by an Asiatic host, however numerous, they would not stand five minutes in level open country against our disciplined troops. On the plains they are as helpless as a shark upon dry land, but on their native hills they are formidable. As a bulwark to British India, a key to lock the gates, and bar all ingress, these tribes are absolutely invaluable to us. We gain nothing by carrying fire and sword in among their homesteads. We only sow the seeds of a blood feud, which no time can obliterate; give rise to deep-seated feelings of revenge and enmity, which will for ever prevent a reconciliation. By showing them that our troops can with comparative ease scale their heights and seize their fastnesses, by a little well-timed severity, but no excessive measures, we teach them that we are strong enough to punish and too powerful to be afraid.

To tame an untamed man or animal, excess of rigour defeats the object. Violence and cruelty will instil fear, but fear alone will not engender confidence. Show that you are able to punish disobedience, and by gentle treatment you may win attachment.

Conquest would not serve our purpose in dealing with this frontier, unless indeed we annex the country beyond these hills; and then nothing but absolute subjugation of the tribes will answer our purpose. When that line of policy is adopted (and we may be pretty sure it never will be), it will be necessary to carry fire and sword into pretty nearly every village and stronghold in the mountains; and no doubt we could do it, if it was to be done. We are quite strong enough to annihilate these people by degrees, to subjugate the country as the Russians have done Circassia; but that measure was imperatively necessary to Russia, because she intended to advance further east, and she dared not leave a formidable enemy in the rear of her advanced posts; and when we take up a similar position here, the same policy will become necessary for us. But in these frontier tribes, strong in their native mountains, nature has given us a shield and a barrier, and it is our own fault if we do not use it.

It should be our policy to establish such a connexion with them that we can, when it suits our purpose to do so, get them to close the passes; and when we have done that, the frontier of British India, from Huzara to the sea-coast of Scinde, will be simply impregnable.

CHAPTER XVI.

THE comparative importance of the subject of education
in India is not to be gauged by the space accorded to it
in a work of the present kind. In every difficulty that
meets us in the consideration or treatment of measures
designed to further the cause of commercial progress or
of political security in India, we involuntarily recur to
the one solution of every problem—education. Is it the
obstacle in the way of an extended circulation of a paper
currency that puzzles the financier? The remedy is education. Are we hampered by a necessary restriction of
expenditure in the matter of public works of general
utility, by reason of the enormous drain upon the resources
of the country for a military establishment without which
it is vain to hope that disaffection can be suppressed and
political excitement subdued? The remedy is education.
Are we dismayed at the slow pace with which liberal
ideas make good their advance against the obstruction
of ignorance, bigotry, and superstition? The remedy is
education. Are we puzzled at the strange anomaly presented by a whole race, or races, preferring the arbitrary
and capricious despotism of native governments to the

organized administration of British rule? We know that
it is to the schoolmaster chiefly we must look to aid in
removing from the mental vision of the people the veil
that shuts out the light. Do we ask how we shall raise
the agricultural population of India to the status of a free
community? The answer is education. Do we ask how
to secure permanent and lasting peace, apart, of course,
from the distant danger of foreign invasion? The answer
is education. Do we ask how we shall break the fetters
of caste that bind millions of our fellow-subjects in social
bondage? The answer is education. Do we wonder how
it is that, after a century and a half of intercourse, the
people of India are still as far separated from us as if
there were scarce the bond of a common nature to unite
us to each other? The answer is to be found in the
slender efforts and the slow progress of education.

Here, as in all other subjects connected with Indian progress, the great difficulty which besets the English reader
is the impossibility of realizing the enormous extent of
country, and the vastness of the area over which our efforts
must extend before we can hope to effect any sensible improvement. And in addition to this, there is the inertness
of the mass we have to move. An Englishman accustomed
to the energy of the Anglo-Saxon or the Celtic character,
the freedom of thought, the signs of activity and life which
beset him at every turn in his own country, can form no
idea of the deadness and apathy of the Asiatic mind. The
difference between national character in the West and East
somewhat resembles that between youth and old age.
In the one there is vigour, energy, self-dependence, a
generous confiding spirit, a looking forward to the future,
a constant struggle to improve; in the other, lassitude, indifference, a tendency to lean on others, to be satisfied
with things as they are rather than undergo the exertion
necessary to effect a change. Unable to help himself, the
feeble octogenarian must have everything done for him;
and if in ministering to his wants his attendants do not

always consult his ease and convenience, he finds fault with all their efforts, grows suspicious, and misinterprets their best intentions.

In so extended a field, and under such conditions, the progress of education must necessarily be very slow. We cannot expect to witness in the present generation many practical results from the efforts which, more especially of late years, have been made in this cause. Progress, of course, there must be among individual sections of the community, which come under the operations of our system of instruction. But, compared with the work of leavening the masses, such progress is infinitesimal. Still it is a commencement of a work whose importance cannot be overrated, for it is nothing else than imparting mental life and vigour to races numbering many millions, whom Nature seems to have compensated for the poverty of physical endowment by the gift of remarkable intellectual powers, which, though now dormant, are capable of being awakened into great activity. It would be vain, however, to look for much fruit from the influence which the present system is gradually working out, in so short a period as ten years. The comparative progress might indeed be shown by long tables of numerical returns, but they would be dry and uninteresting, and in themselves fail to give any real idea of the limits within which education has extended. The utmost I can attempt to do, without wearying the reader with a long array of bare tabulated statements, is to give in as few words as possible an outline of the results already attained by measures introduced since the great epoch of educational history, 1854. In doing this I shall avail myself of the information furnished in a very valuable report composed by Mr. Arthur Howell, of the Bengal Civil Service, now officiating Home Secretary, styled, "A Note on the State of Education in India in 1866-7," recently published.

The following table will show at once glance the present actual results of educational effort.

No. I.—Educational Statistics for 1866-7.

1	2	3	4	5 Colleges			6 Government Schools						7 Aided Schools						8	9 Pupils									10	11
Presidency or Province.	Area in square miles.	Estimated Population.	University.	Government For general educatn.	For special educatn.	Aided Colleges.	Upper.	Middle.	Lower.	Female.	Special.	Total.	Upper.	Middle.	Lower.	Female.	Special.	Total.	Total Colleges and Schools.	Colleges Government.	Colleges Aided.	Government Schools.	Aided Schools.	Female Schools Government.	Female Schools Aided.	Special Schools Government.	Special Schools Aided.	Total.	Proportion of Schools and Colleges to square miles—One in so many square miles.	Proportion of Pupils to population—One in
Bengal	217,331	37,789,430	1	8	8	6	46	127	84	1	32	290	78	987	1,269	257	5	2,596	2,908	1,254	325	19,635	85,414	55	6,168	1,362	972	115,185	74.6	328.
Bombay	137,743	15,775,113	1	2	3	1	9	191	1,357	61	7	1,626	6	13	23	...	12	56	1,687	364	...	104,178	4,954	1,935	1,193	298	143	113,045	81.6	139.5
Madras	104,438	28,276,265	1	2	4	...	14	68	14	...	...	106	16	212	971	75	5	1,279	1,391	185	151	8,042	35,205	8,981	3,109	1,558	616	48,866	75.07	578.6
N. W. Provs.	81,378	30,251,641	...	2	2	1	5	82	3,467	479	10	3,961	21	121	47	68	8	424	4,208	448	...	124,355	16,000	...	2,239	423	87	152,553	19.3	198.3
Punjab	100,466	15,166,157	...	3	...	...	24	10	296	6	8	2,096	7	16	651	2	...	751	2,823	31	10	11,033	6,553	81	14,243	279	107	97,658	35.5	155.2
Oude	20,243	8,320,647	...	...	...	...	10	34	264	6	2	316	4	73	38	12	4	70	386	...	...	70,277	3,416	...	327	293	...	15,154	52.4	549.5
Central Provs.	104,222	8,659,697	...	...	...	...	1	24	658	130	7	819	1	16	238	249	...	257	248	...	...	33,751	20,621	3,621	501	144	...	58,137	96.8	148.9
Britsh. Burmah	67,292	2,129,501	...	...	...	...	1	...	...	...	...	4	1	7	...	...	...	244	248	...	...	440	6,058	...	...	...	...	7,599	271.7	260.1
Hyderabad	17,334	1,586,047	...	...	...	...	23	...	122	2	...	147	4	2	16	8	...	244	147	...	...	6,644	...	...	569	63	...	6,644	117.8	238.7
Mysore	27,003	3,920,735	...	...	...	...	2	8	38	...	...	55	8	...	...	...	...	36	91	...	...	2,974	2,999	...	...	...	...	6,535	296.7	597.6
Coorg	1,800	118,100	...	...	...	...	7	1	24	...	...	25	...	...	...	...	...	...	25	...	...	946	...	...	...	...	...	946	27.	124.8

No. II.—Educational Statistics for 1866-7 (Eleven Months).

1 Presidency or Province	2 Expenditure from Imperial Funds	3 Local Funds	3 Private Expenditure	4 Total Expenditure on Education	5 Direction and Inspection	6 Instruction, including all charges not included in column 5	7 Imperial Expenditure in Government Colleges and Schools	8 Grants in aid, including payments by results	9 Percentage of column 7 on column 2	10 Percentage of column 8 on column 2	11 Colleges Government	11 Colleges Aided	11 Government Schools	11 Aided Schools	12 To Government	12 To other Funds	12 Total average cost
	Rupees.	Rupees.	Rupees.	Rupees.	Rupees.	Rupees.	Rupees.	Rupees.	Rupees.	Rupees.	Rps.	Rps.	R/s.	R/s.	R/s.	R/s.	R/s.
Bengal	13,85,762	4,96,708	4,08,221	22,90,691	2,27,010	20,63,081	6,98,844	3,12,183	50.43	23.97	219.9	64.	20.	3.3	12.	7.8	19.8
Bombay	9,16,678	6,01,629	Not given	15,18,307	1,64,105	13,54,202	4,63,572	76,682	50.5	7.7	181.2	...	3.7	3.1	8.1	5.7	13.4
Madras	6,16,074	1,16,090	...	7,32,164	1,23,495	6,08,669	3,10,911	1,21,271	50.4	19.6	236.1	32.08	27.9	2.9	12.6	2.3	14.9
N. W. Provs.	7,74,009	4,57,286	...	12,31,295	1,78,299	10,52,996	2,51,275	1,36,968	32.4	17.8	1211.5	554.6	1.8	7.4	3.	3.	8.07
Punjab	5,62,654	2,84,847	1,01,562	9,49,063	2,01,432	7,47,631	2,36,376	1,36,252	42.01	24.2	...	...	2.5	6.1	5.7	3.9	9.6
Oude	1,54,078	87,623	Not given	2,42,301	35,408	2,06,893	59,911	41,779	38.7	27.01	...	...	5.2	11.1	10.2	5.7	15.9
Central Provs.	1,56,402	2,34,269	...	3,90,731	70,884	3,19,847	70,030	18,086	44.7	14.1	...	...	1.8	.8	2.6	4.02	6.7
Brish. Burmah								No returns sent in for 1866-67.									
Hyderabad	84,246	...	Not given	84,246	18,579	65,667	65,667	...	77.9	...	...	...	9.8	...	12.6	...	12.6
Mysore	1,20,203	30,610	...	1,50,813	25,031	95,172	52,758	28,228	43.8	23.3	...	...	17.3	8.07	18.3	4.7	23.
Coorg	12,276	220	...	12,496	1,100	11,396	11,176	...	91.7	...	...	...	11.8	...	12.9	.2	13.2

Column 2 = Expenditure from Imperial Funds. Column 3 = Expenditure from Local Sources (Local Funds; Private Expenditure). Column 4 = Total Expenditure on Education. Analysis of Expenditure (cols. 5–8). Column 11 = Average annual cost to State per Pupil. Column 12 = Total annual average cost per Pupil under instruction.

By this we find that there are in all India, in the different establishments, colleges, schools, public and half-public and half-private, 622,342 students, not two-thirds of a million, amid an estimated population of one hundred and fifty-one millions, receiving instruction : a small proportion, though it is something to be instructing half a million of people. But the prospect of one hundred and fifty-one millions who want to be educated, and who mainly look to the Government to provide the means, is truly appalling.

The present system dates from the Despatch of 1854, which, besides sketching out the details of the educational establishment since developed, enforces as its main principle the necessity of Government action in aid of voluntary effort. The Court of Directors who were in power in 1857 were indeed somewhat over-sanguine in looking forward "to the time when any general system of education entirely provided by Government may be discontinued with the gradual advance of the system of grants in aid, and when many of the Government institutions, especially those of the higher order, may be safely closed or transferred to the management of local bodies under the control of and aided by the State." And they confidently expected that the introduction of the system of grants in aid would very largely increase the number of schools of a superior order; and that before long sufficient provision might be found to exist in many parts of the country for the education of the middle and higher classes, independent of the Government institutions, which might then be closed. But this expectation was never realized. In the ten years from 1856-7 to 1866-7 the expenditure of the State upon education increased from 195,494*l.*, when the Imperial revenues were 29,702,854*l.*, to 763,230*l.* in 1867, when the Imperial revenues were estimated at 46,752,800*l.* During the past year educational projects were submitted to the supreme Government involving an increased expenditure of 58,544*l.*, although at the commencement of that year an advance of 100,000*l.* was made upon the vote of the previous year; and the

assignment made at the commencement of the current year
of the report, 1867-8, shows an increase of 72,000*l.* over the
grant of the preceding year.

In the extension of educational efforts, no less than in
that of irrigation and other useful public works, it is of
course necessary to provide against a lavish expenditure
which will only waste the resources of the country, without
producing any adequate fruits. We have seen that the
late Viceroy was fully alive to the necessity of not undertaking larger irrigation works than there was a fair prospect of carrying out to completion, on the sound principle
that when working with borrowed money we ought to be
especially careful of extravagance. And it is doubtful
whether in some parts of India, if more money was placed
at the disposal of the Directors of Education, it could be
usefully employed. At least, in the North-West Provinces,
I am assured by the energetic Director of Public Instruction, Mr. Kempson, that even if Government were to place
more funds at his disposal, it is doubtful if he could find a
useful and profitable field for their expenditure. Yet the
great outcry from all parts of the country is for more
money. The Directors of Public Instruction in Bengal
Proper and Bombay demand that two per cent. of the total
revenue collected in the two provinces should be the State
contribution to education. And, as Mr. Howell very fairly
remarks, were these concessions made to these two provinces, they could not reasonably be refused to the other
provinces, which, excluding the Hyderabad assigned districts and Mysore, would entail an immediate increase of
244,255*l.* from the Imperial revenues. " In the present
state of the finances it is probable that, unless other departments are proportionately reduced, Sir Alexander Grant
and Mr. Atkinson, in asking for so large an increase to the
Imperial grant, are also asking for increased taxation."[1] It
is therefore urged that local agency must be indented upon
to supplement the grants from the Imperial funds; but

---

[1] Note on Education, p. 5.

"local agency" is only another word for taxation, and
whether the money be collected by means of a tax imposed
by an act of the Legislature, or by municipal bodies, makes
very little difference to the people who pay it. There may
be in some places less unwillingness to contribute money
which it is known will be expended in the immediate
neighbourhood, than if it were levied for Imperial purposes;
but it must not be forgotten that in either case the results
to the tax-payers are the same.

If the wealthier classes could be induced to recognise
their duty in this respect, and to acknowledge the obliga-
tion of making some sacrifice and some united effort to
assist in education, this appeal to local agency might come
to mean something very different from what it means now.
At present, throughout the greater part of India, it signifies simply a shifting on to local taxation burdens which
Imperial taxation is not able to meet.

In countries with which the English reader is mostly
familiar a very large proportion of the population will be
in no need of any State education at all. Among the
upper classes the value, the necessity, of education is so
fully recognised, that it is looked upon as one of the
ordinary conditions of life, as indispensable almost as food
and clothing. But in India the case is totally different.
And of the one hundred and fifty-one millions of the
population there are few who are not in want of instruction
as much as the five or six hundred thousand who are
already in the receipt of it. And if we are to go on
increasing our expenditure under this head till we meet
the demand, we must be content to see the whole resources
of the State swallowed up in accomplishing what after all
would be but a mere fraction of the whole task, at the
sacrifice of every other branch of the administration. It
would seem, therefore, that the most prudent course was
to proceed cautiously, being content to wait till the results
of the education now being imparted to the present generation awaken the desire for a further extension of the

benefits, which they will only then learn to appreciate whose minds have been enlarged by the training they are now receiving. Then, and then only, may we expect to see a voluntary effort, in some degree proportionate to the end to be accomplished, by which alone the gigantic task of educating the millions of India is to be achieved.

The principle of the Despatch of 1854 was sound, inasmuch as it recognised the only course which it is open to pursue, viz. voluntary effort aided by the State; that aid being measured by the extent of the voluntary contributions, an equivalent to which is payable in every case from the Imperial exchequer.

In some parts of India very considerable efforts have, indeed, been spontaneously made by the natives themselves in the cause of education. Thus at Lucknow the talookdars have founded a college, called after Lord Canning, in grateful remembrance of that statesman's services to the country, which is now one of the most successful institutions in Upper India, and an annual grant, equal in amount to the endowment given by the talookdars, is made from the Imperial revenues. The merchants of Bombay have contributed largely to similar institutions, and Sir Jamsetjee Jejeeboy's munificent liberality supplied no less than 200,000*l.* to charitable and educational institutions in his native city. Mr. Rustumjee Jamsetjee has offered 10,000*l.* for the promotion of English education in Guzerat and Bombay, besides, in conjunction with his brother, spending 1,200*l.* on the School of Arts in the presidency town. Mr. Chesetjee Furdinjee has founded a school in Surat; and Mr. Mungaldas Nathabhoy has founded a travelling scholarship for Hindoos in the Bombay University, at a cost of 2,000*l.*, and has endowed a professorship of economic science, as well as provided funds for building the Civil Engineering College at Poona.[1] Nor has Calcutta been behindhand in instances of munificent liberality on the part of wealthy natives.

[1] Mr. Algernon West's "Administration of Sir Charles Wood."

There has been a great deal of discussion lately, both in
Parliament and in the press, as to the extent to which the
public service of India should be open to the natives. It
is obvious that if they are to be expected to qualify themselves for competitive examinations for the Civil and other
services, a residence in England is almost a *sine quâ non*.
With the view of encouraging the natives to go to England
to complete their education, scholarships have recently
been established by the Government, worth 200*l.* a year or
thereabouts, in addition to an outfit and passage-allowance,
for those who qualify themselves. As yet, the number of
these scholarships is small ; but if the scheme is found to
answer, it will no doubt be extended. To complete the
design, however, some further step is necessary, in the
shape of a college or institution of some kind in the neighbourhood of London itself, where natives of India can
reside during their stay in England, and where they can be
received and looked after immediately on arrival. It is
worth considering whether some scheme might not be
designed for an Indian Civil Service College, an institution
much required to give the young civilian that special education for an Indian career which, since the abolishment
of Haileybury, has been unattainable, and in which the
natives of India who come to England to complete their
education might be brought up amid the atmosphere of
academical associations, and where they would derive that
benefit from academical discipline, and a regular system of
university training, of which, both in an intellectual and a
moral point of view, they are universally acknowledged to
be much in need.

The intercourse between the native student and the
young civilian could not fail to be most beneficial to both ;
and under such a system the latter would obtain that
which is at present a great desideratum—more acquaintance
with the inner life of the better classes of the natives of
India, and more insight into their social condition, their
habits of thought, and tone of mind. An institution of this

kind would go further than anything else towards levelling
the barrier that now exists beween the races, at the same
time that such a course of education would probably remove
most of the objections now not unreasonably urged against
the more frequent employment of natives in public offices
of trust and responsibility.

The system established by the Despatch of 1854, followed up by a second Despatch in 1859, is thus epitomized
by Mr. Howell :—

"3. The Indian Educational Code is contained in the despatches of
the Home Government of 1854 and 1859. The main object of the
former despatch is to divert the efforts of the Government from the
education of the higher classes, upon whom they had up to that date
been too exclusively directed, and to turn them to the wider diffusion
of education among all classes of the people, and especially to the provision of primary instruction for the masses. Such instruction is to be
provided by the direct instrumentality of Government, and a compulsory rate, levied under the direct authority of Government, is
pointed out as the best means of obtaining funds for the purpose. The
system must be extended upwards by the establishment of Government
schools as models, to be superseded gradually by schools supported on
the grant-in-aid principle. This principle is to be of perfect religious
neutrality, defined in regular rules adapted to the circumstances of
each province, and clearly and publicly placed before the natives of
India. Schools, whether purely Government institutions or aided, in
all of which (excepting normal schools) the payment of some fee, however small, is to be the rule, are to be in regular gradation from those
which give the humblest elementary instruction to the highest colleges,
and the best pupils of one grade are to climb through the other grades
by means of scholarships obtained in the lower school and tenable in
the higher. To provide masters, normal schools are to be established
in each province, and moderate allowances given for the support of
those who possess an aptness for teaching, and are willing to devote
themselves to the profession of schoolmasters. By this means it is
hoped that, at no distant period, institutions may be in operation in all
the presidencies, calculated to supply masters for all classes of schools,
and thus in time greatly to limit, if not altogether to obviate, the
necessity of recruiting the educational service by means of engagements
made in England. The medium of education is to be the vernacular
languages of India, into which the best elementary treatises in English
should be translated. Such translations are to be advertised for, and
liberally rewarded by Government as the means of enriching vernacular literature. While, therefore, the vernacular languages are on

no account to be neglected, the English language may be taught where there is a demand for it ; but the English language is not to be substituted for the vernacular dialects of the country. The existing institutions for the study of the classical languages of India are to be maintained. and respect is to be paid to the hereditary veneration which they command. Female education is to receive the frank and cordial support of Government, as by it a far greater proportional impulse is imparted to the educational and moral tone of the people than by the education of men. In addition to the Government and aided colleges and schools for general education, special institutions for imparting special education in law, medicine, engineering art. and agriculture [1] are to receive in every province the direct aid and encouragement of Government. The agency by which this system of education is to be carried out is a Director in each province, assisted by a competent staff of Inspectors, care being taken that the cost of control shall be kept in fair proportion to the cost of direct measures of instruction. To complete the system in each presidency, a university is to be established on the model of the London University at each of the three presidency towns. These universities are not to be themselves places of education, but they are to test the value of the education given elsewhere ; they are to pass every student of ordinary ability who has fairly profited by the curriculum of school and college study which he has passed through, the standard required being such as to command respect without discouraging the efforts of deserving students. Education is to be aided and supported by the principal officials in every district, and is to receive, besides, the direct encouragement of the State by the opening of Government appointments to those who have received a good education, irrespective of the place or manner in which it may have been acquired, and in the lower situations by preferring a man who can read and write, and is equally eligible in other respects, to one who cannot."

Mr. Howell then proceeds to remark upon four striking and noticeable facts in the progress of education which the tables given above disclose. The first is its extraordinary development in the last twelve years, which has given to

---

[1] Great stress is laid on this point. "We have also perceived with satisfaction that the attention of the Council of Education in Calcutta has been lately directed to the subject of attaching to each zillah school the means of teaching practical agriculture ; . . . for there is, as Dr. Mouat most truly observes, no single advantage that could be afforded to the vast rural population of India that would equal the introduction of an improved system of agriculture."

every province the complete educational agency, and to the older provinces the machinery described above.

The second is the gigantic nature of the task imposed upon the Government by the enormous area and the vast population of the country. Notwithstanding the development of the last twelve years, the remark made in 1854 seems almost equally applicable now, " that the efforts of the State have reached but an insignificant number of those who are of a proper age to receive school instruction."

The third noticeable point to which Mr. Howell draws attention is the limited result of what he calls the " downward filtration of education." The tables given above show that even in the oldest and richest and most advanced province the masses of the people are practically untouched; and this can be no time to propose to limit the action of the State, when in Bengal there is only one institution aided by Government to every 74 square miles, and in Madras only one pupil to every 578 of the population. But this very important portion of the work did not escape the attention of Sir Charles Wood and Lord Stanley. "At a time when there were not 12,000 pupils altogether in the Government colleges and inferior schools for general education in all India, the framers of the Code were of opinion that the efforts of Government had been too exclusively directed theretofore to the higher classes, and that all that then remained for Government to do for these classes was to establish universities to complete the educational machinery in each presidency. After the establishment of universities it is said that the State has done as much as a Government can do to place the benefits of education plainly and practically before the higher classes of India. . . . Our attention should now be directed to a consideration if possible still more important, and one which has been hitherto, we are bound to admit, too much neglected— viz. how useful and practical knowledge suited to every station in life may be best conveyed to the great mass of the people who are utterly incapable of obtaining any education worthy of the name by their own unaided efforts ; and we desire to see the active measures of Government more especially directed for the future to this object, for the attainment of which we are ready to sanction a considerable increase of expenditure. Schools whose object should be, not to train highly a few youths, but to provide more opportunities than now exist for the acquisition of such an improved education as will make those who possess it more useful members of society in every condition of life, should exist in every district in India." This principle was further insisted upon in subsequent despatches from the Home Government, in 1863 and 1864. But Mr. Howell concludes from a survey of the whole operations, that, speaking generally, elementary education is one of the points on which full effect has yet to be given to the Educational Code.

With the view of carrying out this portion of the scheme, efforts have been made in all the different provinces, varying according to the circumstances of each, to relieve the burden upon the Imperial exchequer by local cesses levied in different ways and in different proportions. It is obvious that, with the best intentions, the exertions of the Government must be limited by the means available. Schools for the lower classes must be maintained at the expense of the State ; in other words, of taxes, whether imposed in the form of Imperial taxation or by local cesses. But it is a mistake to view the latter in any case as voluntary contributions.

The fourth branch of the subject to which Mr. Howell draws attention is female education. And the review of the results effected here is not, on the whole, satisfactory. It must, however, be recollected that whatever difficulties attend the spread of education in India, they become multiplied tenfold when the system approaches the seclusion of female life. Here we are met, not by dull apathy and indifference, but by a deep-rooted and active prejudice, grounded on a deeper foundation perhaps than many of us

are apt to imagine. It is not the prejudice of caste, nor
the influence of religious bigotry, but something that has
its root nearer the heart than either of them—the instinct
of human nature as it exists in Oriental character—that
opposes the introduction of education into the zenana.
The fact is, that in the East women fit into their places in
the social system of Oriental life so well, that the other sex
are slow to see the necessity for any change. A very
erroneous notion prevails in England and the West generally with regard to the position and influence of the
Eastern women. They so frequently figure in pictures of
Indian and other Oriental scenes, carrying earthen water-
pots on their heads, that a general notion has arisen that
women in the East never do anything else but carry
water-pots, or at any rate that they are mere slaves whose
lives are spent in menial household drudgery. Among the
poorer classes, as in our own country, a vast deal of household drudgery does fall to woman's lot. But in spite of
their seclusion—may we not say, perhaps in consequence
of it?—the female sex among the upper classes of Hindoos
and Mahommedans exercise as much influence in family
affairs as among ourselves. In India, whatever may be
their condition in other Eastern countries, wives and mothers
are certainly not the nonentities they are generally represented by Western writers. As wives and mothers, they
are treated with just as much respect and consideration as
among the upper classes, certainly, of Englishmen; and the
very seclusion of the zenana, so suggestive of intolerable
monotony to an Englishwoman, is connected with no such
disagreeable association in the East. The bird that is born
in a cage is quite content to live and die there, the more
so if it has been the habit of its kind for countless generations. But in the family circle and the daily round of
domestic duties, interests, and enjoyments the Hindoo
woman has a field for her sympathies and her affections
which puts her quite on a par with her sisters of the West.

If the education which it is endeavoured to impart to

the gentler sex of India were moral and religious training,
there could be no question as to its value; but it is open to
doubt, to say the least, whether a little knowledge of arith-
metic and geography will make Indian women better wives
and mothers. The notion so generally entertained, the
principle on which the advocates of female education in
India ride their hobby, is one derived from our own habits
and customs, the tendency of Western civilization. To see
the women in India occupying the same sphere, and undertaking the same part in social economy, as they do in
Europe, is the result at which their efforts at female education are directed; but people are too apt to forget that
nature has formed different races, each on its own model,
and that when we aim at modifying the national character
of one race in accordance with the ideas of another, we
are in reality endeavouring to subvert the laws of Nature
herself, and to confound distinctions which, in spite of all
our efforts, may turn out to be indelible. There is, indeed,
one broad basis upon which all races of mankind may meet,
and that is the common ground of our relation to a common Father—the reception of religious truth, the recognition of moral responsibility. But to that ground a State
education founded on the essential principle of religious
neutrality has no tendency to lead. Until Nature herself
has changed the fundamental laws which mark the distinction between the national characteristics of different races,
no education in the world will ever assimilate the women
of the East to their sisters in the West. And taking the
two extremes of woman's lot—the tranquil existence of the
Hindoo wife and mother, confined to her circle of home
duties, and the innocent enjoyment of domestic love, sharing
her husband's confidence, and finding thus a full scope
for the play of the purest and holiest of our natural sympathies, on the one hand; or the restless ambition of the
English female, bearding the revising barrister in his court,
and clamouring for her suffrage, on the other—it may be
allowed to remain an open question, at any rate, which of

the two best fulfils the place Nature has set apart in her economy for the wife, the sister, and the mother.

To zenana missions, as they are called, there has been no allusion in the above remarks. The end and purport of those efforts is to impart an education really worthy of the name ; a moral and religious training, which, if efficient at all, cannot fail to purify, ennoble, and elevate the character. I cannot help thinking that it would be well if all attempts at female education in India were confined to this. But it ought to be managed with the utmost delicacy, judgment, and good taste ; and it is to be feared that, in spite of the plausible reports announced from missionary platforms, and published in missionary reports, the system would hardly bear the sifting which ought to be, but rarely is, accorded to the results of every movement originating in enthusiasm. The natives themselves are most jealous of any breach of the seclusion in which they consider they have a right to veil their domestic affairs. They profess to welcome the visits of the earnest and self-denying ladies who brave the dangers and disagreeables of a terrible climate, and a life cheered with but few enjoyments, in the cause of duty. But there is often much fear of giving offence at the bottom of their apparent willingness to open the door of their zenanas; and if I can depend on the accounts that reach me, natives speak bitterly to one another of the overflow of Anglo-Saxon energy that will not leave them even their wives and daughters to themselves. If I may say so without giving offence, I should suggest that too great care cannot be taken in the selection of those who are appointed to this delicate duty—a duty in which, if enthusiasm is necessary to reconcile to its performance, sound judgment is quite as indispensable to its success.

These remarks may appear unfair to those who pin their faith to blue-books and reports, which have from time to time set forth a good deal about the apparent heartiness with which the notion of female education was

at first taken up by the natives themselves, especially in
the Punjab. But those who have studied India and its
people through other media than blue-books know how
much of this heartiness is only skin-deep, and put on to
gratify some man in power, whose favour may be worth
canvassing. The Punjab, for instance, made the first
great start in female education in 1862-3, yet it is thus
spoken of in the Report for 1867-8 by the inspectors of
the Umballa circle: "There is a considerable reduction
in female schools. . . . Some of the schools appear to
have made a certain amount of progress : amongst others,
that at Nizamudeen, under the patronage of Mirza Ilahi
Buksh, was visited by Mr. Hutton ; he was shown some
good specimens of handwriting, and he heard some of the
girls read the Khat i Taqdir and the Wakiat i Hind. He
remarks, however, that it is difficult for an examiner to
speak with any confidence on this point (the progress of
the pupils) when all the girls are *parda nisheen* (behind
the screen), and it is impossible to tell whether the girls
answer the questions or their teachers, or whether they
recite by heart what they are supposed to read."

The Umballa circle is that contiguous to the older provinces ; at the other extremity of the Lieutenant-Governor-
ship, the inspector of the Frontier circle writes: "All the
female schools in the Bunnoo district have been closed,
with the exception of one at Moosakhail, in which 18
girls read Gooroomookhi, but are not making much
progress." .

In the Lahore circle, on the other hand, the number
of schools has increased from 129 to 147, and the Rawul
Pindee circle has maintained a fair average.

In Bengal, as regards Government agency, it must be
confessed, says Mr. Howell, that a beginning only has
been made ; there being but one normal and one ordinary
school. Of the aided schools there were 82 in the Central
Division, with 3,183 pupils, the number in the last five
years having nearly tripled ; but the inspector complains

that the standard of instruction attained is by no means
so satisfactory as the numerical increase, owing to the
early age at which girls cease to attend school after their
betrothal.

The account given by the inspector of the South-East
division is still less encouraging. There are 41 schools,
with 745 pupils, on the grant-in-aid system, and 27
schools, with 348 pupils, that receive allowance under
other rules. We may fear that the account the inspector
gives of these schools might be found applicable to other
parts of the country besides Bengal. "The female schools
which I have seen," he writes, "consist in general of three
to six infants sprawling about and inking their fingers in
copying letters on strips of leaves. Sometimes one or two
could attempt a little reading."

In the North-West division the inspector writes: "I
have not encouraged the establishment of girls' schools,
because I know that competent teachers for this division
are not to be had, and without such teachers schools would
be a delusion." In the North-East division of Bengal the
deputy-inspector states : "It grieves me much, that, instead
of having to record the establishment of some new girls'
schools, I have this year the painful duty of noticing the
extinction of one at Kurpore. But in relief to this[1] I
may mention that the zenana system of teaching is now
being carried on more extensively than heretofore, and the
notions which the people have been accustomed to entertain in respect of female education are rapidly giving way
before the general spread of education. This happy state
of things is in a great measure due to the exertions of the
pundits, who are ever ready to do their very best to
promote the cause of female education. It is no exag-
geration to say, that in almost every village where there
is a school many a Hindoo lady of respectable family has
commenced reading and writing."

In Madras very little seems to have been done at all in

---

[1] Sic.

the matter of female education ; and in the review of the
Report of Government the question is hardly noticed at
all. "All that the director says about the subject is, that
there has been much discussion among the more enlightened Hindoos at the Presidency town, but the results
of the year have been rather in words than in acts."

In the North-West there are 595 schools, with 12,000
pupils ; but the movement seems to have languished during
the year for want of funds and competent inspection. A
step, however, has been taken to remedy the latter defect
by providing a lady inspector : the success of the measure
remains to be seen.

In the Central Provinces the progress of female education, judging by the returns, has been rapid during the
last few years ; but there is nothing to show definitely what
real progress has been made. There were 130 schools and
3,621 scholars, with one normal school, and one private one
unaided by Government. In British Burmah, Mysore, and
Coorg, and the Hyderabad assigned districts, there are
no Government institutions at all for the purpose of
female education.

The Director of Public Instruction of Bombay seems to
have taken a very sound view of the question. He expressed his opinion in 1865-6, "that the public education,
properly so called, of women, is incompatible with the
system of infant marriages, and with many of the existing
prejudices on the most delicate subjects." We believe,
however, that the education and civilization of the male
portion of the people of India, together with the example
of the European community, will inevitably bring on
the education of the women in India—but that this result
will be very gradual, and subsequent to many important social changes. In his last report he states that
Government can hardly be said to have commenced undertaking female education in Western India. Very recently,
however, an impetus has been given to it by Miss' Carpenter's influence, and the intelligent, enterprising, and

philanthropic native gentry of Bombay have come forward
to aid her with their purses and their co-operation in the
most liberal and hearty manner. Summing up the general
results all over India, Mr. Howell remarks : " On the whole,
it would appear that up to the year under review the
frank and cordial support of Government to female education, promised in 1854, had not been given, and that
only a beginning had been made in some Provinces. But
it should be mentioned that the current year has been one
of progress in this direction. Miss Carpenter's visit at the
close of 1866 gave a stimulus to the movement, which had
been warmly taken up in the Punjab four years previously,
and the Government of India has since held out promises
of liberal assistance and support to an indefinite extent,
on the single condition that the genuine co-operation of
the native community can be secured. It will belong to
the record of another year to show how that offer has
been responded to.

" Looking generally at the results which I have recorded,
it would appear that the immediate obstacles to progress
are the want of trained schoolmistresses and of adequate
inspection, and that the greatest degree of success has
been achieved in those Provinces where a personal interest
in the movement has been evidenced most by the district
and educational authorities. It may, perhaps, be considered
a matter of congratulation, and a good earnest for the
future, that any success at all has been achieved in a few
years in a matter which is surrounded by difficulties that
spring from the strongest social prejudices of a nation, the
most tenacious of all prejudices."

Government has very recently[1] made a fresh grant for
the support of normal schools ; and under present circum-
cumstances it is worth consideration whether all efforts at
female education for the next ten or fifteen years had not
better be directed exclusively to the training of competent
female teachers.

[1] 1868.

CHAPTER XVII.

SOCIAL PROGRESS.

Brahmoism— Prospects of Christianity — Caste prejudices — Social intercourse between natives and Europeans—Changes—Great public scandals — Feverish thirst for promotion — Cliqueism — Love of intrigue—Russian system in Asia.

THE history of Indian administration during the last decade would be incomplete without some notice of the general progress and the social condition of the country. No one who has passed twenty consecutive years in India can fail to have observed the great change which attended the transfer of the country to the direct dominion of the Crown. The year of the rebellion, 1857-8, was an epoch in the modern history of India from which future writers will date the commencement of an era of reform. And it is certain that if the administration between 1859 and 1869 has been successful, we ought to be able to trace its results in a general improvement in the condition of the people.

The subject of Indian social progress necessarily resolves itself into two heads : 1st, the condition of native, 2d, that of European society. I shall deal with these two branches as briefly as possible in that order.

Among the classes of the native population which come into contact with European civilization, in consequence of their being located in the Presidency cities and on the great lines of railway, the change during the last ten

years has been very marked. Much of the prejudice and
ignorant confidence of Orientals in their own superiority,
which has always formed so prominent a feature in their
character, has yielded to liberal ideas developed by education, combined with commercial intercourse with European
nations. Even the strongholds of Hindoo superstition, so
long intact, have been unable to withstand the progress of
thought, and the new sect of Brahmos is daily increasing
in influence, and gathering converts in all the large cities
on the Bengal side. The tenets of this new sect are a sort
of compromise between Hindooism and common sense.
Brahmoism more nearly approaches the Deism of Europe
in the earlier part of the present century than any of the
systems of philosophy promulgated in the East. Finding
that the fables of the Hindoo mythology (which formed
no part of the Hindoo religion as inculcated by the
earlier sages) were unable to stand the test of reason, and
were rapidly losing their hold upon the minds of the
people, and unwilling at the same time to embrace Christianity—which came to them recommended indeed by the
preaching of missionaries, but not by the practice of the
bulk of the English with whom they came in contact—the
founders of this school endeavoured to enunciate a philo-
sophic and religious system grounded on those ideas of
natural religion which commend themselves to the reason
and instincts of mankind. The Brahmos are in fact deists,
but they inculcate the strictest observance of the moral
law. As such, it is difficult to perceive, as some writers do,
in the present movement any indication of a tendency
towards Christianity. On the contrary, it would seem as
if the system of State education preserving the strictest
neutrality in religious questions is producing exactly the
results which might have been anticipated. A Hindoo
educated in our schools and colleges finds it impossible
to believe, for instance, that the world rests on the back of
a tortoise or the horns of a bull. Uninstructed in the
Christian faith, he is well acquainted with the history of

modern discovery, and more or less proficient in natural science, having at the same time an innate tendency towards metaphysical speculations. He therefore gladly takes refuge in a system which in its observance of the moral law satisfies the higher aspirations of his mind, and in its speculative tenets on the existence of a divine creator and ruler of the universe is sufficient to fill the void caused by a rejection of the mythological fables which amused him as a child. Practically, for many years, the few thoughtful men among the Hindoos have, I believe, abandoned the superstitions of the Purans; but, fettered by the bonds of caste, and deterred by the bad example of Englishmen from embracing a religion whose followers seemed to ignore the connexion between precept and practice, and unable to find a refuge anywhere, they were content to live and die in the faith of their fore-fathers, believing as much as they could bring their minds not to reject, and leaving the great riddle to be solved hereafter.

In intellectual acquirements and natural mental capacity, the various classes of natives differ very materially. Christianity has very little present prospect of success among the Hindoos and Mahommedans of our older provinces ; but wherever it has been preached among the ruder tribes of the interior, it has generally been received with some enthusiasm. It is of course only natural that the simple minds of the barbarous descendants of the aborigines who are to be met with in mountainous tracts in various parts of the continent of Central India, and in one portion of Rajpootana, in Bengal Proper, and in Burmah, should be more easily impressed with the truths of Christianity than the Hindoo, wedded to a system of philosophy and long inured to the slavery of caste, or than the fanatical Mahommedan ; to either, a system of religion whose great principle is that of self-sacrifice is so utterly foreign that we may cease to wonder at the little effect as yet produced by the teaching of our missionaries.

Caste prejudices, however, are gradually yielding; natives are beginning to understand the value of co-operation, and to see that an irksome system which has been imposed by general consent may by general consent be shaken off. Quite recently a reformer, whose name deserves to be recorded, Peearee Lall, has by persevering agitation succeeded in getting up meetings at all the large cities in the Upper Provinces, and in inducing a large and influential sect of Brahmins to discontinue the old-established custom of expensive marriages, which has involved so many families in debt and ruin.

In many parts of India the natives now have their societies and associations, which meet at stated periods and discuss questions of social science. At these congresses all the forms used among ourselves at public meetings are strictly observed; the members address the chairman, and the proceedings are duly recorded and published at the expense of the association under the auspices of the secretary. In Oude, the Talookdars' Association has a little more of a political character,[1] as they not unfrequently discuss questions having reference to their rights and privileges.

India is occasionally visited by travellers from the continent of Europe—Frenchmen, Germans, Italians—who in the pursuit of business or pleasure spend a few months rambling over the continent. These observers are always struck most forcibly with what is beyond a doubt one of

---

[1] This association was mainly got up by a gentleman whose name deserves to be recorded as a public man very far in advance in many things of the rest of his countrymen, Baboo Dukhinarunjun Mookerjee. A highly intellectual mind, well stored with the treasures of English literature and the teachings of history, can hardly be expected to rest content in a condition of political nullity. Baboo Dukhinarunjun Mookerjee, by the expression and inculcation of liberal ideas, has offended many men in power, and is consequently more or less in disgrace among the official classes. Any government less exclusive than that of the Indian would make use of such a man as Mookerjee, instead of forcing him into the opposition.

the strangest features in our position in the country, viz. the utter absence of anything like social intercourse between the races. Englishmen meet natives in business, and there their connexion ceases. After being upwards of a century in the country, we have never penetrated the barrier of reserve in which the native shelters himself from social intercourse with the Englishman. In Bombay, the attempt at amalgamation has been occasionally made, with very indifferent success. It seems as if there was on both sides a deep-rooted antipathy to meeting on an equality in social position which no efforts can overcome.

One reason of this is the existence of habits and customs which preclude Englishmen and natives from eating and drinking together. It is a theory, not grounded on a very exalted view of human life, but it seems as if it were one of the laws of nature, and one of the demarcations between man and the lower order of animals, that social intercourse among the former should be best developed by the process of consuming food in company. Two men dine together, and become friends : two dogs eat out of the same dish, and the chances are that they fight over their food. The Englishman and the Oriental cannot amalgamate socially, because their habits and prejudices entail on them the necessity of taking their meals apart. Community of interest is a weaker bond than similarity of taste and manner. This is a truism, but it is a truism aptly illustrated in the conditions of life in India, where the Englishman and the native, subjects of one sovereign, originally of one race, with common sympathies and unity of interests, may meet one another many times daily, week after week, year after year, in their ordinary avocations, and yet never advance one step towards real intimacy or friendship.

The extension of the cotton trade and the introduction of railways have undoubtedly done much towards stimulating the commercial industry of the people, and inculcating more active habits of life. The advantages of railway travelling are as thoroughly appreciated in India as in any other country in the world, and may do something in time towards breaking down the great barrier to social progress —caste. There has been a tendency among writers rather to exaggerate the results already attained in this direction, and the reform as yet has reached very little, if at all, below the surface. But social reform in a country where the caste system has been so many centuries in operation, must necessarily be very gradual. Education, and more intimate and more extended intercourse with the Anglo-Saxon, are the most efficient if not the only agents capable of removing the obstructions that now prevent the social amalgamation of the two races.

The changes that followed the transfer of India from the Company to the Crown affected the tone of English society even more than that of the natives. The great influx of fresh regiments, the large number of officers who with their wives were thus brought to India, the breaking up of the old system and social habits of the past generation of Anglo-Indians, the more frequent intercourse between the mother-country and her distant dependency, developed a great improvement in the manners and customs of English residents. Three other causes simultaneously co-operated to infuse a more healthy atmosphere into social life. One was the increasing number of men who had gone out, and in course of time had begun to rise in the official ladder, under the Civil Service competitive system ; another was the formation of the High Courts, and the introduction of barristers and legal practitioners into the Mofussil; and the third was the extension of the educational department, which brought out to India many men of intellectual acquirements and refined tastes from our English universities.

The history of the period under review is scarcely complete without a description of several great public scandals, the echo of which, in one or two cases, has been heard in England. These great public scandals are essentially Indian. They are the cancers and gangrenes that are developed from the unhealthy condition of the social constitution. But aptly as they serve to illustrate the condition of society, they are not pleasing subjects to dwell upon. In the first place, it is undesirable to re-open old sores. Men whose names have already been before the public in unhappy notoriety are glad to let their story be forgotten, even if with oblivion comes despair of getting justice. And, on the other hand, as there are two sides to every story, and as in common fairness a writer who tells the story at all ought to set forth both sides, the description of these illustrative scandals would occupy more space than I can afford. During the decade, Indian society has been stirred to its lowest depths by the excitement consequent on the trial of the Rev. Mr. Long for libel, in a matter connected with the great indigo dispute, where a missionary was made the scapegoat for an official delinquent of high position. There was the Oude case, where two classes of officials fought, a newspaper proprietary being the buffer between them, upon which Lord Canning, who was forced to interfere, published an elaborate minute, dealing censure pretty fairly on both parties. There were the Priestley and the Crawley cases, by which a clique hostile to Sir Hugh Rose attempted to bring about his recall. There was the Agra arms case, in which a perfectly innocent man was almost ruined to save the Government from acknowledging they had been misled by their own servants, and which resulted in the triumphant acquittal by a jury in Calcutta of an officer charged with a crime in support of which there was not a particle of really trustworthy evidence. There is the Jervis case, which set all Simla wild for a whole season; and the Nyn Singh case, in which a flagrant abuse of the judicial office called down on the officials of Kumaon a severe reprimand from the judges of the High Court.

These incidents arise, as has been stated, from the unhealthy condition of the Anglo-Indian social body, which the English reader finds a difficulty in comprehending, because there is nothing which he sees around him that the least resembles it. He cannot appreciate the intense spirit

of clanship and partisanship, rising when excited into a
passion, to which the peculiar conditions of life in India,
perpetuated through at least a century, have given birth.
There, society is cut up into circles and sections, the limits
of each larger circle being confined to the limits of each
branch of the service. The prevailing element in English
society—the upper middle classes, consisting of professional,
commercial, literary men, those engaged in the superior
branches of trade, agriculture, or manufacture, and the clergy
—is totally wanting; at least, these classes form so small a
body that their influence is *nil.* If it were possible to conceive society in England reduced to the judges and magistrates, clerks of the Treasury, Somerset House, and other
Government offices, all belonging to one service and coming
from one college; and the officers of the army, with a considerable number of subordinates in each department, who
are not sufficiently independent to entertain or express
opinions of their own except surreptitiously by anonymous
contributions to the press, or among their own circle of
friends and associates—if it were possible to conceive English society reduced to these limits, the reader would have
no bad counterpart of Indian society as it is everywhere
beyond the limits of the Presidency towns. For, although
one feature in the picture just presented—viz. the unity of
origin of all the members of the Civil Service—may seem
hardly to apply to the present time, when Haileybury belongs to the past, yet its influence and traditional associations are still so strong that, as against the outside world,
the Civil Service is imbued with just as powerful an element
of clanship as if Haileybury were still the only channel
through which the Indian Civil Service was supplied. There
is, practically, no middle class independent of Government,
although by degrees the bar and commerce together are
collecting the material out of which, many years hence,
such a class may be constructed. There is no aristocracy
elevated above the level of the masses, and the interest
awakened by a ceaseless struggle for advancement in the

official world. The clergy, unfortunately, are so small a body that their influence is scarcely felt except among the few who preserve something more than the mere outward forms of religious profession. But at the summit of each department, centreing round the head, is a clique of officials who have the ear of the Governor-General, or Governor, or Commander-in-chief, or general, or head of the department, whatever it may be, who bar effectually all approach to the sole source of professional advancement except through themselves. They resolutely combine to maintain the privilege of their order intact, and to hand it down to their successors unimpaired—the privilege of representing everything to their head, with exactly the colouring it may suit their fancies, or prejudices, or interest to impart. To borrow a figure from physiology in illustration of the anatomy of Indian society, the ganglionic system may be said to permeate the whole official world, from the Viceroy down to the smallest moonshee who draws his pay from the State; that is, a system where a succession of centres of action follow one another, each centre of action having its own subordinate administrators, each of whom is a ganglionic centre in his turn, and has his own subordinate administration : in all cases the subordinate administrator being dependent (as a deputy-judge-advocate-general of the army once said in the witness-box he was) on the breath of his superior for his official existence.

To all these elements of the most artificial and unhealthy condition of the body social it is possible to conceive, must be added the important and invariable accompaniment of female agency, the love of power and capacity for intrigue which are natural to every woman, and which the habits and condition of society in India are so well calculated to foster.

But the picture is not yet complete. Few Englishmen have any idea of the enormous amount of patronage at the disposal of the Indian authorities. A residence in the East is not calculated to suppress the *auri sacra fames* which finds a place in every human breast. On the contrary, the incessant desire to earn a sufficiency to visit England or a competency to retire, the immense expense which the ever-recurring separations of families entail, the education of children brought up away from their parents at expensive schools, and the extravagant habits of Indian life—all these considerations whet the appetite, strong enough in any case, for gold, and stimulate the unflagging energies of the Anglo-Indian official to ever fresh exertions in the race for wealth. And if the struggle is hard, the prizes to be gained are golden ones. Offices, the incomes attached to which would seem to most English professional men princely stipends, are at the disposal of those in power. To win their favour, to make interest with those who are really and literally the dispensers of golden prizes, public functionaries devote themselves with the assiduity of diggers in the Australian and Californian goldfields, only that the instruments they use are not the pick-axe and the shovel. They are, first and foremost, female influence, which is ever actively and unceasingly at work in the saloons of Simla and Calcutta, Nynee Tal and Murree, Madras and Bombay, Mahableshwur and Mount Aboo. Next to this, is the genius for display of talent— above all, a ready pen, and a certain undefinable faculty; which some men have naturally and some acquire, of pushing themselves on by making friends with those in power. In these respects—that is, as regards the means employed for getting up the official ladder—there is probably little difference between India and other civilized countries in modern times. Human nature is much the same everywhere, and similar circumstances beget kindred efforts. But there is this peculiarity about India, that there the field is exceedingly narrowed, while the opportunity for securing prizes is in proportion to the number of competitors, immensely magnified. It is the difference between a battle where large forces are arrayed on both sides, and a duel between two, where in the former, owing to the number engaged and the distance over which the armies extend, there is little or no acquaintance on either side with details on the other, and no such thing as actual combat between individuals. But in a smaller field, where the combatants are few, each sees the other, measures his opponent's capacity for resistance or attack, scrutinizes his weapons, his dress, his physique, and considers how best he shall take him at advantage.

In such a condition of things it is obvious that, unless human nature in India is different from what it is in other parts of the world, the result must be a feverish thirst for promotion, and a terrible temptation to a laxity as to the means by which it is secured. Here and there, of course, are men who rise very far above the average by the force of their genius and a legitimate exercise of it. In India the field for such men is a glorious one, and their rapid elevation to posts of high emolument and great responsibility evinces the truth that real genius, well directed, must assert itself. These are the exceptions. Men so gifted may perhaps scorn the arts and machinations by which less able men climb to power. But below the level, and apart from these few exceptions, the whole official society in India—and it is almost all purely official—is like a mass of some substance in which the process of fermentation is going on, heaving and seething with incessant motion ; each atomic molecule, under the operation of natural laws, urging, pressing, pushing its neighbour molecule, either aside, that it may be out of its way, or forward, that it may take its place, or down, that it may rise upon it. And according to the very varying scale in which moral obligations are regarded by different individual molecules, or by the same molecule at different times, are the means employed to make good the advance. Man's nature must be other than it is, if in such a condition of society the basest motives did not occasionally influence actions, or if the struggles towards wealth and power were always consistent with honour and integrity.

Then again, in addition to the ganglionic system above described, the essential tendency of official life is cliqueism. When a struggle so incessant is being maintained by every individual member of the whole body—and to appreciate thoroughly the motive power at work, it must be understood that there is nothing to prevent an ensign from rising to command an army, or an assistant-magistrate from becoming a member of the imperial council or a proconsul—it will be obvious that the molecules may find it of the utmost advantage to secure the assistance of other molecules working in the same direction. Few can hope to succeed in the struggle unaided and alone. Hence arise cliques, connected together by the strongest bond of union, self-interest. Hence springs a firm, united effort, among the officers of a department, to prevent an abuse from transpiring and coming before the public, even if necessary, by crushing the man bold enough to attempt the disclosure. Hence comes a determined struggle to oppose every effort to introduce reform, because reform inevitably sweeps away some privileges. Hence arises a result often seen in India when fresh blood is introduced into a department, and some new-comer, conscientious and enthusiastic, strives by his own exertions to check abuses, of which he is at first horrified to find himself a passive and involuntary supporter. There is perhaps no creature so obnoxious to the ganglionic centres as an enthusiastic reformer. Any subordinate who is unwary enough to adopt that line, rushes on destruction. He is given to understand that he is expected to carry on the system as his predecessors did, and his suggestions will be called for when wanted. Summary ejection from the department, or a mark against his name as unfit for promotion, is the fate which speedily befalls such an one. This probably is also a characteristic not confined to the Indian official world, but it is very strongly developed there; for the whole country, with its inhabitants, native and European, and its system of government, is the hot-bed of conservatism.

No Englishman can possibly understand the extent to which intrigue goes to make up the business of Asiatic life. What Macaulay wrote in 1841 is true enough now : "An Indian Government has only to let it be understood that it wishes a particular man to be ruined, and in twenty-four hours it will be furnished with grave charges, supported by depositions so full and circumstantial, that any person unaccustomed to Asiatic mendacity would regard them as decisive. It is well if the signature of the destined victim is not counterfeited at the foot of some illegal compact, or if some treasonable paper is not dropped into a hiding-place in his house."

The criminal law in India is the usual weapon to which a native resorts when he wants to revenge himself upon an enemy. No one who has not been many years in the country can realize in the faintest degree the facility with which evidence can be suborned, or the frequency with which a man's ruin is sought by means of plotting and intrigue. It is this more than anything else which has given birth to that deep-rooted hatred which the natives everywhere bear to our rule—a hatred which found expression in 1857, and is only kept silent by overpowering physical force. It is this which makes our dominion appear so unfavourably in comparison with that of native states. In the latter, intrigue can be met by intrigue, one clique can oppose another ; if there is danger of oppression, or of the law being turned into an engine of private animosity, there is always a chance of escape, which our cast-iron system and our rigid codes of criminal law and police, backed up by physical power, do not allow. And the evil is intensified by the character and constitution of the Government, whose heads turn a deaf ear to all complaints, the stereotyped reply to every petition for redress being, that "they see no reason to interfere." Tools in the hands of cliques themselves, they are not to be reached except through channels that convey only those impressions of each case that are agreeable to the men in power, and consonant

with the views of the very parties against whom the cry
for redress is raised.

The Russians have a system of administration very
superior to ours in many respects, but one upon which the
large number of officials for whom we make a point of
finding employ in India would hardly allow us to fall back.
When they occupy a new province, they select the leading
men among the natives, and place the executive authority
in their hands, appointing a Russian officer of rank as
commissioner to superintend the whole, with full powers
to interfere in any or every branch of the public service.
There is thus provided an administration with a court of
appeal perfectly independent of the executive, to which
any aggrieved person may apply for redress. But of
course the two systems, theirs and ours, will not bear
comparison, because it has ever been our endeavour, at
least till very lately, to employ European agency as much
as possible, from the belief that under it the administration
of justice will be more pure and free from the defects of
Oriental character ; while it is theirs to economize, as far as
possible, the European element. Whatever may be the
actual result of the two systems in the success or the
defects of the executive administration, there is no question
that the Russian is the more popular of the two, for with
them the defects are the handiwork of the natives themselves, and those who suffer, suffer from the hands of their
own countrymen and co-religionists ; while the character in
which foreign rule appears is solely that of a restraining,
mitigating element, affording redress of grievances and
constituting a check upon oppression.

CHAPTER XVIII.

THE HISTORY OF LEGISLATION.

The constitution of the Legislative Council—Act VIII. of 1859—Civil Procedure—The Rent Law, and its effects upon society—The Law of Limitation—Special legislation—The effects of civil war—The Legislature confirms acts done in 1857-8 — Stamp Act — Small Cause Courts—The penal code—Penal consequences of adultery—Criminal procedure—Appeals—Police—Abuses of present system.

IN all countries where the representative element exists in the Government, where the action of the legislature is prompted by the ascertained wants of the community, the history of legislation will afford a very fair index of general progress. In such cases the historian who deals exhaustively with this subject has little else to engage his attention, for public feeling and public morals, commercial prosperity and decline, the interests of the different classes of the community, and the general condition of the country, will be reflected faithfully in the deliberations and the acts of the assembly convened for the purpose of making laws. In a country where the government is constituted as is that of India it is not so. There the whole business of the legislature is mainly in the hands of a small clique of officials, who do, indeed, nominally represent the different presidencies and grand geographical divisions of the country, but who are by position and education, in thought and idea, nearly as far removed from the people they legislate for as the gods in Olympus, in the old mythology, were removed above the ordinary concerns of mortal men. The independent classes are also nominally represented, but the influence of their representatives is so small, and their privileges so restricted, that in point of fact they are a mere nonentity, and utterly unable to affect in the smallest degree the official tone which pervades the Indian council chamber.

The *modus operandi* is pretty much as follows. A member of the Council conceives an idea. Perhaps it is suggested to him by some official in high position, in one of the minor provinces; perhaps it is developed from the depths of his internal consciousness. At any rate, he turns it over in his thoughts, and convinces himself that such and such a measure is required. He discusses it, perhaps with a colleague; and after the scheme has simmered a little in his mind, he applies for leave to bring in a bill, having given three days' notice to the secretary. If the motion be carried in the affirmative, the member sends the bill to the secretary, with a full statement of objects and reasons, and any other papers which he may consider necessary. The draft bill is then printed with the statement of objects and reasons, and a copy forwarded to each member. A translation of it is also made into the vernacular, for the use of members who cannot read English. After fourteen days have elapsed, the bill may be introduced; and on that day, or any subsequent day to which the discussion may be postponed, the principle of the bill and its general provisions may be discussed. If the Council so decide, the bill is referred to a select committee for report, and, together with the statement of objects and reasons, is published, in English and the vernacular, in the official *Gazette*. But the publication of a bill may be suspended until it has been considered by the select committee and reported to the Council, if the Council at the time of referring it to the select committee shall so order. When three months have elapsed from the publication of a draft in the *Gazette*, or in any

shorter period that the Council may order, the select
committee to which the bill has been sent shall write a
report thereon. Such report is taken into consideration by
the Council as soon as convenient, but not until a week
after the report has been furnished to the members. If
any member wishes to propose an amendment affecting
the principle of a bill as settled by the select committee,
he must send the amendment to the secretary at least
three days before the meeting of the Council at which the
bill is to be considered. An amendment of which notice
has not been given previously may, nevertheless, be considered if the president decide that such a measure shall
be considered by the Council, at the meeting at which
it is proposed, or be deferred to the next following
meeting. If no amendment be made by the Council in
a bill as settled by the select committee, it may at once
be passed. If any amendment be made, the bill shall not
be passed till next meeting. Finally, the consent of the
Governor-General in Council is required before the bill can
become law.

The fecundity of the Indian Legislative Council may
well strike dismay into the mind of the man whose business it is to make himself acquainted, in order that he may
advise others, with the law of the land. In 1859, twenty-
eight bills became law; in 1860, fifty-three; in 1861,
thirty-three; 1862, twenty-four; 1863, thirty-two; 1864,
twenty-eight; 1865, thirty; 1866, thirty; 1867, thirty-
seven; in 1868, twenty-eight: making a total for the ten
years of three hundred and twenty-three.

The general character of Indian legislation is well illustrated by two very important Acts passed in 1859. It can
easily be understood that a small body of legislators,
whose whole career has been passed in official life, would
be well qualified to deal with any matter of mere procedure, or mere technical detail ; while we should naturally
expect to find them at fault in handling broad questions,
such as involve rights of property, or the nature of obliga-

tions, or any other rights grounded on general principles,
or those difficult complications where statute law has to
step in and interfere with, or modify, the custom or common law. I have before spoken of the veil that is thrown
over the eyes of the Indian official from the day he lands
to the day he sails for England on his return. All this
time he sees exactly as much as those about him wish him
to see, and no more. But the matters that come before
him personally in the transaction of his daily official duties
he cannot help seeing. In these he is not to be misled.
But test him as to his knowledge of the actual condition
of the masses of the people,—of their thoughts, feelings,
sympathies, their wants or grievances,—he will be utterly
at fault. There is between him and them a barrier which
may not be passed over, a barrier of Oriental reserve
guarded by the jealous care of the *amla*, or native subordinates, without whom the minutest fraction of official
routine cannot be gone through. He cannot write an
order for himself : he cannot write a line of one. He
cannot read a single petition presented to him. He
cannot read one sentence in numbers of documents to
which he daily affixes his signature. Accordingly, we are
not surprised to find in the two most important Acts of
1859, perhaps of the whole ten years under review,—viz.
the Code of Civil Procedure, or Act VIII. of 1859, and
the Rent Law, as it is called (though it is in reality
much more than a rent law), or Act X. of 1859;—we are
not surprised to find in these laws, one an enactment of
extreme utility, admirably adapted to facilitate the administration of justice in India, in the other an act which
well illustrates Sir Erskine Perry's remark, elsewhere
quoted, " That the history of British India is full of
examples of the great mischief done by clothing imperfect
theories in the rigid garb of law."

The great value of the Civil Procedure Code is, that
it affords all the technical safeguards which an efficient
administration of the law requires, while at the same time

it is elastic enough to admit a due observance of the
principles of equity. An English lawyer may get an idea
of its scope by conceiving the courts of law and equity
amalgamated into one, with a common code of procedure.
It is in force in all the civil courts in India: in the courts
established by Royal Charter, viz. the High Courts at
Calcutta, Bombay, Madras, and Agra; and the courts
constituted by local enactment, which are the ordinary
civil courts of the Mofussil in the three Presidencies,
including the Punjab, Oude, the Central Provinces, and
Jhansie; the courts of Burmah, including the Recorder's,
the Chief Court of Lahore, and the Court of the Resident
at Aden; as well as the Small Cause Courts, which are
established pretty generally in all the largest towns and
settlements, such as Simla, and Mussoorie in the hills.
The Small Cause Courts of the Presidency towns have a
procedure of their own.[1]

This Act was supplemented by another, Act XXIII. of
1861, which made a few necessary additions and amendments dictated by experience. In one or two minor points
it is still susceptible of improvement.

Act X., or the Rent Law, affecting, as it does, rights in
land over a large part of the continent of India, is one of
the most important in the whole Statute-book. So far as
it deals with procedure, in providing a more efficient
machinery for the speedy settlement of claims for rent
between landlord and tenant, it is, as we might expect it to
be, eminently useful. So far as it deals with general principles, affecting rights to real property, it is, as we might
expect it to be, faulty and mischievous.

It starts with providing that every ryot is entitled to
receive from the person to whom the rent of the land held
or cultivated by him is payable, a lease, showing the
quantity of land, and, where fields have been numbered in
the Government survey, the number of each field, the
amount of annual rent, the instalments in which it is to be

[1] Vide Broughton's "Civil Procedure."

paid, and any special condition that may exist. If the rent
is shown not to have been changed for twenty years, it is
presumed that the land has been held at that rent from the
time of the permanent settlement—that is, in the province
where there has been a permanent settlement, or Bengal
Proper.

One of the theories which our Indian legislature has
clothed in the rigid garb of law is, that the rights of the
ryots were ever in danger of being overridden, and that it
was the especial duty of Government to protect the interests
of this class, even to the extent of conferring by law rights
in the soil which they never held before. No doubt the
principle was advocated in all good faith by the men who
held office at the time when new provinces, now old, had
just passed under British rule. It was the pet hobby of the
orthodox Haileybury school, handed down from father to
son, with all the prestige that attaches to traditional policy.
To detail the different landed tenures in vogue throughout
India would occupy in itself several volumes, of little
interest to the casual reader. The general character of such
tenures, and the system of revenue settlement in the different provinces and presidencies, may be stated broadly as
being, in Bengal Proper, a zemindaree tenure under the permanent settlement which was made in Lord Cornwallis's
time; in Madras and Bombay a ryotwarree tenure settlement,
being made, when practicable, with ryots or actual cultivators
of the soil. In the North-West Provinces and the Punjab the
village tenure mostly prevails, settlement being made when
practicable with the whole village community under the
head man. The revenue system introduced into Oude on
the annexation, and modified after the reconquest of the
province in 1858, has been elsewhere mentioned. Nothing
could be more sweeping than the enactment in 1859, which
gave to every ryot who has cultivated or held land for
twelve years a right of occupancy in the land so held, so
long as he pays his rent. There are exceptions made in
the case of land called khāmār, neejjote, or seer. And the

I 2

holding of the father or other person from whom the ryot inherits is deemed the holding of the ryot. But this does not apply to a lessee whose tenure is intermediate between that of ryot and landlord, and who therefore acquires no right of occupancy by a twelve years' tenure.[1]

A right of occupancy was of course but little worth, unless the ryot was protected from having his rent raised. The Act therefore goes on to provide that the rent may not be enhanced unless the rate is below the prevailing rate payable by the same class of ryot for land of a similar description and with similar advantages in the places adjacent, or unless the value of the productive powers of the land has been increased otherwise than by the agency or at the expense of the ryot, or unless the quantity of land held by the ryot has been proved by measurement to be greater than the quantity for which rent has been previously paid.

This principle, which has coloured the policy of our civil administration ever since we acquired dominion in India, is calculated to extend one of the greatest evils under which the poorer classes in the country labour. Whenever a settlement is made in a province newly handed over to British rule, the instructions given to the settlement officers are to inquire into and to confirm for the time being existing rights, leaving claims not supported by actual possession to be decided afterwards in the civil courts. This is all very well in theory ; but how men's minds may be swayed by pre-existing ideas and a long-established mode of regarding revenue questions, is well shown by the settlement in Oude immediately after the annexation, to which allusion has already been made. If civil officers are determined upon finding " rights," we may depend upon it the rights will be found. And the extent to which an idea can lay hold of the mind and warp the views of even able men, may be seen by the recorded opinions of one or two of our most experienced civil officers in the North-West. Mr.

---

[1] Raja Teekum Singh *v.* Hurlall; Sudder Dewanny, Agra, May 11, 1863.

George Campbell, who has acquired a well-earned reputation in India, writes on the 3d May, 1861, with reference to the Oude land tenure question : " My own impression is, that under all tenures and all systems in all parts of India, at the bottom of all a strong tenant right exists." One would expect, however, in a country like India, where all rights in land are so jealously watched, the existence of tenant right, where it had any existence, would have been susceptible of some more satisfactory proof than the mere impression of a civil officer that it did lie somewhere out of sight, buried under the superincumbent tenures of another character.   Another civil officer of great repute in his time, Mr. Martin Gubbins, who was selected to conduct the settlement of Oude on the annexation, had in the earlier stage of his career been deputed to effect the settlement of a large district in the North-West, called Etawah.   Here he found, and he honestly recorded the finding, that there were generally no such things as hereditary cultivators—an idea so hideously strange and foreign to the civilian school, that a revenue officer who subsequently took charge of the district, horrified at finding such an opinion recorded, declared that Mr. Martin Gubbins had persuaded the people to abandon their rights.   Now, if there is anything a native in India will not abandon, it is a right in land.   And the Board of Revenue accepted this explanation, and ruled that the declaration by the cultivators formally recorded at the settlement in open court, that there were no hereditary cultivators, could not affect the indefeasible rights of all who had held the same land for a stated period to be considered, and thereafter treated, as hereditary cultivators.   Here there was a case "where the ablest of settlement officers and the most faithful recorder of village customs had found that no tenant right existed.   The people themselves declared that they were not hereditary cultivators, but the revenue system required that hereditary cultivators there should be, and accordingly the Board and the revenue officers created them."

Sir C. Wingfield bears witness to the same point, in a despatch dated 15th December, 1862, where he says, at par. 4, that hereditary cultivators and the rights they possessed were unknown in the North-West till we created them.[1]

There is nothing more dangerous than legislative interference with rights to real property. In every civilized country in the world, more especially in India, where custom dates back literally to time immemorial, the inhabitants, both landed proprietors and their tenants, or cultivators, will always be found to have among them some well-established and well-recognised principles by which the tenure of land, and the relations of the agricultural community generally towards one another and towards the ruling powers, are regulated. It is true that for many years previous to our acquisition of dominion in India the country had passed through a period of great anarchy. But it is wonderful how little political revolutions in India affect the agricultural classes. The land may be overrun by a conquering army, the landholders may be plundered, the peasantry slaughtered, but the survivors, as soon as the hurricane has swept by, return to their villages, and resume their occupations, regardless of the cares of State, or who wears the crown. This was frequently observable in 1857, when British dominion was for a time trembling in the balance: when troops were marching, and countermarching, and fighting every day, within sound of the cannon of the contending armies the peasant might be seen ploughing up his land, or sowing his crop, as quietly and unconcernedly as if there was nothing unusual going on.

The result of the Rent Law, as it is called, will be to increase what is already the bane of India, a vast pauper population; it will tend to sever the connexion between the peasant and his natural superior, protector, and supporter; to destroy the landed aristocracy, the best safeguard to British rule; and to deteriorate the value of land,

---

[1] *Vide* a series of articles on tenant right, republished from the *Delhi Gazette* in 1865.

by making it over to a class too poor to improve it, and
ever liable, in the event of a bad year, to succumb beneath
the pressure of famine. The cultivators themselves do not
want the rights thus forced upon them. One of the ablest
revenue officers in India is without a doubt Sir William
Muir, the present Lieutenant-Governor of the North-West
Provinces. A civilian of civilians, he is not likely to bear
witness unnecessarily to any shortcomings of the class of
statesmen to which he belongs. In a minute upon the
Oude tenure question, written when he was senior member
of the Board of Revenue, North-West Provinces, 29th May,
1863, he says, "I am afraid Act X. of 1859 has not left the
question of tenant-right upon a basis on which it can be
permanently maintained."

But tenant-rights and rights in land are awkward matters
to legislate upon prematurely. A change in the essentials
of a law like that of Act X. reaches the lowest stratum of
society. If the agricultural population of the country are
made to feel that every ten years or so the Legislature, by
some new enactment, or some amendment of an old one,
will work an agrarian revolution—at one time creating rights
in the soil, and at another uprooting them—it is impossible
they can have any confidence in the stability or the justice
of the Government. There are some errors in administration which it is less mischievous to leave alone than to
remedy. Sir William Muir continues : "The law providing
a possessory prescription for simple occupancy for twelve
years can, of course, only be sustained on the ground that
it is required by the custom and practice of the people.
Had the recognised custom and practice been clearly to
this effect, I should not have sought to re-open the question
on any grounds of expediency, because I think that our
legislation should be based on the existing status of rights,
and the popular feeling and conviction in respect of their
acquisition or growth. I do not think that legislation in
matters connected with the occupancy of the soil can hope
to succeed unless it is built upon the habits and axioms of

the natives. . . . I believe that there is no clear custom on the subject " (*i. c.* of a prescriptive title arising from a twelve years' occupancy), " and that, on the contrary, the sense of the proprietary body is, that if we have not imposed a new custom to their disadvantage, we have at least imposed an old one with a stringency and imperativeness as to its sudden development which was unknown before."

After citing a number of authorities, he says: " I think it has been abundantly shown from the foregoing recapitulation of authorities, that there is no certain evidence in favour of any fixed period as giving a title to prescription."

The general tendency of the enactment is to destroy the power and influence of the landed aristocracy for the sake of the tenant or the ryot. If we could be sure that the position of the latter would be improved in proportion as that of the former deteriorated, there might be some show of reason in a measure which benefited the many at the expense of the few. But whatever may be the experience of other countries as to the system of a peasant proprietary, one result of it in India will be that the cultivators, deprived of the support of their natural protectors the large landed proprietors, will fall into the hands of the money-lenders and corn-dealers, a race whose tender mercies are cruel, whose influence is already far too great, and whose oppression drove into rebellion the Sonthals a few years ago. Nor must we shut our eyes to the results of this system upon ourselves. While the political and moral influence of the cultivating class in India is *nil*, a well-affected landed aristocracy would be the strongest possible support to British dominion. The tendency of our legislation has been to destroy the power of that class altogether. In fact, even now, there is scarcely such a thing as a landed aristocracy in Upper India at all. As time goes on the few remnants now left will disappear. In their place will be a race of pauper cultivators, bound hand and foot to a comparatively few very wealthy money-lenders, usurers, and corn-dealers. Oude, of course, forms an exception. And that province,

which has cost us so much to conquer, will one of these
days be one of our strongest and most secure possessions.
The feelings of the present generation may be embittered
by a recollection of recent strife, but when time has effaced
the memory of 1856 and the few succeeding years, and left
a landed aristocracy influential and, it is to be hoped, tolerably contented, we shall find, should need arise to rest on
any other defence—under Providence—than our own strong
right hand, that the system built up by Lord Canning, or
restored by him, will form the most powerful support to
the British Government.

Another very useful procedure Act was passed in this
year, the Limitation Act, or an Act to provide for the limitation of suits. By this legislative measure, suits for the
recovery of rights in real or immoveable property must be
brought within twelve years, reckoning from the date when
the cause of action arose. But the period within which
petty debts may be recovered—which, of course, concerns
the greatest number of litigants, and affects the bulk of the
community—was cut down to three years, instead of six, as
it was before and is in England. It is not very easy to
understand the object proposed to be gained by this. As
a general principle, it is advisable, of course, to narrow the
limits within which in point of time claims for ordinary
debts may be kept alive. For the interests of the European
trading community in India this law was not well adapted,
because in that country changes of residence are common ;
men quit India for years together and at a few days'
notice, and there is generally a want of stability about the
character of society that interferes with the speedy realiza-
tion of accounts and collections of debts. Of course, the
Act provides for what are called legal disabilities to pro-
secute a claim ; but still, in spite of that provision, I do not
think the introduction of the three years' clause was beneficial. In other respects this law, like other acts regulating
procedure, is the offspring of official experience ; and the
matter, being within the scope of the actual observation of

the members of the Legislature, has been on the whole, with the exception of one or two imperfectly expressed clauses, efficiently and practically dealt with.

Another Act passed in this year deserves notice as illustrating that special legislation which is sometimes necessary in India. In a part of the Madras Presidency there are a class of desperate fanatics, called the Moplas, who not unfrequently break out into some wild fits of excitement, under the influence of which they will commit the most shocking outrages, utterly regardless of the consequences to themselves. Accordingly, the preamble of the Act (XX. of 1859) states that in the district of Malabar, in the Presidency of Madras, murderous outrages have been frequently committed by persons of the class called Moplas, the offenders in such outrages intending thereby to sacrifice their lives; and as the general law of the country is not adequate to suppress such outrages, a special enactment follows, containing stringent measures of more than ordinary severity against the perpetrators of these crimes.

This was passed in 1859, specially directed against the Moplas. There is therefore very little force in the argument used in support of the Disarming Act passed in 1860, viz. that it was necessary to avoid special legislation, and that Europeans and Christians could not be exempted in an Act passed to disarm the population generally. If the Moplas were worthy of special legislation on the side of severity, one does not see why the European and Christian community might not have been deemed worthy of a clause exempting them from the operation of so ungrateful a measure as the " Disarming Act."

Several measures of the Legislature in 1860 deserve especial notice. The first in order of time is the Indigo Act, already mentioned. This was in force for six months, and provides for the assembly of a committee of inquiry into the system of indigo culture. Any ryot having received an advance for the cultivation of indigo during the current season, and not cultivating it according to agreement, may

under this Act be summoned before the magistrate, who
may assess damages, and order payment or specific performance of the contract, and may attach the land to be
cultivated if described in the contract, or in default may
order the ryot to be imprisoned, and damages levied on
his property. It also provides for the summary punishment of any person intimidating a ryot into breach of
contract, or maliciously destroying or damaging indigo
crops; and no appeal is to lie from the decision of the
magistrate. It was limited to Bengal Proper as regards
area, and to six months as regards time. It was another
instance of a special Act passed for a special purpose.

It is hardly necessary to notice in detail the Income
Tax Bill which was passed in this year, but an important
measure received the assent of the Governor-General in
August 1860, upon which it is necessary to offer a remark
or two. It was an Act (XXXIV. of 1860) to indemnify
officers of Government *and other persons* in respect of fines
and contributions levied and *acts done* by them during the
disturbance.

After the rebellion of 1857 was over there succeeded
a reign of terror. The natives certainly learnt a lesson
which, for the present generation at least, will not be
effaced from their memory. They had played for high
stakes and lost. In the hour of their short-lived success
they had known no mercy, and they had no right to look
for any at the hands of the victors. Great as are the evils
of civil war and the miseries it entails, not the least of
its bad consequences is the demoralizing effect the spirit
of strife produces on the mind, blunting the feelings and
kindling evil passions which for the time almost transform
human beings into wild beasts; and Lord Canning has
been much praised for the calmness he preserved amid
a period of general excitement, and for not yielding to the
clamour of those who, it is said, were thirsting for wholesale revenge upon the native population. The European
community in India were accused by the English press,

and by speakers in the House of Commons, of advocating indiscriminate slaughter, and a general confiscation of property. No doubt at the time, under the excitement which prevailed amid the heat of the conflict, men placed too little restraint upon their desire for revenge ; but it may be doubted whether anything so bloodthirsty in its tone as some articles which appeared in the columns of leading London journals was ever published in any Indian paper. But in truth more than half the clamour raised against Lord Canning and his government was not on account of this " clemency " or leniency in dealing with the rebels, so much as the persistence they showed in releasing and rewarding men who ought not to have been rewarded, and punishing men who ought to have been released. Every allowance is to be made for the circumstances under which the Government or its officers had to act, and it might have been difficult at the time to discriminate between the innocent and the guilty. Unhappily, there can be little doubt that out of those who were punished in the rebellion a large proportion were innocent, while the guilty escaped. Thus at Cawnpore, when it was retaken by the column under Neil and Havelock, and Renaud's detachment first marched into the ruined cantonments, when the bodies of the victims that had been thrown down the well were still quivering with the last remnants of vitality, the soldiers were for destroying all the natives they found in the place. The fact was, they were too angry to discriminate at the time, or to understand that all who had been concerned in the rebellion and massacre had fled and concealed themselves. Only those remained who from their sympathy, or their neutrality at least, felt that they could regard the approach of an English army of retribution with confidence. It was the same everywhere. The guilty took care to get out of the way, the innocent were seized and had to suffer.

But another great evil sprang out of the general excitement to which the civil war had given rise. Not only did the antagonism of race intensify men's passions, but among the natives themselves society was unhinged. No man could trust his fellow, no one's life or property was safe. It was said to be a common thing for debtors to get their creditors hanged by the simple process of charging them with rebellion and murder. Wholesale confiscations followed the restoration of order as a matter of course. And grievous were the errors committed for want of patient and judicial investigation, or inability to find out the truth. It was a grand time for gratifying old animosities, and getting rid of creditors. Witnesses were to be had, as they always are in India, for a few rupees ; and if Ram Singh had a grudge against Ely Bux, or owed him more than it was convenient to pay, he had but to go to the Commissioner and denounce him as a rebel, taking care at the same time to have his witnesses ready, and not forgetting to fee well the moonshee or jemadar through whom the Commissioner was in the habit of conducting his private inquiries. If Ram Singh managed properly, he would soon have the satisfaction of seeing Ely Bux either hanged or beggared for life. Again, there were many such cases as the following. There was a family out of which one perhaps joined the rebels, the rest kept aloof. No matter : they dared not come forward to declare their innocence. They preferred beggary to the chance of being hanged. They trusted that, when the excitement had passed over, they might be able to prove their innocence, and recover something from the general wreck. It was not safe to trust to any evidence of non-complicity. The only safe anchorage was the friendship of the native subordinates and *amla* of the commissioners' or the magistrates' court. The injustice and hardship that resulted was wholesale. Nor would the Government deny that such was the case. In a conference with one of the members of Sir John Lawrence's council on this very subject, he admitted that instances of unjust confiscation and spoliation were so numerous that the Government dare not grant redress in one lest it should be inundated with similar claims. All this was owing to the system on which the Indian Government will persist in carrying on the executive administration. Special commissions were appointed to conduct these inquiries into charges of rebellion. But it was impossible for special commissioners and magistrates, accessible only through native moonshees, clerks, informers, or servants, to find out the truth. Intrigue and corruption ran rampant ; and after the thirst for blood had been slaked, and there were no more victims for the gallows, the most reckless system of confiscation of property began, the confiscated property being bestowed upon loyal characters, the main difference between the loyal and disloyal being that the one had managed to play his cards better than the other.

It is true that in 1858 an Act was passed creating a summary method of procedure for the recovery of estates confiscated by mistake, and special commissioners were appointed under it to adjudicate upon all such cases, and by this tribunal some remedy might have been applied, but it was a very inefficient one. Men were afraid, and it actually was not safe for them, to come forward at that time to assert their innocence. They did not know what evidence might not be arrayed against them. If they had landed property, there were next of kin or some harpies ready to pounce upon it, waiting to see the owner hanged or transported in order to take possession. If during the rebellion a zemindar had absconded to escape the violence of either party, his return was at the risk of his life. Some informer would give evidence against him ; he would be seized as implicated in the rebellion, and if he had much property, and it was desirable he should be hanged, he would be accused of complicity in the murder of Europeans. Numbers preferred to abandon their estates altogether, with the chance of recovering them when passion had cooled down, rather than run that risk.

A country cannot of course go through the horrors of civil war without suffering for it. An unsuccessful attempt at insurrection always entails terrible consequences on the vanquished. The swell of the ocean after a storm is in proportion to the strength of the hurricane. And after such a terrible outbreak of national hatred, and long-pent-up broodings over wrongs, it was not to be wondered at that the subsidence of the storm should be attended by much individual suffering, and that in all cases the victors were not able to discriminate very nicely between the innocent and the guilty, or between degrees of guilt. But there was assuredly no necessity to perpetuate errors committed in the hour of excited passion.

Yet it was to stereotype such a condition of affairs that the Act of Indemnity was passed in 1860. It provides, " that all fines, penalties, assessments, and contributions imposed since the 10th May, 1857, in respect of the destruction or injury of Government or other property, or on any other account connected with the late disturbance, shall be deemed to have been duly levied, and all officers of Government are indemnified from liability therefor." The clause adds rather illogically, " provided that nothing in this Act shall authorize the levy of any fine, penalty, assessment or contribution not already levied." The second clause " confirms" and " makes valid" all acts done since the 10th May, 1857, in connexion with the late disturbances, by officers of Government or by persons acting under their authority or otherwise in pursuance of an order of Government.

It was under this Act that the Government, whenever a case was brought to its notice in which some illegal confiscation had been made or unjust sentence passed, took shelter, and declared itself unable to interfere.

So far as the Act of Indemnity went, no one will find fault with the measure. An Act of Indemnity was indeed most necessary. But it was altogether unnecessary at so short a period, that is, when the rights of property were in question, to confirm the confiscations and the grants that followed. If it had not been for this Act numbers of mistakes

that were made through inadvertence or ignorance during
the excitement of the rebellion and of the period subsequent
to it might have been rectified, and where injustice had
been committed a remedy might have been applied, and
redress or compensation granted. But it appeared as if
the Government had not the courage to look into its own
acts, or as if it dared not review the past history of those
few years. Like a spendthrift who will not examine his
accounts to see how he stands with the world, but closes
his books and determines to continue the course he has
entered upon, it shut itself out from all possibility of doing
justice by giving the sanction of the Legislature to the acts
done between 1857 and 1860.

Act XXXIV. of 1860 is a blot upon the Indian statute-
book which never could have found a place there had there
been an independent member in Council who was practically acquainted with the condition of the country and the
feelings of the people. We are not well versed in the history
of Russian legislation with respect to Poland, but I doubt
whether there is a page in it so black as that which stereo-
types in the rigid garb of law, and places it thereby beyond
the power of the executive to cancel, acts done and sen-
tences passed in the height of the passion aroused by civil
war and the flood-tide of excitement consequent on victory.

From the frequency with which Indian legislators have
of late years amended and altered the stamp duties, it
would appear as if a member of Council, whenever he had
nothing else to propose, suggested a new stamp law to
keep his hand in. Changes in stamp duties occasion a great
deal of vexation, trouble, and annoyance which ought never
to be unnecessarily inflicted on a population like that of
India. Yet in 1860 we had a stamp law, No. XXXIV.,
repealing former provisions, and laying down a new scale
of duties altogether. This was passed on the 2d August,
and in the following month a second Act amends the former,
and makes certain alterations and additions. The amended
Act, however, did not remain in favour very long; for in

1862 another (Act X.) repealed it altogether, and laid down an entirely new scale of duties. Again, five years later, we have the old story repeated—" Whereas it is expedient to amend the law relating to stamp duties," &c. This last regulation proved so faulty that it has been found necessary to supersede it by another enactment, noticed further on, and passed in 1868.

In this year, Small Cause Courts, which answer pretty much to the county courts in England, were extended. These courts for the recovery of small debts, from the decrees of which there is no appeal, would undoubtedly be a great convenience if, as in England, efficient judges could be found for them. But the pay is too small in relation to the usual rate of salaries in India, for civilians of any standing to be appointed. For the same reason, no barrister with a tolerable practice would take the office ; and the consequence is, that Government has been forced to appoint in many cases, as judges of these courts, clerks and subordinates—any one, in short, who had a little interest, totally irrespective of their fitness to conduct the duties. It is, of course, not so in all cases. In some cities these courts are under the superintendence of most efficient officers, but these are exceptional instances. And the mischief of having inefficient men is aggravated by the constitution of the courts themselves, which allow of no appeal. To decide promptly in suits that come before a Small Cause court in a large town requires no insignificant knowledge of law. A judge must have his law at his fingers' ends, for he has not time to study and to write elaborate judgments. In other courts, from which there is an appeal, a lawsuit in India takes so long in running its course that a judge has time to work up the question, and even if he errs it is not of so much consequence, because the Court of Appeal will set the matter right. It very often happens that a small sum of money is of as much importance to a poor man as a large sum or a landed estate is to a rich one ; and to force the poor man who has to recover

a small debt, of great consequence to him, into a court
where the decisions are guided frequently neither by law
nor common sense, and from which there is no appeal, is to
legislate in one way for the rich and in another for the
poor. The establishment and extension of these Small
Cause Courts has been much belauded as a wise and
useful measure. From the mode in which justice is administered in many of them, I know they are a source of
the utmost dissatisfaction, and frequently of the grossest
injustice. The Government could easily afford to raise the
salary of the judge of a Small Cause Court to 1,000*l.*
or 1,200*l.* a year, and for that a barrister or a solicitor
with a legal education and some aptitude for his work
might almost always be obtained.

The English reader must not forget that the course of
justice in the Mofussil is not watched, as it is in England,
by the press. The papers could not, if they tried, publish
reports of all cases ; and if they were to, it would be their
ruin, for such matters are not to the taste of most Indian
readers. There is therefore absolutely no check upon an
inefficient and ignorant judge of a court from which there
is no appeal. Either efficient judges should be appointed,
or the law should be altered, and special appeals on
technical points allowed.[1]

The most important Act of all, perhaps, that was passed
in 1860, was the Indian Penal Code. As a code it is very
complete, and the remark is very commonly made that
Indian legislation is far in advance of that in England, in
that it possesses a complete and exhaustive code of
criminal law and procedure. It is very comprehensive,
and it has been wittily said of it, that a man, for almost
any action of his every-day life, might be brought under
one or other of its sections. This is, of course, an exag-
geration. But there can be no doubt that it is an
effective weapon in the hands of a vindictive man, and it

[1] This, in fact, it has been found necessary to do by an enactment,
which will be noticed in its proper place, passed in 1867.

has been found to be so. A stringent code of criminal law was, indeed, necessary for India, and we have got it ; but the High Courts of Judicature ought to watch its operations very closely, and check any approach to abuse of the formidable power it puts into the hands of police officers and magistrates. It was commenced as long ago as 1833, and completed by the Indian Law Commission, which has numbered among its members some of the ablest and most experienced Indian jurists of the day.

The propriety of making Englishmen in India subject to the criminal law has been the battle-ground for incessant strife between the official and non-official classes for years past. Any attempt to make the European British subject amenable to a native magistrate's court in criminal matters has been resisted hitherto, happily with success. It will be a bad day for English residents should such a procedure ever be adopted ; it will be a bad day, indeed, for India altogether, for there is no doubt the attempt would be forcibly resisted. The framers of the Penal Code, and its supplement the Criminal Procedure Code, seem to have intended to make European British subjects amenable to the ordinary courts of the country, when, in Section 25 of the latter Act, they lay down : " No person whatever shall by reason of place of birth, or by reason of descent, be exempt from the rules of criminal procedure contained in this Act. Provided that nothing in the section shall be held to authorize the trial or commitment for trial before any criminal court, of any person who in respect of the offence with which he is charged is not subject to the jurisdiction of that court."

But this is not held to make them amenable to the Mofussil courts, although there was a very general opinion that it did. In introducing the European Vagrancy Bill in 1868, Mr. Maine remarked : " The Code of Criminal Procedure, though it does not apply to European British subjects beyond the Presidency towns, except so far as it regulates the procedure of the High Court, Agra, and the Chief Court, Lahore, has a certain modified application to Europeans who are not British subjects, and to Americans." And in a very recent case the High Court, Agra, has ruled that, even as respects maintenance of an illegitimate child, the justice of the peace has no power to compel a European British subject to make a payment on that account. Strange as it may seem, there is at the present moment, even after all that the Legislature has done, and the number of cases that have transpired, the greatest uncertainty as to the criminal law to which the European British subject is amenable in the Mofussil, except in cases that come before the High Courts.

An instance of the working of the Code may be mentioned, as it has often been argued that the Englishman in India should not be subjected to pains and penalties to which the English law does not subject him in his own land. The Penal Code makes—and very properly makes—seduction of a married woman a penal offence. No doubt the framers of the law at the time they penned these clauses had in their mind's eye the peculiar constitution of native society. It is possible they may have had also in their mind's eye the character popularly attributed to Anglo-Indian society. However, there the clauses stand, and the Englishman is amenable to them as much as the native. One or two cases have occurred recently in which an Englishman has sued in the Civil Court for damages against the seducer of his wife, and got them, and then afterwards laid a charge against him under the Penal Code, and the unhappy libertine has had to pay for the indulgence of his licentiousness, and to suffer imprisonment besides. Of course, in these cases, the maxim, " Nemo bis vexari potest," &c., is always pleaded, but without effect; for there is nothing in the law to prevent the seducer from being amerced in damages in a civil suit, and nothing in the Penal Code to prevent his being tried criminally. At the same time, it cannot be denied that in such a case we have a distinct instance where a man "bis vexatur pro unâ et eadem causâ."

But the enactment is very salutary. A general and growing open disregard to the laws of morality is one of the most formidable signs of the decay of a nation. In England there is sufficient respect for the moral law, even amid the growing dissoluteness of modern times, to place a restraint upon the commission of this offence.

Among a certain class, and doubtless a large class, the seducer of woman's virtue meets with but little discountenance and discouragement; but everywhere out of the circle of his own associates his conduct is regarded with abhorrence, and called by its right name. In India, unhappily, society has not yet outgrown the evil effects of the laxity and immorality of a former generation. And not only that, but there are growing up in India, like festering sores in the body politic, communities of men and women calling themselves Christian, who in laxity of morals bid fair to surpass the lowest classes of the heathen by whom they are surrounded. A low style of Englishmen, with blunted perceptions of right and wrong, given to habits of intemperance, are intermarrying with native and half-caste women, who have been brought up with no religious instruction, and no attention to those safeguards which the good sense of the community among the better-educated of the same or an equal class in our own country have erected around the decencies and the obligations of domestic life. The glimpses which our criminal courts occasionally afford of the moral condition of these classes is something appalling. Neither the judges of our courts nor the public have an opportunity of seeing into the depth of these abysses of immorality, but those who are compelled occasionally to look behind the scenes can testify to the ugly revelations of depravity and moral laxity which they thus unwillingly obtain. As to this particular offence, withdraw the penal consequence of it, and you withdraw absolutely the only barrier against the breach of the laws of nature—

of human nature at least—and the law of God. If the writers who advocate the non-application of the penal clauses against adultery knew what they were writing about—at least, if they knew anything of the condition in which large masses of the Anglo-Indian and Eurasian community are living—they would be the last to weaken the barrier which the Legislature has most prudently and wisely erected against a prevalent, and an increasing, and most debasing vice.

The year 1861 was not characterised by so many legislative enactments of general importance as its predecessor. The Criminal Procedure Bill was passed this year, which may be said to have completed what was wanting in the Penal Code. The Procedure was the work of the same master-hands that framed the sister code ; and although at its first introduction an imperfect acquaintance with its provisions, and a misunderstanding of many of its clauses, on the part mostly of inefficient and indolent magisterial officers and judges, caused a little confusion, it is exceedingly simple and at the same time comprehensive in its character. I think, considering the great inefficiency we often meet with in India in judicial officers, the proneness to become mere tools in the hands of some astute native, and the readiness with which the Code can be used as a weapon of offence and an instrument of vindictiveness, there ought to be an appeal always open to the High Courts, on points of law as well as of fact; such appeals being admitted only when cause is shown, and not as a matter of course in every case. Many cases may be finally disposed of by the lower courts, and when the appeal has been preferred to the district court the resources are exhausted. I am quite alive to the evils inherent in a system that permits incessant appeals, more especially in criminal matters; but as long as the Indian climate is what it is, it will be impossible to provide a sufficient number of qualified revenue and judicial officers to get through the work properly ; and as long as this condition of affairs lasts it will be impossible for officers to devote so much time to the study of law as to make them efficient judges. And if we want to provide India with a sound administration of justice, it is necessary to open out as much as possible channels of appeal to the High Courts, where the law is administered by trained and experienced officers, whose decisions alone are regarded with confidence by the native suitor. And any law, regulation, provision, or order that checks that resort to the only courts in India where a man can be sure of getting justice, is *pro tanto* mischievous and unsalutary.

One of the most difficult questions connected with the administration of criminal law in India is the police. In 1861 the Legislature endeavoured to provide for an efficient police system in Act V.

The old police which existed before the rebellion had been broken up. Its dissolution was attended with no regret on the part of those who had watched the method of its working, and many experienced men hold to the opinion that much of the disaffection which came to a head in 1857 was to be attributed to the extortion, intrigue, and oppression exercised by the police. Since 1857, various systems—at least, modifications of systems—have been tried, and all have proved faulty. The truth is, the establishment of an efficient and trustworthy police in India is one of the most difficult tasks that the Administration encounters. You have no good material to work with. In the first place, the class of men from which you must draw your constabulary are not to be trusted out of sight of their European superiors. The native of India is by nature cruel, unfeeling, avaricious, and an adept at intrigue. I am not trying to run down the native character. I believe that, intellectually, the native of India is as a rule nearly equal to the European. Nor do I wish to draw any unfavourable comparison in point of morals, for I believe that it often happens that one race lays claim to superior morality over another, while all the time the superiority may be accounted for on the principle that we

are all apt to condemn in others those particular faults
to which we ourselves have no inclination, while the sins
that we "have a mind to" are passed over among our
own class leniently. Leaving this question to the ethno-
logist or the philosopher, I am safe in asserting that the
native of India is by nature cruel and unfeeling. He
will inflict pain and suffering on other men, as well as
inferior animals, without the least remorse. He will take
life, when he can do so with impunity, with comparative
indifference. At the same time, he will himself undergo
pain and suffering, even loss of life, with an amount of
patient endurance and stolid apathy which often astonishes
the European spectator. He is avaricious, and will undergo
great risk for the sake of a probable gain. For love of
intrigue there is, I suppose, no race in the world so prone to
it as the Asiatic, and among Asiatic nations none in which
it forms so prominent a characteristic as the Indian. The
native does not regard truth in the same light that we do,
nor does he consider that any disgrace attends the being
convicted of a falsehood. At the same time he is clever,
sharp, and astute at getting up a story, and with it all, very
easily intimidated.

With men whose character has been formed in such a
mould, it may easily be understood how exceedingly
difficult it is to organize an efficient and trustworthy
police force. The police officer can never be sure that the
case reported to him has not been fabricated to secure
some private ends. Vindictiveness forms as prominent a
feature in the Indian character as any of the qualities I
have mentioned. If a man loses a lawsuit, it is a common
thing for him to revenge himself on the successful suitor
by advancing a criminal charge. Perhaps he adopts an
artifice to which resort is very frequently made, and places
opium or some contraband article in the house or on the
premises of his adversary, and then goes and gives information to the police. These articles are, of course,
discovered where they were placed. What can the house-

holder urge but that he did not put them there himself? He cannot *prove* he did not, and there is the fact of the discovery against him. In such a case, his only course is to give a *douceur* to the native inspector of police, who, if sufficiently well paid, will tell the magistrate that the man bears a good character, that it is a very common trick to put such articles on another man's premises and then inform against him, and the magistrate probably gives the prisoner the benefit of the doubt.

Since the introduction of the Penal Code, and the facilities it offers for bringing charges, the power in the hands of the police in India has increased enormously. When a criminal charge is brought against a native, the very first thing the attention of a legal adviser of the accused is directed to, next to the facts of the case, is the motive and character of the accuser. From what I have seen of the practice of Indian criminal law in subordinate courts, I should never look upon the fact of a conviction being obtained as *per se* any proof of the guilt of the prisoner. Natives themselves do not so regard it. It is simply a game that has been played out, in which the accused party, now the prisoner, has lost. It is very much to be desired that the ticket-of-leave system should be introduced into Indian jails, and prisoners convicted of petty crimes allowed to go out on good behaviour. The fact of their being there is of itself no imputation upon their moral character; and were it the custom to allow them to go out on ticket of leave, society would have a guarantee for their good behaviour, for the fact of their freedom being conditional would be a strong inducement to honesty, and that of their being convicts under sentence would have but little weight with any one who knows how easily criminal charges are got up, and established to the satisfaction of magistrates and sessions judges. The police, as at present constituted, can get any native convicted of almost any crime they like, provided the crime has been committed in the first instance; but even this is not always necessary, for it is not very difficult for them to instigate the commission of the crime and then discover a criminal.

That such a state of affairs should exist is very appalling, but it is nevertheless true, and any native independent enough to express his opinion freely will corroborate the assertion I have made, extravagant though it may seem in English ears.

A curious instance illustrative of this occurred not long ago at Lahore. A robbery was committed on the premises of the Lieutenant-Governor, the locality selected for the crime having given it a prominence it would not otherwise have enjoyed. Seven men were arrested. The case was "got up," as it is called—that is, prepared—by the inspector of police. Witnesses were brought forward, and the evidence appeared most conclusive. The case was tried before a careful officer, Mr. Aitcheson, of the Civil Service, who was convinced on the evidence adduced of the guilt of the prisoners, and sentenced them to seven years' penal servitude. After they had been a short time in jail, it was discovered that these men were not the criminals at all. They had nothing whatever to do with the robbery. But five other men were apprehended, the crime was brought home to them, and when they found that escape was impossible they confessed. This occurred at Lahore, the head-quarters of a province, one of the centres of European population, within sight of the chief court, and Government-house itself was the scene of the crime. To these accidental circumstances it owes its publicity. How many cases of a like kind would be brought to light were there any means of bringing them to light, all over the country, where men very inferior to Mr. Aitcheson, who is one of the best officers in the service, have to administer the criminal law unchecked by any supervising authority ?

One of the most objectionable clauses of the Penal Code enables a magistrate, upon the report of the police-officer, to enter in a list the name of any resident of the town or district who may be represented to be a bad character.

These lists are not confined to the magistrate. Police-officers make them for themselves; and in point of practice it is not the most difficult thing in the world for a native who has a grudge against his neighbour, to get his name entered in this list. A refusal to lend a policeman money, or a determination in a man to keep his wife to himself, will not improbably result in the money-lender or the hus-band's name going down in the book of bad characters. The consequences it entails are serious, for in practice the procedure usually adopted in the event of a crime being reported is as follows :—Suppose a robbery, for instance, has taken place at a certain village, and is reported to the police-officer. He sends a native inspector out to institute inquiries. What the native inspector does is to seize the persons in the place whose names are down in this list and keep them in custody. Under the present system a police-constable gets credit and promotion in proportion to the number of convictions he obtains. The consequence is that in most cases, after these wretched people have been in the hands of the police a day or two, the constable or inspector reports to his officer that one of them has con-fessed. What means are used to extort that confession is a dark chapter in our Indian administration. The charge is stoutly denied by all officials, from the governors of provinces downwards, but from the reports that reach me on all sides there is too much reason to fear that in a great majority of cases violence and torture are used to elicit confessions. Sometimes—very rarely—these matters ooze out, and are brought before the public. They do so very rarely, because the easily intimidated native will run the risk of jail and hard labour, and of seeing his family starve, rather than give evidence against the police, whose power is so great that the only thing to which it can be compared is the police system in France under the monarchy, as represented in the pages of Dumas and other romance-writers. It is hardly too much to say that the whole country is absolutely groaning under this oppression, for

the police, in combination with the *amla*, or subordinates
of the magistrates' courts, are all-powerful. A general
impression, a universally received opinion, a belief entertained by a whole community of people who are of course
versed in the customs and practices observed among their
own fellow-countrymen, is seldom found to be without
foundation. There is but one opinion among the natives.
I speak from experience of the North-West and the Punjab
only, but there is no reason to suppose the same remark
would not apply to other provinces, for a system similarly
constituted is calculated to produce similar results in all
parts of the country.[1] A case transpired the other day at
Hooghly, which is close to Calcutta, where a man was
seized by the police, and in order to induce him to confess
to a crime of which he had not in reality been guilty, a
brass vessel called a lota, full of wasps, was fastened on his
stomach. The crime was brought home to the perpetrators
in this instance, and they were punished. This occurred
close to Calcutta, as in the other instance that transpired
at Lahore, within the jurisdiction of the High Court, and
within sight almost of Government-house, and within the
reach, as it were, of the press. What may we not suppose
is the condition of the people in villages and places distant
from European supervision? In the face of the stout
denial with which the assertion is met by every civil and
police official almost in India, I can scarcely expect credit
for the assertion of the existence of the system without
adducing special instances in proof of the charge against
the Indian police. There is, however, the universal belief
of the people. There are the revelations made by the
Madras Torture Commission in former years; and no one,

[1] Even in Bengal, our oldest province, within the jurisdiction of the
High Court of Calcutta, and within reach of the press, where education
has made the greatest stride among the natives, the Report of the
Police Administration for 1867, at p. 122, vol. ii., informs us that 1,570
men in the force were judicially convicted during the year of the crimes
of extortion, receiving stolen property, violence, criminal assault,
bribery, theft, &c.

I presume, would be found to say that the present system is less calculated than the former was to foster this abuse. It is, on the contrary, calculated to foster it a great deal more. Formerly the police were a semi-organized body, to whom the success in obtaining convictions held out no certain rewards and no particular benefits beyond, perhaps, the favourable notice of the collector and his subordinates, and such contingent advantages as might occasionally follow; but now it is almost the only road to promotion.[1]

The *à priori* arguments for the existence of the system are borne out by the instances that now and again crop out and come before the public, and symptoms of it have appeared with sufficient frequency in cases that have come in appeal before the High Courts, to lead some of the judges, if I am not mistaken, to pretty much the same conclusions as those I have formed myself.

The frequency with which criminal convictions are supported and mainly depend upon the confession of the accused, ought long ago to have put magisterial and judicial officers on their guard. Men do not commit crimes and then go and confess them. Now and again we hear of instances where a criminal who has the burden of some tremendous crime upon his conscience, unable to bear the mental agony which he endures, confesses it; but it is contrary to our experience of human nature to suppose that in a large majority of instances criminals should confess, especially when their confession is the principal means of bringing the guilt home to them.

To obviate so terrible an evil I should advocate, first of all, the abandonment of the present practice of making so

---

[1] What promotion in the police means may be exemplified by the instance of one man I knew, who, five or six years ago, was drawing four rupees a month as a common chiprassee, or messenger, and is now, owing to a rapid rise consequent on his getting into the good graces of the magistrate, a wealthy man with landed property, and a terror to the whole district.

much of prisoners' confessions.   Secondly, the more sparing
exercise of the powers conferred by the Criminal Code of
entering names in the lists of bad characters.   Thirdly, the
total abandonment of the practice of retaining accused
parties in custody, which is constantly done all over the
country, in direct opposition to the law.   Fourthly, I would
visit with much severer penalties than are usually inflicted
the crime of illegal detention and the use of violence to
extort confession.   But above all it is necessary that magisterial officers should set their faces against the system, and
let their subordinates understand that they will incur their
very severest displeasure and the heaviest penalties if convicted of it.   So far from doing this, we generally find
that when a charge of illegal action on the part of the police
is made, the European officials, from the magistrate down
to the lowest grade of police-officer, unite all their efforts
to stifle inquiry from a mistaken sense of *esprit de corps.*
It is, however, sufficiently notorious to be undisputed by
any one who has the least practical acquaintance with the
ordinary method of procedure in criminal cases, that illegal
detention in custody of suspected persons for days and
weeks together is carried on openly over the whole country.
Magistrates will not deny it ; on the contrary, many of
them boldly avow that if it were not for this process they
could never apprehend or convict any criminal at all.

What the fate is which the unhappy wretches undergo
during the period of this detention, may be guessed from
the fact that it generally ends in a confession, which is followed by a conviction of the prisoner and the reward of the
police.   I annex in a note[1] a list, in English, of a few of

---

[1] Binding the arms across the back.
Neck and leg torture—fastening the feet to the neck.
Applying venomous insects to the tender parts of the body.
Holding the head over a vapour of chillies.
Burning with red-hot copper coins.
Causing to stand in the sun, or with a heavy stone on the head.
Causing quantities of salt to be eaten.   [Abrading

the tortures common enough in India to have regular names given to them. Most of them are of such a character as to leave no visible marks or impression on the person of the sufferer. Many are unfit for publication.

The police, naturally enough, are much disliked by the native gentry, because they bring the executive power of the law, as it were, to their very doors. Still, it is inconceivable that the feeling against the present system could be so universal, that the testimony of respectable citizens and wealthy men could be so unanimous as to the corruption which exists and the excesses which are committed, unless there were some foundation for it. We might expect to find the evil-disposed, the unruly and disorderly classes of the community—thieves, vagabonds, and swindlers—to be inimical to any system that brought them within reach of the law ; but it is not conceivable that the better classes —deputy-magistrates, bankers, merchants, and others— who have everything to gain, and nothing to lose, from a vigorous executive, should bear testimony to the existence of such abuses, if they were not persuaded that they were practised.

A great deal of what is faulty in the present system is undoubtedly owing to a bad class of police-officers. When the Mutiny had left a vast number of military men unemployed, it was thought an excellent opportunity for providing work for many of them to draught them into the police. Now a military officer does not make a good police-officer. He will look after the drill of the men, and take pains with their get-up and equipment ; and so far as military organization goes, he is the best man to impart it. But, on the other hand, he will generally be found very jealous of interference, prone to fall into the hands of some clever, designing native, who makes his superior believe he is honest, intelligent, and trustworthy. Still worse is the class

Abrading the skin and applying chillies.
Tying up by the thumbs, by the legs, by the ear, hair, or moustache, &c.
      (*Vide* Fallon's " Legal and Commercial Dictionary.")

occasionally employed—private soldiers who have taken or purchased their discharge. Here and there you find an able man fit to be trusted, but, as a rule, they are inefficient. Magistrates, on the other hand, and assistant-magistrates, have no time to attend to police work, having a great deal more than they can do properly in their legitimate field of labour.

The best class to employ are a class generally under-rated, but nevertheless possessing qualities that especially adapt them for this kind of duty. I mean men born in the country, of European parentage or mixed descent. Many of them are men well developed physically, and they have many characteristics, both intellectual and physical, which render them peculiarly fitted for Indian police work. There are several in the lower grades of the force already scattered throughout India, but they are, as a rule, kept down, never allowed to rise above the lower grades, merely because the higher appointments, endowed with better pay, are reserved for those who have a claim on the patronage of the Lieutenant-Governor or the Inspector-General. It is the fashion in India to despise the class, to treat them with every slight and indignity, and to regard them with far less consideration than is accorded to the pure natives. There are among them numbers of high-principled, honourable men, wanting perhaps in some of the features of English and American character, but nevertheless well capable of serving the State, and deserving of a great deal more consideration and promotion than they ever get.

Above all, it is necessary that the importance of an efficient police for India be fully recognised. It is one of those institutions that brings the Administration into close contact with the people. It is the coupling-iron that unites the locomotive with the train. Given a perfect judicial system and courts presided over by efficient and well-trained judges; given a good revenue system, fair settlements, and just taxes; given an army that affords just the amount of protection it ought to afford to the country without interfering with the civil rights of the people; given conscientious and hardworking magisterial officers; given everything that can contribute to the happiness and comfort of a well-governed country: but if the police are corrupt the people are oppressed, and a just and liberal administration is turned into an instrument of tyranny.

As my excuse for dwelling so long upon this subject, I must urge its great importance; for the police, as at present constituted, are not only a source of danger to the State, from the fact of their being an organized body scattered over the whole continent, being readily armed, far removed from effective supervision, with many facilities for communication and co-operation, but the abuses alluded to render them dangerous in another way. It is the British Government and its officers who get the blame of the oppressions exercised by them in the name of the law. They have it in their power to foster disaffection, to organize rebellion, to bring from their own ranks a drilled army one or two hundred thousand strong into the field, and, what is of much more consequence, they could secure the co-operation of the great body of the people.

From what I have said, it will be clear that one-half the power of evil possessed by the Indian police would be removed if the detective element were eliminated from it; for it is in employing men as detectives that so wide a field for oppression and corruption becomes open to them; and it is in attempting the difficult work of detectives that the officers, always untrained and generally inefficient at such duty, become tools in the hands of men who in power of intrigue, astuteness, and cunning are as far superior to the European officer as he is to them in physical development.

At the same time, it is very desirable that there should be a detective police in India; and a body of men for this particular service might be formed under the supervision of some officer of experience. A nucleus for a force of this kind exists already in the establishment for the suppression of dacoitee, now under Colonel Hervey. The duties of this department are essentially detective, and the system only requires a little modification to render it well adapted for all the purposes for which a detective police in India is required.

Above all, the system of employing paid informers, which exists extensively in many parts of India, should be put down with a strong hand ; and as long as there is a debt and credit account kept at the head-quarters of every district of convictions and acquittals, and men and officers are led to believe that their prospects in the service depend on the proportion which the former bears to the latter, so long will means be used to secure conviction which cannot but result in the utmost possible oppression, and the subservience of the law to private ends.

CHAPTER XIX.

THE HISTORY OF LEGISLATION (*continued*).

Amendments in criminal law—Religious endowments—Foreigners The Whipping Act—Coolie emigration—Trustee Act—Indian Marriage Act—Non-regulation provinces—The Indian Succession Act—The grand jury abolished—Petty juries—Natives on juries— The Parsee Marriage and Succession Acts—Summary procedure on bills of exchange—Indian Joint Stock Companies Act—Partner-ship Act—Marriage of converts—Patchwork legislation—Small Cause Courts—Summary procedure for the suppression of outrages in the Punjab—Administrator-General's Act—New Stamp Act— —The law an engine of private malice—The Municipal Committee Act of 1868—Shams and fictions—Oude Tenancy Act—Punjab Tenancy Act.

THE principal enactments in the year 1862 of general interest were directed to the improvement of the criminal law. In the beginning of this year the new Penal Code and Procedure was introduced, and it became necessary in consequence to repeal previous regulations and laws upon the subject. Some idea may be gained of the extent to which the criminal law of the land was simplified, and its procedure facilitated, from the fact that an Act (No. XVII.) passed on the 1st May, 1862, repealed no less than the enormous number of one hundred and fifty-seven entire enactments of previous years, and portions of seventy-three others. No greater commendation than is implied in the simple statement of this fact can be given to the framers of the Penal Code and the Criminal Procedure.

This Act was followed by another passed the same day, 1st May, regulating the powers of the High Court of Calcutta in respect of the administration of the criminal law, giving it certain powers of amendment of indictments, and of finding a prisoner charged with a higher offence guilty of a lower one in the same category, regulating the disposal of prisoners, &c.

In the following year a useful enactment was passed amending the existing law with regard to merchant seamen, defining the relations between masters of vessels and their crews, their respective liabilities, &c. And on the 10th March in the same year, 1863, the Indian Government, by Act of Legislature, divested itself of the charge of the management and control of all religious endowments.

Up to this time, the heavy burden had been laid upon Boards of Revenue, who appointed local agents under them in the different large cities. By this Act the Government, for once and for ever, washed its hands of all responsibility on these matters, and made over the endowments to trustees or committees, selected from the residents of the city or neighbourhood professing the religion to which the endowments belonged. The committee is to be formed in accordance, so far as can be ascertained, with the general wishes of those interested in the maintenance of the mosque or temple, or other religious establishment; and in case of any dispute as to the right of disposal of such endowment, the parties are referred to the ordinary court of the district. With these exceptions, the years 1862 and 1863 were not marked by many acts of the Imperial legislature involving any important principles of administration.

Early in the following year, 1864, it was deemed expedient to introduce some sort of control over the residence of foreigners in India. To prevent any unnecessary interference with the resort of foreigners to its shores, the Act (No. III. of 1864) passed on 12th February contains a clause empowering the Governor-General in Council to put it in operation in any part of India by means of a notification in the *Gazette*, the official medium of communication: foreign ministers and consuls of course being excepted.

By this law, the Government of India, or any local government, is empowered to order a foreigner to "remove himself out of India," as it is rather quaintly expressed ; and if the foreigner shall remain on being ordered to remove himself (which, by the way, he *might* be physically incapable of doing), he is liable to be apprehended, detained, or deported, as the authorities may determine. Certain specified officers are empowered to board vessels and ascertain if there are any of the dreaded or obnoxious foreigners on board, or to require commanders to give information.

I have never heard an instance of the Act being put in operation. It is not difficult to conceive circumstances under which the powers conveyed by it might be exercised with salutary effect.

A great deal of discussion in the public papers and private circles preceded the introduction and passing of what is called the Whipping Act, and which became law in the same month, February.

This is a salutary measure authorizing the punishment of whipping for certain offences, or under certain restrictions. Such offences as theft, or extortion by threat, or dishonestly receiving stolen property, are punishable in this way for the first offence ; and for the second offence, such crimes as giving false evidence, in certain cases, assaults on women, robbery, dacoitee, &c. There can be no question that the punishment is a most suitable one in many cases. But notwithstanding the restrictions that are laid down, and the obvious intention of the Act, it is occasionally abused by inexperienced or hot-headed magisterial officers, and its application ought to be carefully watched. It is not intended to be used where the criminals are men of superior position, high caste, and respectability ; for in such instances the disgrace incurred, which it is not the object of the law to inflict, is of far greater consequence than the pain the criminal suffers. A case has unhappily occurred within my own experience, where the punishment has been inflicted on wealthy men, bankers of repute and position, who were, after the completion of the sentence by which they suffered indelible disgrace, shown to be entirely innocent.

It has been the custom in India ever since the establishment of our law courts, for the presiding judge to have the assistance of Mahommedan and Hindoo law officers, as they were called; in the former case kazees, in the latter pundits. The foundation of the Mahommedan law is to be found in the Koran,' the Hindoo in the Institutes of Menu. Both these sources became, of course, enlarged during the long lapse of time that has ensued since the enunciation of the two systems, by the additions of commentators, and collections of rulings, decisions, opinions, and dogmas of the different authorities, of more or less value, in proportion as they were regarded as orthodox teachers and expounders of the law of their respective systems of religion. The existence among the Hindoos of various schools, holding each its own tenets and interpretation of the sacred texts, within certain specified limits, added much to the responsibility and difficulty of giving judicial decisions in cases that are guided by Hindoo law; and in the earlier days of our Indian administration these questions were deemed so abstruse that it was considered more than could be expected from a judicial officer that he should be competent to decide them, so he was assisted and relieved of the responsibility by the appointment of a Hindoo and Mahommedan law officer attached to the Sudder or chief court, whose opinion might at any time be asked on cases submitted to them by the court. As time went on, and Hindoo and Mahommedan law came to be studied and better known, and the rulings of the superior courts in India and of the Privy Council had settled so many principles and afforded so many precedents, it was considered unnecessary any longer to retain the Hindoo and Mahommedan law advisers, and they were accordingly, in a brief enactment of this year, abolished. The best proof that they were no longer wanted is found in the fact that since their abolition they have, so far as my experience goes, never been missed.

It seems strange that in a country like India, where there are so many thousands of miles of uncultivated lands lying idle, and where the most barren waste can be turned into fertile fields by the simple process of digging wells and irrigating the thirsty soil, the system of emigration should be found in vogue. We are accustomed to regard emigration as the last resort of an overcrowded population, as the natural means which people adopt when their native country affords no field for labour. Yet in spite of this, emigration of labourers, or coolies as they are called, from India to the West Indies and the Mauritius and other places, went on to such an extent that the Legislature was forced to interfere to prevent those abuses which almost always attend the wholesale emigration of the poorest classes.

Several laws had been passed in former years, regulating the conditions under which coolies were to be shipped off to foreign lands. But in this year, 1864, an Act (XIII.) was passed, consolidating and amending the existing enactments on this subject. The geographical limits within which the emigration was recognised are defined in clause 4, which provides that contracts may be made with natives of India to emigrate to any of the British colonies of Mauritius, Jamaica, British Guiana, Trinidad, St. Vincent, and to the Danish colony of St. Croix. The local governments at those places are empowered to establish their agents at Calcutta, Madras, and Bombay, and the local governments at the sea-ports are authorized to appoint for each of the ports an officer called Protector of Emigrants, whose duties are sufficiently intimated in his official title, and who is assisted by a medical inspector.

Such an office can be no sinecure if the duties are properly performed. But, considering the condition of India itself, the call for labour in many parts of the country, the ignorance and utter inability of the native coolie to take care of himself, the liability of his being ill-treated and starved, and his utter helplessness in a foreign land, it is a question whether Government would not be acting more in accordance with the principles of humanity, and more to the interest of India, were emigration of coolies to be restricted as much as possible instead of encouraged.[1] It is an object, of course, with many colonies to get labour from India ; and in that view there is some safeguard for the protection and humane treatment of the emigrants, for a report of ill-treatment might have the effect of deterring others from following in their footsteps. It is very well to talk of free-trade and the liberty of the subject. But when we consider how easy it is to impose upon an illiterate ignorant native of the lower class of India, and to induce him by golden promises to leave his home and country for a foreign land ; when it is considered that at the best he can never realize what it is he is undertaking, or to what risks he may not be exposed ; it is very doubtful, I think, whether the Legislature ought not to interfere to prevent means being used to persuade the people to emigrate. At any rate, the system which I know is resorted to, of sending agents into the Mofussil and enticing large numbers of men to desert their homes, or repair to the seaport and thence to emigrate, ought to be discouraged or put down. The men, under such circumstances, are not free agents. It is

---

[1] This subject has recently (1869) engaged the attention of the Legislature. During the discussion on the new Bill, Mr. Gordon Forbes stated that in the last quarter of a century 455,200 adults had emigrated from Calcutta and Madras alone to different colonies ; and he proceeded to show that the proportion of males among these represented the entire adult population of an ordinary Indian district.

absurd to pretend that they know what they are about to do, and whither they are about to go. If it was impossible for them to obtain their living in India by labour, it would be another thing. But the crying want throughout the country, next to capital, is labour; and to drain the land of its resources in this respect, or to allow it to be drained by emigration agents, appears to me to be bad policy, and an unnecessary sacrifice to the principle of free trade.[1]

A most beneficial enactment, as regards the European community in India, was passed in this year. It has been found necessary in England to relieve trustees of the heavy burden of responsibility with which they frequently found themselves laden, often without the least knowing the risk to which they were exposed, by accepting some trust imposed on them. In India, the character of society is such that it was next to impossible to find people willing to undertake the office of trustee at all. There, society is ever changing; life is more uncertain than at home, and almost all who can, leave the country as soon as they have acquired a competency, either in the shape of a pension or of money saved. The consequence was, that it was most difficult for a man who possessed any property in India to know what provision to make in the event of death. He could certainly appoint his friends trustees, but there was almost always a certainty that they would leave the country as soon as they were in a position to do so, never to return. There was the great uncertainty of life, and the general unwillingness to accept the responsibility of a trust in a country where among the bulk of the people the rights and liabilities of property are so little understood, and so little confidence placed in the courts of law. Under these circumstances the appointment of an official trustee was a measure of the highest wisdom.

---

[1] If these emigrants are asked where they are going, they reply "Chin," or China. Whether it is for service in the West Indies, or Mauritius, or elsewhere that they have been engaged, they are always told, and believe, they are to go to " Chin."

A previous enactment of the year 1863 had, indeed, provided for the appointment of an official trustee in certain cases; but the Act No. XVII. of the present year, 1864, extended the benefit to all classes. By this Act the appointment of official trustee rests with the Chief Justice of the Presidency, by whom he may be removed or suspended, as well as appointed. Such official trustee is to be sole trustee ; he cannot be appointed to act with another. The great advantage of the arrangement is that the interests of the *cestui que* trust are looked after by a professional man, who knows how to carry out the duties that devolve on him, and who in fact never dies or goes away. For should the existing incumbent pay the debt of nature or leave the country, his office is taken charge of by his successor, under the authority and supervision of the principal judicial officer of the Presidency. The official trustee is remunerated by a percentage. I think the measure ought to be extended, and in every presidency or province where there is a High Court an official trustee, as well as administrator-general, should be appointed, under the supervision of the court. At present this is not the case, but I hope that before long the Legislature will remedy the defect.

In this year the establishment of Small Cause Courts was very much extended, but as I have already noticed this subject there is no necessity to dwell upon it in this place. And an Act, also of this year, entitled "An Act to provide further for the Solemnization of Marriages in India of persons professing the Christian religion," was passed on the 9th April, 1864, to be repealed and superseded by a more comprehensive enactment in February of the following year. The constant repetition of the unsatisfactory process of passing Acts, and then immediately afterwards amending or repealing them, is a symptom of that haste and inconsideration which characterises Indian legislation, and is productive of great public inconvenience and a prolific waste of time. The Indian Statute-book would comprise

a volume of about half its present bulk if it were not for
this incessant patchwork, which is undesirable in most
things, but especially to be deprecated in legislation.

This Act (V. of 1865), though called the Indian Marriage
Act, yet has reference only to Christians. It provides that
marriages shall be celebrated by clergymen of the Established, or Roman Catholic Church, or of the Church of
Scotland, according to the ceremonies or customs of those
Churches, or by a marriage registrar or by any minister
of religion who may obtain a licence, and between native
Christians by any persons duly licensed to perform such
marriage. A clause was added giving validity to marriages
which had been solemnized previously by persons not
especially ordained. This was necessary to legalize matri-
monial connexions which ministers of dissenting denomina-
tions located as missionaries in various parts of India had
been frequently in the habit of effecting.

Parties who are to be married by a minister of religion
not an episcopally ordained clergyman or a clergyman·of
the Church of Scotland, must give notice according to a
form prescribed, stating names and length of residence
and the church or chapel in which the ceremony is to be
solemnized. Marriage may be performed any time between
6 A.M. and 7 P.M.; and if desired to be held in a private
dwelling, notice is to be sent to the marriage registrar, to
be affixed in a conspicuous place in his office. But no
clergyman of the Church of England may solemnize a
marriage in a private dwelling if there is a church at the
place, without licence from the bishop. The consent of
parents or guardians is necessary in case of a minor, not
being a widow or widower ; and the person whose consent
is necessary may prohibit the marriage. As regards native
Christians, the law is somewhat peculiar. Any person,
being a Christian, may be licensed by the local government,
or the Chief Commissioner of a province, to perform the
ceremony, which consists in the parties coming before the
person so licensed, or in the presence of two witnesses

repeating the following formula :—" I call upon these persons here present to witness that I, in the presence of Almighty God, and in the name of our Lord Jesus Christ, do take thee to be my lawful wedded wife (or husband)," or words to the like effect.

This is almost as simple a process as that which tradition ascribes to ceremonies conducted by the blacksmith of Gretna Green. In these cases the age of the man must be above sixteen, and that of the woman thirteen.

An important power was conferred by the Legislature upon the Governor-General in Council in this year, viz. of extending any of the acts and regulations to what are called non-regulation provinces, or provinces heretofore not under the regularly established law of the land, but under special regulations, and the half military, half civil domination of a Chief Commissioner, who again acts under the direct supervision of the Supreme Government of India.

The non-regulation system is to a certain extent an anomaly. When a province has recently come under British rule, usually by conquest, there are obvious reasons why the new administration imposed upon it should be of a more simple character than that which experience has shown to work the most efficiently in those parts of the empire which have been for years under British rule. After the excitement of war is over and the sword has been sheathed, and a whole province submitted to a conqueror, it is desirable to heal as fast as possible the wounds which have been inflicted by military operations. In the older provinces, where British rule has been long established, the work of administration is necessarily conducted through the ordinary machinery used in all civilized countries. The work of government could not be carried on without. Each branch of the administration must have its own department—law, revenue, finance, police. No longer unsettled by war, the population betake themselves to cultivating the arts of peace ; commerce and agriculture thrive, and the conflicting interests which the various circumstances

of life in individual classes and members of the community
beget, require the establishment of courts of law and a
fixed system of civil and criminal jurisprudence. The
theory is, that a province should progress gradually from
a condition of semi-barbarism—in which war, if it does not
find, at any rate too often leaves it—to a state of civilization, in which an elaborated system of administration
under a code of laws is absolutely indispensable. Hence
has arisen in India a practice of always subjecting a newly
annexed country to a rule whose elements are two-thirds
military and one-third civil. A Chief Commissioner is
generally appointed at the head of the government, who
is assisted by deputy-commissioners in charge of large
divisions of the province, under whom a host of assistant-
commissioners of various grades conduct the details of the
executive. In the Punjab, as is well known, this system
was introduced after the conquest in 1849, with this slight
modification, that instead of a chief commissioner there
was a board of administration appointed, consisting of
three officers, two of whom were Sir Henry and Sir John
Lawrence. It was found that the board did not work so
well as a government, one and undivided, and Sir Henry
Lawrence, a military officer, was removed, and the third
member of the board otherwise provided for, leaving Sir
John (then Mr.) Lawrence, Chief Commissioner. The
officers under him were selected, some from the army and
some from the civil service, as is generally the case in non-
regulation provinces. There is no regular scale laid down
to determine the proportion in which the two services
contribute to the *matériel* of government. But there is
this peculiarity about all non-regulation provinces, which
is too often overlooked by those who have not a practical
knowledge of our Indian system, viz. that in such provinces
the officers are all *selected*. Very many of them are military
men ; and as the step from military employ and pay to
civil is a most advantageous one for them, these appointments are always much coveted : and although they are

occasionally given away on the principle which too often
regulates the disposal of patronage in India, viz. favour,
yet as a rule the military officers appointed to civil posts
are above the average. I do not mean by this remark to
cast any slight upon the regimental officers. Great offence
was taken some years ago at a passage in the *Edinburgh
Review*, where, speaking of the old system in vogue before
the Mutiny, the writer laid down the law that "the *élite*
of the native army were selected for the staff, and the
refuse only left with their regiments." This remark was
exceedingly unfair to the regimental officers ; for so far
from men being selected for genius or ability for the staff,
it is well known that no such principle was in reality
observed, but that those who were lucky enough to have
interest managed to get posts on the staff, and those who
were unlucky and had none remained with their corps,
going through the drudgery of regimental duty on half or a
quarter the pay which their more fortunate comrades were
receiving in staff employ. Still the effects of the system
were much the same as if a selection had been made. For
an officer taken out of his regiment and appointed to any
particular special duty, turns his whole attention to that
duty. He knows that his prospects in the department to
which he has been removed depend upon his efficiency,
and that if found inefficient or incapable he will be
inevitably remanded to his regiment without a hope of
ever having another chance ; so that although not selected
for any *spécialité* at first, or for any particular genius or
ability, he is yet in the same position as if he had been
so selected. There is a field for his ambition in which he
may rise to the head of his department, and, compared
with his less fortunate comrades, with their colours he has
many more opportunities for distinguishing himself and
bringing himself into notice. This is the secret of the
great success which almost always attends the government
of a non-regulation province at first. Almost all the
principal offices are filled by selected men, by men who

have already more or less distinguished themselves. In the inferior posts, although the selection may not be actually made for any efficiency, yet when a man is once appointed the effect upon his character, so far as stimulating him to exertion and animating him with a praiseworthy spirit of emulation is concerned, is the same as if he had been selected by merit and not by favour. There is a field opened before him full of rich prizes, such as might awaken any man's ambition. And the result is zeal for the public service, which speedily develops itself into *esprit de corps* throughout the whole administration.

Under what is called, in contradistinction, the regular system, on the other hand, there is no such healthy principle at work. There the administration runs on in a groove. Everything goes by rule. It is seldom in the power of the Government to make any selection for particular offices. Seniority claims its due, and an officer who, if he has shown no particular talent, has nevertheless done his duty creditably in the lower branches of the service, is entitled to promotion when it comes to him in the ordinary course of things. This system bears much the same relation to the non-regulation as that of regimental duty does to the staff. There are certain grades, and certain duties required of officers in those grades. So long as an officer does that duty ordinarily well, there is no law or precedent for keeping him out of promotion when it falls to his lot to find it. In the non-regulation provinces, on the other hand, if a man distinguishes himself, he may be advanced to a higher appointment without reference to any rules of the service regulating promotion by seniority. It is obvious that while as an exceptional arrangement the non-regulation system is found to work admirably, it is just because it is an exceptional arrangement that it is capable of being adopted. You could no more introduce the non-regulation system everywhere than you could introduce the practice of promoting junior regimental officers over the heads of their seniors on account of some gallant conduct in the field, or the display of some peculiar administrative ability in garrison or quarters.

Many writers who have seen the success of the non-regulation principle in new provinces, have become so enamoured of it that nothing will satisfy them but its universal introduction. These men forget its real character altogether, and overlook the fact that its introduction would at once upset all established rules and rights of promotion, and occasion the utmost possible confusion in every department of the service.

But the non-regulation system is not without its faults. At first it is no doubt admirably adapted for a newly-annexed province. It serves to introduce gradually a much more complicated system of revenue and judicial administration than that to which the people have been accustomed ; there is more personal communication between the governing and the governed classes than is possible in the regulation provinces, where the machinery of government is more elaborate, where the ordinary routine of departmental labour must be observed. It is a sort of half-way house between the despotic and capricious rule under which the people have lived prior to annexation, and the scarcely less despotic but less capricious government to which they have henceforward to be subject. But beyond a certain time there is little doubt this system, if persisted in, becomes a clog upon the progress of the country. After the first flush is over, there is danger of the non-regulation provinces falling back. Routine asserts its influence over the minds of officials. The men under whom the province first made such rapid strides towards development, retire, and are succeeded by a second generation of officials, who have not the same inducement that their predecessors had to exertion. It is in the essence of zeal to grow cool with lapse of time. When everything was new, it was comparatively easy to work up to a high standard. Upon the unformed mass of clay every effort at design left its impression ; when the whole has been manipulated, and the design complete, it is comparatively dull work maintaining the fabric in the condition to which it has been already brought by the labours of predecessors. In the course of a few years the stimulus given to trade, commerce, and agriculture in a province rich in maiden resources, gives rise to those innumerable complications of rights that eventuate in lawsuits. Property has increased tenfold in value, and claims to it are fought out with efforts proportionate to its value. Intricate questions of law have to be decided in the courts, and the judges are military officers or civilians, who have had little or no training in judicial matters. Every branch of the public service has grown in importance, and accordingly requires greater administrative ability, and more acquaintance with general principles of law, revenue, and police, than the officers, who worked well enough when their task was that of reducing to order a newly-conquered territory, perhaps possess. It is necessary to introduce laws and regulations, codes of procedure, and technical restraints. To work with these new principles grafted upon the old is far more difficult than to carry on the administration in a long-established groove. For these and similar reasons it is not to be wondered at that the non-regulation system, excellent at first, after a while halts : it is well if the progress be not in the wrong direction.

That such is the case will be clear to those who have any practical acquaintance with provinces which have been long under our rule, and for some cause or other not brought under the regulation system. There are several districts in this condition scattered over India, and I am persuaded that it would be advantageous were it the rule in dealing with a newly-annexed province, to bring it, after the lapse of a certain time during which the non-regulation system has been allowed to work, under the regulations. To advocate, as some do, the extension of the former system all over the country is to ignore its essential characteristic, which is the principle of selection.

One most important Act was introduced in 1865—the second contribution to the Indian Statute-book made by the Law Commission. It is intituled "The Indian Succession Act;" but as such a law necessarily interferes with long-established customs, it has been deemed advisable at first to confine its operation to classes other than Hindoos, Mahommedans, or Buddhists. To one accustomed to English law, some of the provisions of this Act seem strange innovations. For instance, it starts by declaring that no person shall by marriage acquire any interest in the property of the person whom he or she marries, nor become incapable of doing any act in respect of his or her own property which she or he could have done if unmarried.[1] Succession to immoveable property is regulated in this enactment by the law of the place where the property is situated, to moveable by the law of the place of domicile. The husband and wife respectively have the same right in regard to the property of the other dying intestate, and this rule applies to a person not domiciled in India marrying in India a person domiciled there. In the matter of construction of wills, the law of legacies, duties of executors, &c. this Act mostly follows the English law. The Act is clear and comprehensive, and forms a valuable addition to the Indian Statute-book.

An Act passed in this year, called "The High Court Criminal Procedure Act," gave rise to a good deal of discussion at the time, and involves one very important principle. Up to this time the procedure as regards Englishmen in India accused of crimes was much the same as that in vogue in England; that is to say, a bill was submitted to a grand jury before the case was sent up for trial. This Act (No. XIII. of 1865) abolishes the grand jury altogether. Perhaps it was found inconvenient to assemble a grand jury; perhaps it was thought that when High Courts were increased and established in

---

[1] Since this was written a bill has been introduced into Parliament regarding the rights and property of married women.

certain places in the Mofussil, it would be difficult to find material for grand jury at all. And there is a good deal to be said in support of the second suggestion; it would be difficult to supply a grand and a petty jury at places like Allahabad and Lahore, for instance. It is, however, very necessary that there should be somewhere or other a machinery to effect that for which it is the custom in England, and was the custom in India, to assemble grand juries. A provision is indeed inserted in the Act, which gives the judges of the High Court the power to act in some measure in place of the old grand jury; for it lays down, that if when the charge has been sent up to the High Court it shall appear to be clearly unsustainable, an entry to that effect may be made any time before trial, and such entry shall have the effect of staying proceedings, but shall not operate as an acquittal of the person so charged until after the expiry of three years, during which period no fresh charge shall have been brought forward in the same matter. So that in effect a man in this position who has been committed on insufficient grounds is, as it were, remanded for three years, being at liberty of course, but liable to be apprehended and committed again if anything else turns up to render his committal on the old charge practicable. Such a law is open to great abuse in India, where a criminal charge is under the Penal Code a very common weapon of revenge or animosity, and where, with a police so easily open to corruption, fabricated evidence is not difficult to procure. The court very seldom exercises this power, perhaps for this very reason, deeming it more fair to the accused that he should be tried and acquitted altogether than that he should lie under the ban of a criminal charge for three years in a measure at the mercy of his enemies. I have only known this power exercised once, and that was in a case where the committal was made on most insufficient evidence; in fact the charge was totally unsustainable, but it was palpably made from a vindictive feeling on the part of the committing officer, who

had the satisfaction of causing a man against whom he
bore a long-established grudge, to travel two or three
hundred miles at much personal inconvenience, and drag
a number of witnesses all the way to attend the summons
of the High Court. All the satisfaction he got was that
he was told he might go back again, and I believe the
expenses of the witnesses were defrayed by the State.
An old Act passed some years ago protects magistrates or
justices of the peace from any penalty for exceeding their
duty or making illegal commitments, provided they acted
bonâ fide, and of course it is next to impossible to show
there was not *bona fides* when the person whose action is
impugned declares there was. Still, cases of the grossest
abuse of power on the part of magistrates constantly occur
in India ; and it is very common indeed to hear an officer
having magisterial powers, under the excitement of anger
promise himself revenge for some slight insult or wrong,
imaginary or real, by bringing the offender up under some
section or other of the Penal Code. Indeed the criminal
law has become a great deal too much a weapon of
offence instead of what it ought to be, a protection to
society.[1]

This Act regulates the assembly and constitution of juries
before which European prisoners are tried. Here one or
two innovations have been made on the English system.

In this Act as well as other Acts regulating the procedure of High Courts, in trials of European British

---

[1] An amusing instance of the abuse of power has been brought to
my notice since this was written. In the neighbourhood of the Hill
settlements it is the custom for native sportsmen,—" Shikaries " they
are called—to shoot pheasants, partridges, and other game, and sell
them to travellers passing by their villages. The Deputy Commissioner of Simla was anxious to introduce some restrictions in the
shape of game laws upon the practice of destroying game out of
season. One day when he was at a village a few miles from Simla,
one of these shikaries brought him a brace of partridges, or a
pheasant, either for sale or as a present. He got very angry, abused
the man for killing game out of season, and then and there ordered
reg him off to jail.

subjects, it is laid down that out of a jury of twelve the
concurrence of nine is sufficient for conviction; that is to
say, provided the judge concurs with the opinion of the
nine. If less than nine or more than three vote for
acquittal, the prisoner is acquitted. Another innovation
upon what would be considered in England, I think, the
right of an Englishman under our constitution, is the
admission of natives on the juries that try European
British subjects. The prisoner may insist that the
majority shall be Europeans or Americans, or seven out
of the twelve. This, I think, is objectionable. There are
many reasons why it is injudicious to put natives upon the
jury in such cases. In the first place, it is by no means
necessary to do so. In every place where European British
subjects are tried there are always plenty of Englishmen to
form a jury. The law allows officers or non-commissioned
officers of the army to be empannelled when necessary.
Now in every large station, certainly wherever there is a
High Court established, there will be found quite a sufficiently large community of English or American residents
to supply any number of jurors; and should by any accident
these fall short, then there will be at least one regiment of
infantry or a battery or two probably of artillery, from
which any number almost of jurors may be taken. There
can, therefore, never arise a necessity for empannelling
natives.

It is not often that out of the Presidency towns we can
find natives sufficiently well versed in the English language
to act as jurors and adjudicate on cases conducted in
English. A very different standard of linguistic knowledge
is required to enable a man to understand and follow legal
proceedings in a criminal case, the speeches of counsel,
the questions and answers of witnesses, and the judge's
charge, to that which is usually attained by natives who
know enough English to keep accounts and copy letters.

In addition to this, the practice needlessly gives rise to
an immense amount of dissatisfaction, for no Englishman

will ever submit except by force to be tried by a jury upon which natives are sitting. And lastly, it is objectionable on principle, not so much on account of distinction of race or colour as of religion. And I am of opinion that no Mahommedan or Hindoo should be allowed to sit in judgment upon a Christian. Were the natives converted even to an outward profession of Christianity, as the blacks for instance of Sierra Leone, who are allowed to sit on juries for the trial of white men, it would be different. As it is, I consider that an Englishman is debarred from that which he has a right to claim certainly in any British colony or dependency, a fair trial, by the practice of allowing Mahommedans and Hindoos, and men of other heathen religions, to sit upon their trial as jurors.

By this Act the High Court may direct the trial of a prisoner to take place in another than the usual place of *i*ts sitting, when one of the judges repairs to the spot indicated and holds the trial. And the Government of India, or the governors of the minor Presidencies, may associate with the judge of the High Court a sessions judge or a barrister of upwards of five years' standing, who is called the associate judge; but this power is not extended under the Act to the High Court, North-West Provinces, or the Chief Court, Punjab.[1] I never knew of a case in which the right was exercised.

A special enactment providing a certain class with the luxury of a divorce law, and defining the law of marriage, was passed in this year, at the instance, so it is stated, of the people themselves. It is called the " Parsee Marriage and Divorce Act," and is confined, of course, to the class

---

[1] As long ago as 1862, the system of trial by native juries was introduced as an experiment in six districts in Bengal Proper. But it has been found not to answer. No sooner are the summonses for the jury issued, than all sorts of efforts are made by the friends of the prisoners awaiting trial to tamper with the jurors. The official reports on the administration of justice complain that it is almost impossible to obtain a conviction before a jury in cases of false evidence and forgery.

indicated. This was followed by a " Parsee Intestate Succession Act;" neither of which, however, call for any special
notice in this place, further than to show that the principle
of special legislation for particular classes is fully and
amply recognised by the Indian legislature whenever any
particular class of natives require a special enactment to be
passed to suit their views, prejudices, or interests.

Early in the following year, 1866, a bill was passed
providing a summary procedure for the recovery of money
due on dishonest bills of exchange, &c. ; and the preamble
goes on to say, that as inconvenience is felt in consequence
of the laws of British India being in some particulars
different from those of England in matters of common
occurrence in the course of trade, it is intended to remedy
that inconvenience by amending the law. Under this Act
a defence to a suit upon a bill of exchange or promissory
note, not more than six months over-due, may only be
made by permission of the judge upon defendant's paying
the amount into court and showing a good defence on the
merits, and after judgment the court may under special
circumstances stay execution. The Act was at first to be
in operation within the jurisdiction of the High Court ; but
a clause in it permits local governments to extend it to
the jurisdiction of the courts within their respective
provinces.

The great stimulus given to commerce by the joint-
stock system all the world over has been communicated
to India perhaps even in a larger proportion than to other
countries ; and accordingly we find that the Indian legislature has uniformly followed at a short distance of time
the English in regulating the action of joint-stock companies.

The statute of 1844 was followed in India by Act XLIII.
of 1850, and the provision of the winding-up Acts of 1848,
1849, also embodied in the Act XLIII. of 1850. Again,
the Limited Liability Act of 1855 and 1856 was followed in
India by Act XIX. of 1857, which embodied the provisions

contained in the English statute of 1855 and 1856. Act
No. X. of the present year, 1866, called the "Indian Companies Act," which was introduced by Mr. Maine in 1865,
is a copy of the English Companies Act of 1862, with
certain alterations necessary to adapt it to India. The
most important of these modifications are,[1] for instance : in
the place of an examination of the affairs of a company
under the orders of the Board of Trade, in India inspectors
are appointed by the local government. The provisions in
the Indian Act relating to reference to arbitration are taken
from the Railway Companies Arbitration Act, 1859, and
the Companies Clauses Consolidation Act of 1845 ; whereas
in the English statute "both these sets of provisions are
only introduced by reference." In India, the time within
which notice is to be given to the registrar of the consolidation and division of the shares of a company, or of
the conversion of its capital into stock, is limited to fifteen
days; in the English statute there is no such limit. The
provisions in the Indian Act as to annual balance-sheets
and audit are compulsory; in the English Act, optional.
A penalty is imposed in India on any director, officer, or
contributary of a company being wound up who fraudu-
lently secretes books, papers, &c. ; this offence is not provided for in the English law. Section 45 of the old Act
XIX. of 1857, relating to contracts made on behalf of a
company, stating that they may be made under the
common seal of the company, or without, merely bearing
the signature of a person, or made verbally by one acting
under authority, express or implied, of the company, has
been reproduced in the present Act, although it is not
inserted in the English Companies Act of 1862. And
finally, as regards the examination of the affairs of a
company by Government inspectors, the Act does away
with the distinction made by the statute between banking
and other companies having a capital divided into shares.
Mr. Whitley Stokes remarks—and I concur with him—

---

[1] *Vide* "The Indian Companies Act, 1866," by Whitley Stokes.

that it is much to be regretted that the Indian legislature has continued the winding-up jurisdiction conferred by the old Act XIX. of 1857 upon the district courts.

A new Post Office Act was passed this year, which does not call for any particular comment. But this was followed by another, amending the law of partnership, which is of more importance. In this it was enacted that an advance of money by way of loan, under a contract in writing that the lender shall receive a rate of interest varying with the profits, shall not of itself constitute the lender a partner. An explanation was added which perhaps was not unnecessary. If a retiring partner, for instance, is entitled to receive payment of a share in the capital or other proceeds of a business, and after the value of such share has been ascertained he agrees in writing to allow the same to remain or to be used for the purposes of the business, he shall be construed to have made a loan which does not lay upon him the responsibilities of partnership. The same principle is applied to a servant or agent, a widow or child of a partner, the two former of whom may be remunerated by a share in the profits, and the two latter receive an annuity from the profits, without being held to be partners.

In every country where the prevailing religion is a heathen one which allows polygamy, and Christianity is making progress, more or less, a great difficulty has always arisen as to the mode of dealing with a convert who has more than one wife. It is no new difficulty, for it beset the earliest preachers of Christianity even so far back as the times of the Apostles. Dr. Colenso proposed to overcome one phase of it by permitting the Christian convert who was a polygamist before conversion to retain the privilege after baptism. This plan, however, which rather yielded to than overcame the difficulty, did not meet with approval, and the crisis became one of such frequent occurrence in India that, after a great deal of discussion, the Legislature of that country resolved upon making an endeavour to meet it. Accordingly, Act XXI. of 1866 provides that, if a native husband becomes a convert to Christianity, and in consequence of this his wife, being a native, deserts or repudiates him for the space of six months, he may sue her for conjugal society, and similarly if the wife be the convert. But a somewhat peculiar construction is given by the Act to the word "native;" a native husband or wife shall be held to mean a man or woman domiciled in British India who shall not be a Christian, a *Mahommedan*, or a *Jew*. "Native law," in like manner, means any law or custom having the force of law of a person domiciled in India other than the three classes mentioned. No appeal lies against the order of the court, which, if it be not the High Court, must be the principal court of the district. By the Act, cohabitation as man and wife is to be held presumptive evidence of marriage, and refusal to cohabit proof of desertion, and of its being in consequence of change of religion. If either party be under age, the suit may be dismissed, but may be revived again within twelve months. If the desertion is found to be the result of cruelty or adultery, the suit is to be dismissed ; and when a male petitioner has two or more wives, the suit is to be dismissed if he is cohabiting with either of them. In the procedure under the Act, the Legislature seems to have followed the model of the French divorce law. Thus, when both parties are before the court, the judge interrogates the respondent as to whether he or she refuses to cohabit with the petitioner; and if the respondent be the woman, and she refuses, the judge may order the case to be adjourned a year, directing that in the interim the parties shall see one another at a time and place fixed by the judge, and in the presence of any one he likes to permit to be present, with the view of ascertaining whether or not the respondent freely and voluntarily persists in the refusal. At the expiration of this period the petitioner appears again in court, and shows that the desertion or repudiation has continued, upon which the respondent is again interrogated by the judge, and if she still refuse to cohabit with the petitioner the judge shall dissolve the marriage. If the petitioner is the wife, the husband is interrogated, and on his refusal to cohabit the case is adjourned for a year, as before, but no provision is made for the meeting of the parties unless at the wish of the wife. At the expiration of the year the marriage is to be dissolved if the respondent still refuse to take his wife back.

When this Act was before Council, there was a considerable amount of excitement and agitation regarding it. The Mahommedans were the first to take alarm at what they considered an infringement on their religious privileges and social customs having the sanction of their religion. They held meetings and got up petitions praying to be exempted from the operation of the Act, and their prayer was granted, as it is stated that the Mahommedans are not affected. When the Hindoos saw that the Mahommedans had gained the point, they also began to agitate. They held meetings at many of the principal cities in Upper India, and petitioned Council, but without effect ; the Government being of opinion that they only moved in the matter because they were encouraged by the success which attended the Mahommedan agitation, and the Hindoos declaring that the Legislature exempted the Mahommedans because we were afraid of them, but did not regard the prayer of the Hindoos because they are a less formidable body politically ; and I am inclined to think that the Hindoos were not far from the truth.

Since the Act became law, I have not heard of any discontent or dissatisfaction expressed with regard to its operation, and the excitement on the subject, so far as one can see, has subsided.

Another very important measure of this year was an enactment conferring on the High Court much the same powers as those exercised by the Court of Chancery in England with reference to property vested in trustees, the

operation of the Act being confined to cases to which the
English law is applicable.

The legislation of 1867 was essentially patchwork legislation.   Out of thirty-seven Acts passed this year, with the
exception of nine or ten, all were amendments of former
laws, or measures passed to supplement something which
had been omitted by neglect or a hasty oversight.   Thus,
Act IV. was passed to define the meaning of the word
"offence" in the Penal Code, and to indicate how certain
sections of the code were to be construed.   The next,
Act V., extends the Penal Code to the Straits Settlements.
Act VIII. exempts horse-racing from the operation of a
previous enactment of 1848 for avoiding wagers, but places
the limit at which a subscription or contribution to a purse
shall be recoverable at law at 50*l.*   The next Act makes
" further provision " for suits by and against the " Comptoir
D'Escompte " of Paris.   Again, we have the Small Cause
Courts patched up in Act X. of 1867, by an enactment
which provides that in a suit for a sum above 50*l.*, if a
point of law arises the judge must refer it to the High
Court.   If this is acted upon, it must entail a great deal of
work upon the judges both of the Small Cause Courts and
High Courts.   It is an obvious makeshift to supply the
place of an appeal.   The great principle of the Small
Cause Court, so much belauded, was that there was to be
no appeal from it.   I have pointed out how injudicious
such a measure is in India, and so we find in 1867 that the
Legislature, fully aware of the injustice which is often
perpetrated by ignorant judges of these courts, though
it will not cancel that part of the court's constitution
which precludes appeal from obstinate adherence to a
false principle, goes a roundabout way to secure the advantages of some sort of supervision by enacting that
in all cases for above 50*l.* where a point of law arises,
it must be referred to the High Court.   It is difficult to
see the superiority of this measure over the old practice
of allowing an appeal when the parties who must be

the best judges of their own interests are desirous of appealing.

Then we have an Act XII., amending the law relating to the custody of prisoners ; an Act to remove doubt as to the legality of certain judicial appointments ; another patching up of the Licence Tax Act passed three months previously ; another amending the Currency Act of 1861, and empowering the Governor-General to transfer, for currency purposes, any town from one presidency to another. Act XXXI. supplies an omission in the Railway Act and Penal Code, and makes railway *employés* public servants. Act XXXIII. amends the law levying fines for smuggling. Act XXXV. enables the Lieutenant-Governor of the Punjab to appoint an additional financial commissioner. The reason of this was, that the arrears of work in the Financial Commissioner's office had accumulated to such an extent that there was no prospect of the single commissioner being able to get through it, and the consequence was grievous injustice to the suitors, who could not get a decision without ruinous delay. The only peculiar circumstance about it was the fact that most of the arrears accumulated under Sir Donald MacLeod, the Lieutenant-Governor's, own tenure of office as Financial Commissioner. The object of Act XXXVI. was to remedy "an error" in a former enactment—"Whereas the said Section number ' XII.' is an error, and it is expedient to correct the same, it is briefly enacted as follows," &c.

In addition to this patchwork legislation, one or two measures were passed this year which require especial notice. Five fiscal enactments may be dismissed without discussion: the Moulmein and Bassein Port dues ; the Pandhari Tax, a native licence-tax of two per cent. upon incomes ; the Customs duties ; and the Licence Tax and drawbacks on transhipment Acts.

In Act XXIII. of 1867 we have another instance of that special legislation which I have shown is at times necessary in India, but the principle of which is always scouted whenever any special legislation is solicited for the European community. The frequency of assassination in the Punjab, and the insufficiency of the existing machinery to suppress the practice, showed the necessity of some more stringent measures than the ordinary operation of the law. This enactment sanctions more summary procedure : forfeiture of all property belonging to the fanatics (a very useless provision, seeing that the only property this class of men are usually possessed of is the knife with which they take their victim's life, and a few rags to cover their nakedness), and disposal of their bodies as the Commissioner shall direct, which refers, of course, to the burning of the bodies of Mahommedan fanatics. Execution immediately follows sentence, and no confirmation is required as necessary under the ordinary procedure.

The objection to Act XXIV. of 1867, or the Administrator-General's Act, is that it appoints only one officer for the whole of the Bengal Presidency, whose head-quarters are of course in Calcutta ; the consequence of which is an overpress of work, which leads to all sorts of ruinous delays, and an utter inability for persons in the Mofussil, concerned in estates which fall into the hands of the Administrator-General, to get their business attended to. They are helpless in the hands of the subordinate clerks of an enormous office, who may, by postponing their business, ruin them. Unless some change is made in a few years' time, the abuses arising from delays and disappointments in this branch of the public service will rival those of the English Courts of Chancery in former years, before the besom of reform swept out the dust which had accumulated in the holes and corners of our system. There is a High Court for the North-West Provinces and a Chief Court for the Punjab ; why should not these large and important provinces have their own Administrator-General ? The limits of the Presidency of Bengal are now merely nominal. The North-West Provinces is as much a separate Presidency as Bombay or Madras, only the use of that word " Presi-

dency "—a foolish and unmeaning term at any time—has
served to perpetuate the results of conditions which no
longer exist. The appointing of one Administrator-General
only for Bengal, the North-West Provinces and the Punjab,
Oude and Central Provinces, in order that the profits from
the whole field may be swept into the coffers of one office,
is a job which could only occur under a government like
that of India.

The only other act of general importance passed in 1867
was the Stamp Act. I have before alluded to the frequency
with which the stamp duties in India have been altered
within the last few years. The Stamp Act of 1867, which
relates only to fees on suits, and legal processes, is of very
questionable advantage. It is highly unpopular, and very
much disapproved of by certainly one-half the officials, who,
from their connexion with the judicial bench, are able to
judge of its effect. The stamp required on institution of
suits is so enormously high that it has had the effect already
of suppressing litigation in a very marked and a most
dangerous degree—dangerous, because in a country like
India, where the people are in many parts just emerging
from a state of semi-barbarism to one of civilization, there
is always a tendency to recur to the wild and lawless
habits of their predecessors, and to settle disputes by
the arbitrament of the club and the sword, rather than
by that of the law. More especially is this the case
with regard to agrarian differences; and the dues levied
by the new Stamp Act upon suits for lands are peculiarly heavy.

A discussion took place upon this Stamp Act in Council,
on the 20th March, 1868, when the Licence Tax was under
debate, and some valuable opinions were expressed with
reference to remarks which fell from Mr. Massey during
his budget statement for 1867-8, which I shall briefly
detail, both because they are a concise embodiment of
my own views, and because, coming from men who have
passed most of their lives in an official career, they will

naturally carry more weight than might be accorded to a
simple exposition of my own sentiments.   Mr. Massey had
stated that the new stamp duties on legal processes were
calculated to yield £680,000 to the revenue.   But he added
that the committee appointed to draw up the scale of
duties gave a very different opinion as to the estimated
revenue to be derived from this source, and admitted that
the result was doubtful.   The proceeds of the new scale of
duties realized £400,000 only.   Alluding to this, the Hon.
Mr. Minchin, whose official career has been passed in the
Madras Presidency, remarked that the stamp law weighed
with peculiar severity upon two classes, the rich—or, he
should rather say, those who had contingent claims to great
wealth—and the very poor.   With reference to the first
class our old stamp law was very moderate: there was a
limit to the initiatory fee, which could in no case exceed
two hundred pounds.   At present the initiatory fee was
practically without limit.[1]   He had heard of a case which
had occurred in Calcutta since he had been there the last
few months.   A suit was brought for the inheritance of
valuable property; the suit was dismissed on a point of
law, not fact, viz. that a certain person through whom
the claimants inherited their rights was found not to be in
existence, and the right had not devolved in the way that
was claimed.   That person was in existence, and was
desirous to come forward and give the necessary right, but
the case could not be re-opened without the payment of a

---

[1] When the property the subject of the suit exceeds 2,000l. and
does not exceed 10,000l., the initiatory stamp is 105l. plus one rupee
per cent. on the difference between 2,000l. and the amount of value
sued for.   When the value of the property exceeds 10,000l. the rate
increases at eight annas or half a rupee per cent.

In suits for immoveable property the amount of duty is to be computed according to the market value of the property in suit.   In suits
for immoveable property paying revenue, when the settlement is
temporary, eight times the revenue is payable, and when the settlement is permanent, ten times; and in suits for immoveable property not paying revenue, twenty times the annual net profits of the
property shall be taken to be the market value.

second initiatory fee of £8,000, which the parties could not afford to pay. In another case, in Burmah, a suitor had paid £1,250 as an initiatory fee, and the suit was dismissed on the ground of no jurisdiction." Mr. Minchin added that he supposed he should not be far wrong in estimating the diminution of suits under the new Act at 25 per cent. " In ordinary commercial affairs this would be an excellent stroke of business, but when we consider that the article of which we had sold less and for which we had charged more was presumed to be justice, he did not think it was a matter for unmixed congratulation."

Another objectionable feature in this Act was the extending of stamp duties on all ordinary petitions and on petitions in criminal proceedings. In Madras, as Mr. Minchin shows, "the first would have struck at the root of our whole system of administration, and it had to be got rid of by an order which the Government then passed, an order ruling that all petitions connected with the land revenue should come under the exemption for petitions relating to matters connected with a settlement pending its formation. Such an order was absolutely necessary for the due transaction of the revenue work in that Presidency, unless it was intended to employ revenue officers solely as machines for collecting eight-anna stamps." The stamp on petitions in criminal proceedings was justified by Mr. Maine on the ground of acting as a safeguard against false and vexatious criminal complaints ; and here, I think the impost of a small duty a salutary measure. " Bengal Proper was the great litigating province of British India, and it was established that the result of taking the stamp off complaints in criminal cases was that out of 177,000 persons charged with offences in the single year 1864, 105,000 were never brought to trial and more than half the rest were acquitted. Mr. Justice Hobhouse (Calcutta High Court) had explained to the Council last year how these 105,000 cases never came to be tried. There was a quarrel in the village ;

an angry villager went to the court, paid one of the persons
hanging about there a few pice (copper coins) to write a
complaint in which the name of his bitterest enemy was
put down as defendant to a criminal charge, while the
persons whom he hated with an only moderate hatred were
named as witnesses. The defendant and witnesses were
thereupon summoned by the police: the complainant
never appeared, and the charge was dismissed. But the
defendant and his witnesses went home, having lost two
or three days' work, and labouring for life under the discredit (which it was honourable to the Bengalese to
consider a discredit) of having been brought up before
the court on a criminal charge."[1]

The reconsideration of this Stamp Act was after some
discussion postponed till next year, 1868.

The practice of employing the law courts as an engine
of private malice in India is very common indeed. The
intense dislike which every respectable native has to be
summoned to a court ; the fear of being insulted by the
police and subordinates, perhaps of meeting with dis-
courteous reception from the overworked officer presiding ;
the delay ; the distance to be traversed there and back, and
consequent waste of time ; the hatred that all well-bred
natives have for the *amla* of the courts—who are, generally
speaking, men belonging to the lowest station of society,
who have improved their worldly position and raised
themselves in life perhaps by successful intrigues, by
interest, by accident, by superior education at Government
colleges—all combine to make forced attendance at court
what it ought not to be, in spite of Mr. Maine's assertion,
a degradation. Too often European officers avail themselves of this to make some man who has perhaps defied
their authority or rendered himself obnoxious in some way,
smart for his independence. Much more frequently do
the members of the *amla* avail themselves of it. There
is therefore, every reason why a petition of complaint

[1] *Gazette of India* (official), March 28, 1868.

involving the attendance of persons either as defendants or witnesses, should bear some charge. And in an extreme case, or cases where real poverty might prevent a complainant from presenting a petition, a verbal representation can always be made to the magistrate.

Of the legislative enactments passed in 1868, there are but few that require any detailed notice. Several of them are of a mere technical character, others relate to local matters, while two or three of more general interest, and of a more important nature, have already been noticed in previous chapters. The first bill passed during the year was for " Shortening the Language used in Acts of the Governor-General in Council, and for other purposes." The " other purposes " relate to matters of detail, and are of no interest to the general reader. The second Act of the year was on the subject of duty leviable on Cochin pepper; the third authorized the Local Government of the Punjab to invest petty officers with certain powers ; the fourth had reference to certain villages in the Bombay Presidency belonging to certain chiefs, exempting them from the operation of the regulations in force in that Presidency ; and the fifth authorized the Local Government to delegate certain powers to the Commissioner of Sind.

Act VI. of 1868 is also of a local character, affecting only the North-West Provinces. Those provinces, however, contain thirty millions of inhabitants ; and the enactment, therefore, which is called " The Municipal Improvement Act," and involves some weighty principles, is of too great importance to be passed over without notice. The main principle it enunciates is to render the municipal organization compulsory. Up to that time the voluntary system had been maintained ; that is to say, municipal committees were imposed on those towns only which intimated a desire to be placed under their authority. By the present measure the Lieutenant-Governor has power to extend the provisions of the Act, by a notification in the local Government Gazette, to any

town in the territories under his government. The Lieutenant-Governor appoints the members. It is, indeed,
provided that he may direct these appointments by
election; but in India, where no machinery exists for any
kind of representation of the people, this privilege of
election is a mere dead letter, and in effect the members
of the committee are nominees of the Lieutenant-
Governor. He also appoints the official members, who
are not to be more than one-third of the whole; he
appoints the president and vice-president; and the shadowy
fragment of independent action alone is left to the committee, who are allowed to select their secretary! Indeed,
as Mr. Massey remarked in the debate on the bill, the
committee, "so far as it professed to assume the status
of an independent body, was a phantom and a fiction."
In its executive character, however, the committee is by
no means a phantom, for it wields the formidable power
of defining the persons and property to be taxed, and the
amount and rate of taxes to be imposed. After all that
has been said and written lately about the duty of
teaching the natives the art of self-government, it might
be supposed, perhaps, that the engine of taxation would
in some measure be under the control of the people, or
that they would have some voice in the matter, and something to say to the mode in which the money is expended.
Such a principle, while it accords well with the theory of
Indian government, as represented to the English reader
in official minutes, ministerial journals, and the speeches
of Secretaries of State, is totally opposed to the practice.
The Lieutenant-Governor appoints the committee, the
Lieutenant-Governor nominates the president and vice-
president, the committee impose the taxes, and the
Lieutenant-Governor sanctions them. The whole Act,
which was framed on the model of another Act of a
similar character for the Punjab, passed the year before
as an experimental measure, is in effect nothing but a
machine to invest the head of the local government with

powers he would not otherwise possess, and by the fiction of a sham committee lessen the responsibility which would otherwise rest upon him alone.

These municipal committees, which are now in operation pretty well all over India, are—except in Presidency towns, and in a few exceptionally situated settlements in the Punjab, where the official element is weak and the independent European element abnormally strong—the merest fiction it is possible to conceive. The collector, magistrate, or commissioner, or one of his subordinates, attends the meetings, and signifies his wishes, to which the native members bow acquiescence. Should there happen to be a non-official European member present, he is immediately out-voted if his views in any way differ from those of the official president ; and finding himself a mere dummy, if he is a wise man, or a busy one, he does not waste valuable time by attending a second meeting. Entertaining very crude notions of political economy, these committees wield, often with fatal power as regards the interests of trade, the tremendous machinery of taxation with which the Legislature has armed them. The octroi system, condemned universally by every political economist, has been introduced into almost every town in Mofussil India, and by its extension in the shape of transit duties has perpetuated in our own provinces the mischievous system which British officials are so eager to condemn in native States. The money wrung from the poorer classes—for it is they who suffer mostly from octroi duties levied on the necessaries of life—is often spent in useless ornaments, the construction of elaborate municipal commission offices, and other buildings adapted to Western tastes and Anglo-Saxon ideas of municipal requirements, but very little appreciated by poor natives who have to stint their families of food and clothing in proportion to the impost levied on their daily food. Sir William Mansfield, in the course of the debate, described his visit to a "town of some ten thousand inhabitants, in which there was a beautiful new market-place, a handsome dispensary, a new square, and a cross erected at the meeting of certain roads," all out of the public funds. In other towns some scientific member of a municipal committee will exhibit with pride a museum full of stuffed birds or animals, prepared at the expense of the stomachs of the poorer classes, who must have sacrificed, it is certain, some portion of their daily food to provide the wherewithal to stuff specimens for the museum which a chance visitor may go to see once in six months, and write his name in a book. Woe betide the poorer classes of the towns and cities whose collector or magistrate has a taste for ornamental building, gardening, or the collection of curiosities! Here and there the funds produced by the octroi, in the hands of a thrifty official of sound judgment and some knowledge of engineering, of physics, and of the principles of sanitation, are well spent in measures really adapted to the wants of the citizens. The roads are kept in repair, order and cleanliness preserved in the streets; but too often—such is the infirmity of human nature—the tendency is to the square, the market-place, and crosses Sir William Mansfield speaks of, which catch the eye of a Lieutenant-Governor on a tour of inspection, and secure the rapid promotion of the energetic district officer who has evinced so much public spirit.

Of course, strictly speaking, the octroi duty should be leviable neither on articles in transit nor on those which have already paid duty, such as import duty, elsewhere. But in many places the transit duty is avoided only by the greatest possible inconvenience—timber, for instance, being taxed if it is allowed to remain in the neighbourhood of a town more than a few hours, although it is merely lodged there temporarily *en route.* Cotton and piece goods are with equal difficulty, inconvenience, and expense cleared without having to pay a duty, and in some places are not allowed to escape at any cost. The whole business of a town in the North-West was ruined in a few months by

the tax upon cotton in transit, which used to be taken to
the place for screwing and forwarding by rail. The cotton
agents and screwers left the spot, and set up their screws
elsewhere, and the tide of commerce was regularly turned
aside into artificial channels. Such abuses, of course,
could not exist in England, or in any country where the
voice of public opinion could make itself heard ; but in
official-ridden India, unless some English resident, or travelling cotton-speculator, or merchant should happen by
chance to have his attention drawn to the matter, there is
no hope for the native, who could not get his complaint
heard even if he had the courage to prefer it. The official
members of these municipal committees attend the meetings, put resolutions to the " vote," and gravely record the
proceedings, as if they were not conscious of the ludicrous
burlesque they were enacting. The whole thing is regarded
as a laughable farce, a matter for unceasing amusement
to all outside the walls of the Commissioners' office, who
watch the solemnity with which the fiction is kept up ;—
except indeed to the poor, who can provide a few rags the
less for their wives and children in the biting cold of the
winter months of Upper India, a few sticks the less to cook
their scanty meals, and who have to stint their half-filled
stomachs daily of one anna's worth of grain, ghee, and
sugar cut off by the octroi duty.

Undoubtedly improvements have been effected in most of
the towns where this system has been in operation for some
time—improvements, that is, which strike the eye of the
visitor. The new market-place, and the square, and the
museum are improvements, present a pleasing appearance,
and convey a favourable impression to the traveller on the
look-out for objects of external interest. But there is no
record of the cost at which these improvements have been
effected—cost, not in money, but in the sufferings of the
poverty-stricken classes who form the bulk of the population in every native town. The whole system is far in
advance of the times ; it is a crude and premature effort to

engraft the ideas of Western civilization, and the habits of
advanced communities of people born and bred under free
institutions, upon the dry and withered branch of Oriental
pauperism, not only of substance, but of public spirit.
Half a century hence, if English capitalists were encouraged to invest and settle in the country, and teach the
people to think and act for themselves, municipal institutions might not be out of place. At present they are a
fiction and a sham, and fictions and shams never yet
answered any useful purpose.

Act VII. had reference to procedure in the Chief Court
of the Punjab. VIII. repealed former enactments now out
of date, to the extent—such is the fecundity of Indian
legislation—of 296 entire Acts, and portions of almost as
many more. Act IX. was the Licence Tax, which has
been noticed elsewhere. Act X. related to the refund of
certain customs duties. XI. exempted timber from impost
dues. XII. amended the law of military courts of requests.
XIII. exempted the King of Oude from the jurisdiction of
the civil courts ; a measure of very doubtful expediency,
inasmuch as no one living within the limits of British
territory ought to be exempt from the jurisdiction of the
courts. XIV., called "The Indian Contagious Diseases Act,"
placed brothels under wholesome restrictions and regulations. XV. had reference to stamps and fees in the High
Court ; XVI. to the appointment of subordinate native
judicial officers. XVII. appointed the commission to inquire
into the affairs of the Bank of Bombay, and empowered
them to take evidence on oath. XVIII. related to Small
Cause Courts in the Neilgherry hills in Madras ; and XIX.
was the famous Oude Tenancy Bill.

The most important feature of this enactment was the
provision for compensation for tenants' improvements. By
these provisions, a tenant who has made improvements on
his holding may not be ousted, nor have his rent raised till
he or his representatives have been compensated by money,
or the grant of a beneficial lease, or by both, for such

improvements; provided the expenditure for improvements has been made within thirty years of the date of such proposed enhancement of rent or ejection. This, of course, applies also to any one from whom the tenant has inherited. It is an important question, what are improvements ? and they are defined to be such works as increase the annual "letting value" of the land: "the construction of works for the storage of water, or the supply of water for agricultural purposes, for drainage, and for protection against floods ; the construction of wells, the reclaiming and clearing of waste lands, and *other works of like nature*." In case a landlord tenders to a tenant a twenty years' lease of the land in occupation, at the annual rent then paid by the tenant, or at such other annual rent as may be agreed upon, such tenders, if accepted, will bar any claim to compensation. A tenant, with right of occupancy, is defined as one who within thirty years of the 13th February, 1856, has been in possession as proprietor in a village or estate ; in such case the tenant has a heritable, *but not a transferable, right* in the land which he cultivated or held in such village or estate on the 29th August, 1866, provided that such land has not come into his occupation for the first time since the 13th Feb. 1856 ; and provided also that no such tenant shall have a right of occupancy in any land in which he or any co-sharer with him possesses any under-proprietary right. No tenant having a right of occupancy can have his rent increased, except on the ground that the rate is below that usually paid by the same class of tenants for land of a similar description in the same village; or that the rate paid is more than 12½ per cent. below that of rent usually paid by tenants of the same class not having a right of occupancy for land of a similar description in the same village ; or that the quantity of land held by him exceeds the quantity for which he has previously paid rent. Tenants-at-will, of course, must pay according to agreement, or, if there is no agreement, according to the rate paid the previous year.

The part of the Act which gave much dissatisfaction to the talookdars and landlords was that relating to distress for arrears of rent, the provisions of which section of the Act are deemed too favourable to the tenant.

The six following enactments were of a local character. Act XXVI. empowers municipalities to provide Lock hospitals within their jurisdiction; and Act XXVII. exempts certain instruments from the provisions of the Registration Act. The next, No. XXVIII., was the only other important legislative measure of the year, entitled the " Punjab Tenancy Bill." This defines a tenant having a right of occupancy as one who has paid no rent or service in respect of his holding, and whose father and grandfather, uncle and grand-uncle, have occupied the same holding free of rent or service ; or as one who has involuntarily parted with proprietary rights otherwise than by forfeiture, and who has continuously occupied such land from the time of parting with his right in it ; or as one who is the representative of a person settled as a cultivator in the village in which the land occupied by such tenant is situate, along with the founders of the village ; or as one who is, or has been, a jageerdar of the village, or any part of it, in which the land occupied by him as tenant is situated, and who has continuously occupied such land for twenty years. It adds the important provision, therein differing from the most objectionable features of Act X. of 1859, that no tenant by mere lapse of time shall acquire a right of occupancy. The provisions relating to compensation for improvements of the tenant are the same as in the Oude Law. The Act confers important powers of alienation upon tenants with occupancy rights, that power being limited only by the landlord's right of pre-emption, a right which is open to him for a month only.

The agitation that was caused by the discussion on these bills has been alluded to in a previous chapter.[1] There is

---

[1] Chapter XIII.

a society at Lahore, consisting of the leading and influential native gentlemen of the Punjab, who meet at stated intervals, read papers, and discuss questions of public interest, and their proceedings are published in a journal, or sort of magazine. The following paragraphs, extracted from a resolution or memorial which the society drew up and forwarded to Mr. Brandreth, who brought in the first Punjab Tenancy Bill, contains matter well worthy of perusal. The evil noticed by the memorialists lies at the root of the whole present system of Indian legislation :—

" 4. We would respectfully desire to state that in our opinion no propositions can be more unfounded than those lately advanced : *firstly*, that there was no such thing as property in land in the Punjab in former days ; and *secondly*, that there were no recognised customs affecting the relations between landlord and tenant. We affirm that such customs are clear and generally recognised by the people, and that property in land has always existed in the Punjab. The report will show that, in our opinion, there are no such customs as to give to a tenant adverse rights of occupancy against a landlord.

" 5. We would, with the utmost confidence in the generosity and benevolence of His Excellency and the Legislative Council, beg to recall the words of Her Most Gracious Majesty the Queen, in her Proclamation of the 1st November, 1858, and to point out that in accordance with her gracious promise, our ancient rights, usages, and customs should be duly regarded :—

" 'We know and respect the feelings of attachment with which the natives of India regard the lands inherited by them from their ancestors, and we desire to protect them in all rights connected therewith, subject to the equitable demands of the State ; *and we will, that generally in framing and administrating the law due regard be paid to the ancient rights, usages, and customs of India.*'

" 6. In conclusion we would desire to observe, that, on this and on other occasions, great injury has threatened to fall on the people of this province, from important measures being passed or introduced in Council without the feeling of the people having been sought or ascertained : we would respectfully request that no measure affecting materially the social relations of the people, or their ancient rights, usages, and customs, be introduced into the Legislative Council before the Lieutenant-Governor of the Punjab has been empowered to call together a Local Council, and has thus ascertained the opinion of the people and the facts of the case.

" We deprecate, however, all and any legislation which disturbs ' ancient rights, usages, and customs.' "

Several other very important bills were introduced into Council at the latter end of 1868 which will probably become law during 1869 : such as the new Law of Evidence, a draft drawn up by the Indian Law Commission ; a new Stamp Act, most urgently required, although there have been so many alterations in the stamp law of late years ; the Land Improvement Bill for the North-West Provinces, introduced by the Hon. John Strachey, with reference especially to a recent ruling of the High Court, Agra, to the effect that a tenant under Act X. of 1859, and in accordance with local custom, is liable to be ejected for digging a temporary well or planting trees without permission of the landlord—a ruling which to the socialist legislators of India seems to be unjust in the extreme, whereas it is not only in accordance with law and custom, but with equity too ; for if a tenant may dig one well without permission of his landlord, he may dig ten or twenty till he has drained the circumjacent land and rendered it hopelessly barren.   But these measures at the close of 1868, being in embryo, do not call for discussion in a chapter on Legislation, which might not inaptly have concluded with the last sentence of the resolution of the " Anjooman " or Debating Society of the Punjab, so far as it has reference to real property: " We deprecate, however, all and any legislation which disturbs ' ancient rights, usages, and customs.' "

CHAPTER XX.

Mr. Wilson's policy — Extravagant expenditure — Retrenchment — Loans — Mr. Wilson's review of Lord Canning's war policy — The tariff modified — Income Tax — Salt Tax — The opium revenue — Mr. Laing's budget — Disappearance of the deficit — Failure of Mr. Wilson's measures.

THE history of Indian Finance, as a system, may be said to have commenced with Mr. Wilson's appointment as Finance Member of Council, or Finance Minister, as the post should, properly speaking, be called. The year previous to that, indeed, Lord Canning had published the budget statement for the first time, thus showing that he was the first of Viceroys to recognise the existence of the governed class as an element in the commonwealth. But Mr. Wilson was the first to reduce the financial administration of India to a system. He laid the foundation upon which his successors raised the walls of the edifice.

It would serve no purpose, in reviewing the history of the past ten years, to dwell upon the details of the annual budgets as they came out, each correcting the errors of the preceding one as the regular estimate tested the accuracy of the budget estimate. Still less would it be worth our while to enter into a discussion of the difference which has frequently arisen between the accounts as presented to the Indian public, and as laid before Parliament by the Secretary of State. But it may not be uninteresting or uninstructive to glance at the general features of Indian financial administration, tracing the absorption of the enormous deficit Mr. Wilson found on his arrival, and pointing out briefly the principal method by which the accounts were reduced to their present condition of average equilibrium, reviewing as we go on the main features in the policy of the different administrators who have successively tried their hand at the difficult subject of Indian finance.

The difficulty of the task that lay before Mr. Wilson has been very much overrated, and in reality the deficit was reduced to equilibrium more by simple retrenchment than by any elaborate system of finance. In the earlier part of the period under review, that is to say in the year 1860-1 and 1861-2, the course which the Chancellor of the Indian Exchequer had to pursue was very plainly marked out indeed. India was in the condition of a country gentleman who had for years neglected to look after his affairs, or if he had looked after them he had done so in such a slipshod and unpractical manner that he had failed to realize the extent to which he was involved. So long as he had a balance at his banker's available for current expenses, he cared not to inquire how his account was kept at credit. Whether the money was realized by loans or mortgages on his property he never paused to inquire, nor until he called in the aid of a man of business was he aware of the extent to which he had been living beyond his income, mainly in consequence of the extravagance of the establishment his steward kept up. To the enormous deficit that awaited Mr. Wilson's consideration there was but one remedy—retrenchment.

The finances were burdened with large, overgrown, useless institutions, on which public money was being squandered in a way that can only be pronounced reckless. Costly military and naval establishments were devouring the resources of the empire. The superfluous part of the one was an actual source of danger to the State; the advantage derived from the other was wholly out of proportion to its

cost. The great benefit that India derived from the
appointment of a financier straight from home was that
when he set to work vigorously to use the shears in cutting
down expenditure, there was no influence in the country
strong enough to oppose him. Aware, as the Indian
Government must have been, of the necessity for retrenchment, it is doubtful if it would have had the strength of
purpose and the energy to deal effectively and summarily
with vested interests. It would indeed have used the shears
here and there, cut down expenses in this department and
that, but its measures of reform would have lacked that
energy and vigour which a financier enjoying the confidence
of. the Government at home, and backed up by public
opinion, could freely exercise. The labours of the Military
Finance Commission, to which Mr. Laing alludes in the
most flattering terms in his budget speech for 1861-2,
must not be overlooked. But the Military Finance Commission, with a Wilson or a Laing to back it up, could
do a great deal more than if it had to wage the war against
vested interests, aided only by the countenance and support
of Indian civilian statesmen.

Mr. Laing thus alludes to the services performed by this
commission : " If the future historian of India should have
occasion to mention that in the year 1861 India was saved
from a great financial danger, that history will be very
imperfectly written if it omits the names of Colonel
Balfour and his colleagues Mr. R. Temple and Colonel
Simpson. Nor would I willingly omit to mention the
name of Captain Rennie, to whom, in conjunction with the
civil and military finance commission, it is mainly owing
that we have been able to effect important reduction in the
navy and marine."

Without in the least seeking to undervalue the services
rendered by these officers, it would be affectation to pretend
not to see that of all duties that can fall to the lot of public
men in office, that of cutting down expenditure and reducing establishments *on paper* is about the easiest. They

have no responsibility, because the onus of carrying out
their recommendation for reduction does not fall on
them. Their duty, in fact, is limited to looking through
the list of establishments and recording their opinion
as to what may, with the least sacrifice of efficiency, be
struck out.

There was not much room for hesitation in 1860-1.
During the campaign that succeeded the breaking up of
the old Bengal native army in 1857, an untold number of
native troops were enlisted. In spite of the patent fact
that we had very nearly lost India altogether in consequence of the disproportionate strength of our native army
when compared with our European, not two years had
passed before we had a much larger native force on the'
rolls than before the Mutiny.

In April 1857, or immediately before the Mutiny, the
total strength of the Indian army, including the Queen's
troops, was—Europeans, 45,522 ; natives, 266,852 ; maintained at a cost of 11,500,000*l*. a year in India, besides
1,250,000*l*. in England : but this was below the proper cost,
as this limit was only attained by allowing the effective
European force to remain dangerously below its established
strength. The real cost should have been about 12,000,000*l*.
in India, and 1,500,000*l*. in England. In 1858-9 this item
alone rose to 21,000,000*l*. in India and 3,750,000*l*. in England, showing a total increase of 11,000,000*l*., to which
must be added a million more for military police. Meantime, another million a year was being thrown into the sea
by the maintenance of the Indian navy, an establishment
than which probably none more utterly useless was to be
found within the limits of the British Empire and its
dependencies. To say that the native army as it stood in
1858-9 was useless is only to state half the truth. It was
a positive evil, not only eating up the resources of the
country, but a real source of danger. We had hordes of
undisciplined levies recruited from the lowest classes,
draughted into corps of police and told off in regiments,

and officered with some of the numerous remnants of the commissioned ranks of the old Bengal army, who were drifting about after the general wreck in search of employ-ment. The rabble, after being drilled for a short time, and armed and dressed in "Khakee rung" (as their uniform, a dust clay-coloured dress, was called), were marched off to occupy stations formerly garrisoned by the old Bengal sepoys, or despatched when they could be trusted in the field in pursuit of some remnant of the rebel army seeking cover in the jungle. What with disbanded native soldiers, the old army which had mutinied, and new levies and police, the country was overrun with military of all sorts.

In one sense, the second native army may be said almost to have grown up of itself. During the height of the storm, when amid the strife of elements the captain's voice could not be heard nor could any gain access to him, each man was constrained to do his best to confront the danger that immediately beset him. And this is where the individual character of the officers belonging to the Indian services, both the army and the civil service, come out so strongly. On a sudden, struck by the shock of a great emergency, men who had before shown no genius for com-mand, still less for diplomacy, evinced all the qualities of experienced leaders and prudent statesmen. Thus num-bers of officers all over the country raised bands of men of greater or less strength, either on their own authority, or with that of their immediate superiors, depending for eventual confirmation by the Government of an act which the emergency alone could justify. The Government did confirm all such measures, and not only confirmed, but kept on the men so raised in the pay of the State. The bodies of troops, however, so got together were far more efficient than the levies raised *en masse* by Lord Canning's order, who were for years afterwards the greatest rabble, probably, that ever appeared on a regimental parade-ground.

The purpose these levies were intended to serve is very doubtful, unless the opportunity for giving employ to a

number of unemployed officers could be regarded as a justification for the expenditure. Weeded, and worked up into
something like military organization, these levies eventually
formed the nucleus of the bulk of the present native army.

Of a different class altogether were the Goorkha, Sikh,
and Pathan regiments, raised by several old Punjabee
officers, who, from the extraordinary influence they possessed over the natives with whom they came in contact,
were enabled to inspire their men with daring intrepidity
and almost servile attachment. Men of these races commanded by really good officers are worth any number of
the Hindoostanees, who can never be depended upon. The
history of India is full of instances of battles lost and
dynasties overthrown by the treachery of Hindoostanee
soldiers ; and if we had studied history to any purpose, we
should not have been taken by surprise in 1857.

But the increase in the cost of our military establishment was not confined to the Bengal Presidency. Mr.
Wilson, speaking in February 1860, says : " If I compare
the increase of military charges alone in the three Presidencies at the present moment as compared with 1856-7,
the increase in Madras and Bombay is as great as it is in
Bengal. And if I compare the number of troops, according
to a return recently furnished to me, in 1857 and at the
close of 1859 in the different Presidencies, I find the increase
in Bengal barely five per cent. ; in Madras it is fifty per
cent., and in Bombay thirty per cent. But these returns
do not include the military police, the civil corps, and new
levies in Bengal, nor the new police in Madras ; they are
confined to the troops under the Commander-in-chief of
each of the three Presidencies."

This army consisted in 1859, including military police,
of 353,783 men, being an increase of 60,000 upon the
native army of 1857.

To reduce this enormous military establishment within
reasonable limits was a most salutary, indeed a necessary
measure of reform, but it is absurd to contend that it

called for any great financial skill. It was simply cutting
down the weeds which had sprung up during the ab-
normal condition of the country in 1857 and 1858. It is
likely enough that the operation was performed far more
effectually and speedily under the supervision of the new
financial member of Council, than it would have been without his aid and support. Without the stimulus imparted
by the energy and independence of men straight from
England, the bureaucratic and clique-beridden Government
of India might have played with the task, and lingered
over it for years. The disbanding of corps and reduction
of establishments necessarily entailed loss of emoluments
to commanding officers and others, each of whom would
have set in motion the complex machinery which in a
government like that of India controls the disposal of
patronage. To save this regiment and that levy from the
shears of the Financial Commissioner, the powerful influence which at times is exerted with so much effect in
Calcutta and Simla drawing-rooms would have been
directed to spare this tree and that from the axe of the
woodman. With men like Mr. Wilson and Mr. Samuel
Laing at the Governor-General's right hand, men who were
held responsible by the Government and people of England
for the state of the Indian finance, the work of wholesale
reduction was carried on without interruption. The reduction, however, it is fair to add, had been commenced
before Mr. Wilson's arrival. In 1859-60 the military
expenditure in India was brought down to 17,750,000*l.*,
and in England to 2,750,000*l.*, making a saving of 4,250,000*l.*
In 1860-1, under Mr. Wilson's supervision, a further saving
of 2,500,000*l.* was effected, and in the following year a
further reduction of 3,220,000*l.*

It was on the 18th of February, 1860, that Mr. Wilson
put forward his statement, which was looked for most
anxiously by the whole European community of India,
and that section of the English public who felt any
interest in the condition of our Eastern empire. After

alluding briefly but eloquently to the recent disturbances and the subsequent military successes, Mr. Wilson prefaced his statement with the following remarks :—

" Severe as was the storm, and numerous as were the wrecks strewed over the land, it is now restored to complete tranquillity, and the Indian political atmosphere was probably never at any former time so settled and clear. But though this is undoubtedly the case, though by the power of our arms and the courage of our civil administration a well-founded feeling of greater security pervades India than at any former time, yet it is unfortunately no State secret that an evil of the greatest magnitude is corroding the very heart of our political existence. Sir, if we have surmounted one class of difficulties, we have still to grapple with another class, which, if not so exciting and alarming, is still of the most pressing and urgent character. It would be in vain that we could boast of the success of our arms, of the restoration of peace and tranquillity, if we could see no end to that financial disorder which so notoriously prevails at this moment. That our situation is serious, that it is even worse than I expected, I am bound to admit."

On the 1st August, 1859, the Secretary of State had told the House of Commons, that the deficiency of income, as against expenditure, for the year ending 30th April, 1860, would be 10,250,000*l*. In the following month, another statement, drawn up in India, showed a deficit, including the Home charges, of 6,499,981*l*. This rapid decrease in the amount of the deficit was hailed as a good omen ; and it was said in England that the neck of Indian financial difficulties was broken. Mr. Wilson then proceeds to dispel this illusion. He shows that whereas the income of the year was 37,706,209*l*., the charges, including the value of stores from England, was 41,770,008*l*., leaving a deficiency of 4,063,809*l*., which, however, was reduced by the net profits of railway receipts to 3,783,109*l*. In addition to this there was a sum due on Home charges of 5,507,020*l.*, raising the whole deficit to 9,290,129*l.* This was an improvement, however, upon the former year, for the deficit on the 30th April was upwards of 13,000,000*l.* In the three years dating from the commencement of the Mutiny, the net deficiency of income as compared with expenditure was upwards of 30,000,000*l.*, which added to the deficit of 1860-1, after making allowance for reduction of expenditure, and increase of revenue by the fiscal measures then sanctioned, amounted to 38,410,755*l.*; and this, as Mr. Wilson takes care to impress upon the attention of his hearers and the country at large, is the sum to be debited to India on account of the Mutiny.

The ruinous system of loans by which it had been the practice to supplement the deficiencies of the Indian exchequer had resulted in burdening the country with a debt of no less than 97,851,807*l.* involving an annual charge for interest of about four millions and a half. Of this system Mr. Wilson speaks as follows :—" Our deficiencies have been supplied by loans in England and in India, and what has been the result ? And here I claim the special attention of every one, native and European, who feels a real interest in India. What was the state of our debt before the Mutiny, and what is it now ? and let us ask, what will it soon be if we are to resort to the miserable, the disreputable expediency of continuing to borrow in time of peace ? Loans may be justified in time of war, and, as the consequences of war, for a year after ; but even then they should not be exclusively relied upon." In another place, he adds that by returns furnished to Parliament the last Session, out of fifty-nine years which elapsed in the present century, in no fewer than forty-four of those years have considerable, often large, additions been made to the Indian debt, while in fifteen only have diminutions taken place ; so that the normal state of Indian finance may be said to be deficiency of income and addition to debt.

No one will, of course, for a moment think of disputing

the accuracy of Mr. Wilson's opinion condemnatory of the
system of incessantly resorting to loans. But there is one
argument in favour of Indian State loans which cannot
apply to other countries, and it is that the wealthy classes
among the natives, the independent chiefs and others, are
thereby induced to give a guarantee for their fidelity to the
British Government. By investing largely in Government
securities, they become personally interested in the preservation of peace and the maintenance of British power. The
ideal of British dominion in India is that of the power
paramount standing like some lofty building in the midst
of a cluster of minor edifices, each in proportion to its size
and strength contributing to the solidity and the ornament
of the whole design. The connexion between the grand
central structure and its outworks is such, that although
they add to its beauty and stability, acting as bulwarks to
protect it from the effects of weather, the violence of floods
and winds, political agitation from within and danger from
without, yet their strength and durability, though they
contribute to the solidity of the whole building, is not
necessary to its existence. On the other hand, the massive
centre-piece is indispensable to the existence of the cluster
of minor structures which, without their mainstay and support, would fall together and crumble into ruin. Anything
which serves to cement this union between British dominion
and the independent states should be fostered and encouraged. Were that union solid and complete, the British
Indian Empire would contain such an element of stability
that it might defy the influence of internal discord, or the
power of external foes. And the more the rulers and the
people of these states feel that their interests are bound up
with those of the British Government, the firmer will be this
union. I know no better means of cementing it than for
the British Government to borrow largely from these states.
There are no friends and well-wishers like creditors. It is
astonishing how interested they are in the welfare of the
debtor who is involved to an immense amount, but who

will, there is no doubt, if he only retain his health and
flourish in his business, pay his interest regularly, and
liquidate his liabilities in full eventually.   Under such
circumstances a creditor becomes almost as attentive and
sympathising as a lover.   There is perhaps no power in
the world—at any rate, there is none in Europe—situated
as the British Indian Government is in respect to the
native states.   And it is not to be wondered at that a
statesman just from England, accustomed to deal with
questions of European politics only, should have overlooked
this unique feature in our situation in India, and when
condemning the system of resorting to loans to meet
current liabilities, even in time of peace, should have overlooked the fact that there is one strong argument in favour
of the system in India which does not hold elsewhere.

This exceptional advantage, however, which results from
the practice of resorting to loans in India, is contingent and
accessory merely.   It was not, probably, with any such
object in view that the different Governors-general have
adopted this idle and easy method of avoiding financial
difficulties.   The practice is in itself pernicious and un-
statesmanlike.   And Mr. Wilson's wholesale condemnation
of the habit of perpetually resorting to loans in time of
peace was founded on the most commonly received axioms
of political economy.   But in reckoning the expense incurred by the war of 1858-9 as a deficit, he seems to have
overlooked the fact that war expenses are in no country
and under no system of financial administration charged to
revenue.   There is not a government in the world that
does not consider itself justified in saddling posterity with
a share, at any rate, of the burden incurred by war.   And
the principle is essentially a just one when the war is forced
upon a people by necessity, and the expenditure is incurred
in purely defensive measures.

It may be interesting to note briefly the comparison
instituted by Mr. Wilson between the expenditure incurred
in former wars and that of 1858-9.   Lord Amherst, who

came out shortly after the conclusion of the Nepal and
Mahratta wars, had to meet an accumulated deficiency,
during nine years, of three millions. Lord William Bentinck, who came out in 1828, after the first Burmese war,
had to cope with a deficiency during five years of fourteen
millions. Even the Affghan, Sind, and Gwalior wars,
together with the two Sikh wars, covering a period of
eleven years, left only an accumulated deficit of fifteen
millions and a half. . During the four years from 1849
to 1853 there was a surplus of 1,700,000*l.* But the
four years preceding 1861 left a deficit of thirty-seven
millions. " In making these comparisons we cannot
help being struck," says Mr. Wilson, " with the greatly
increased cost of the recent occasion. In one respect,"
he adds, alluding in terms of high commendation to
Lord Canning, " I must own that I found in this, one
of the redeeming points to reconcile us to the financial
difficulty in which we now find ourselves. The future
historian of India, when recording the occurrence of the
last three years, if he be a man of fine discrimination,
will dwell with pride upon the fact, that at that moment
India was governed by an English nobleman, who in the
midst of the greatest peril never for an instant allowed his
judgment to be swayed by passion, or his fine sense of
honour and justice to be tarnished by even a passing feeling
of revenge. For perhaps the first time in any Asiatic war,
Lord Canning adopted throughout the whole of this campaign the most scrupulous principle of integrity. Whatever
service was performed, whatever provisions were supplied,
were strictly paid for : and when under the vigorous
administration of the Punjab, money contributions were
exacted, the obligations have been all acknowledged and
faithfully repaid. Sir, rely upon it, however much such a
mode of conducting a campaign may add to present expenses, the statesman who pursues it is far more than repaid
in the permanent stability which he thus gives to an empire ;
and I cannot avoid the opportunity of saying, that however

much some may have differed with the policy which the
Governor-General pursued, yet that the time is not very
distant when even they, and I am sure the public at large,
will do justice to the calm and dispassionate, but truly
courageous discrimination which the noble Earl has exhibited throughout these trying occurrences; and I cannot
but believe that we are already reaping the benefit of it in
the great repose which has now spread itself over India,
and which, I am convinced, will enable me the more
effectually to deal with our present financial difficulties."

Without wishing to qualify the eulogy which Mr. Wilson
in these words passes upon Lord Canning's policy, justice
to the past generation of administrators demands that we
should bear in mind that this has ever been the policy of
the British Government in India in all its wars. We have
never adopted the plan of supporting our armies at the
expense of the people with whose rulers we were at war.

There were other sources of confidence besides this.
Railway traffic receipts bade fair to increase beyond the
most sanguine expectations; the renewal of peace was
followed by a reaction of commercial impulse; the people
seemed awakened from a state of lethargy to one of unprecedented activity. Since 1834 the total value of exports
and imports together had increased progressively from
13,847,289*l.* in 1833-4 to 60,219,660*l.* in 1858-9. The demand
for country produce had stimulated the energies of the
cultivators of the soil. The arrears of land revenue, which
in 1834 amounted to four millions, had dwindled down to
an almost nominal sum. The increased demand for labour
had caused the rate of wages to rise in many districts two-
fold, in some threefold, within the few preceding years;[1]
and, in spite of the desolating wars of 1858-9, Mr. Wilson
could hazard the remark, that every class of the community was in a condition of unparalleled prosperity.

One of the first things Mr. Wilson had to do was to
correct a grave error into which Lord Canning's govern-

---

[1] This was not the case, however, with agricultural labourers.

ment had fallen just previous to his arrival, from want of
acquaintance with, or in consequence of disregarding, the
very first principles of political economy. An excessive
impost always results in the repression of trade. How
Lord Canning could have fallen into so great a mistake as
to raise the tariff upon certain imposts from five to twenty
per cent. at one swoop, it is difficult to understand. The
enormous increase had the effect of checking trade to such
an extent that the revenue derived from the duty on these
articles, instead of rising to four times the amount, fell at
once to nearly one-half. Mr. Wilson at once rectified this
by reducing the tariff to ten per cent. from twenty. At
the same time, with the view of encouraging as much as
possible the development of country produce, he remitted
the export duty altogether on certain articles—wool, hides,
hemp, jute, flax, tea, and the import duty on books, maps,
prints, &c., which remission in the aggregate would, it was
calculated, entail a loss of 82,000*l.* The duty on saltpetre
it was proposed to raise to 5*l.* 10*s.* a ton. The quantity
exported from Calcutta was about 800,000 maunds of eighty
pounds, and from Bombay about 100,000 maunds, and the
duty was expected to realize 180,000*l.*

For the eleven months ending with the conclusion of
1859 the export of cotton-piece goods to India had reached
the large amount of 11,041,000*l.* against 8,497,000*l.* of the
previous year. The export to India of cotton yarn in the
same period had amounted to 2,306,000*l.* against 1,763,000*l.*
of the previous twelve months. The duty on the manu-
factured article was ten per cent., and Mr. Wilson now
proposed to fix a similar duty on the raw material, cotton
yarn and twist, which was expected to give an addition of
67,461*l.* to the revenue. A revised system of valuation of
duties was expected to realize an increase of 150,000*l.* or
200,000*l.*

The income-tax, together with a licence-tax (which,
however, was not passed), was the next measure proposed.
The former was to extend to incomes of 200 rupees a year.

Incomes from 200 to 500 rupees a year were taxed two per cent.; above that the rate was four per cent., of which it was intended to expend one per cent. in local improvements.

As regards the zemindars of Bengal, in behalf of whom it was urged that they ought to be wholly exempt from the income-tax, Mr. Wilson, overruling the arguments adduced in support of their position, decided that it would be a fair rate to assess this class at one-half the rent they paid to Government as their profits in respect of land. All who paid less than 400 rupees became thus exempt.

We have now to see how far these measures were successful. The income-tax was expected to produce about 2,500,000*l.*, which was to have been supplemented by the proceeds of the licence-tax to the extent of 1,000,000*l.* The latter, as we have seen, never became law ; and the income-tax only realized 1,400,000*l.*

Mr. Laing's financial statement for 1861-2 was delivered on the 27th April, 1861. His figures represent a deficit of 6,000,000*l.* The actual deficit at the end of the previous year 1861, according to the regular estimate drawn up in February 1861, was 6,678,000*l.* It will be recollected that Mr. Wilson's statement showed a deficit of about nine millions when he first took office. His prospective deficit for 1860-1, estimated at six millions and a half, was not far wrong. This he had proposed to meet partly by reductions and partly by drawing on his cash balances, which were then unusually large, owing to the success of recent loans. Unfortunately, of these anticipations the last only was realized. The actual deficit of 1860-1 was 6,678,000*l.*, and it was partly met by a corresponding reduction of the cash balances in India and England, which on the 30th April, 1860, stood together at 19,000,000*l.*, and on the 30th April, 1861, about 14,500,000*l.*[1]

The deficit, therefore, not having been met by Mr.

---

[1] *Vide* Financial Statement by the Hon. Samuel Laing, 27th April, 1861.

Wilson's measures, stood over for his successor to deal
with; and the first thing to which Mr. Laing had recourse
was reduction in military expenditure.[1]   By this alone
a saving was effected of 3,220,000*l.*   The net annual profit
of the income-tax he rated at 1,400,000*l.*   The increased
duty on cotton yarn, which Mr. Wilson calculated to produce 67,000*l.*, only realized half that amount, and the duty
was reduced again to five per cent.

It is remarkable that all throughout what may be called
the financial experiments of the last ten years, the tendency
has been to undo the work of the previous government,
and to return to the old system, which long experience
had taught Antediluvian[2] administrators to be the best
for practical purposes.

In 1869 a slight increase had been made in the salt-tax,
which had realized 1,000,000*l.*, or two-thirds as much as the
income-tax, without, as Mr. Laing said, being felt by any
one.   The increase in duty, it was shown, had had no effect
whatever upon the consumption; indeed, owing to the
general progress of the country and the rise in the rate of
wages, an increase of consumption had gone on concurrently
with the increase in duty.   Encouraged by this fact, Mr.
Laing proposed a trifling increase in this impost (which
already, in 1860-1, brought to the revenue 3,391,630*l.*, and
in 1861-2, 3,980,000*l.*), calculated to give an increase of
598,370*l.*

The condition of the Indian opium trade, and the system
by which so large a revenue is derived from it, has for

---

[1] It must be recollected in justice to Mr. Wilson, that the reductions
instituted under his auspices had not begun to produce any sensible
effect when his lamented death carried him away from the scene of
his labours.

[2] The era of the rebellion, 1857-8, often goes by the name of
" the Deluge " in India.   All before was " Antediluvian."   And indeed
the storm swept away so many antiquated systems, and wrought such
a complete revolution in others, that those who have known India for
the last twenty years can see many features which render the simile a
not inapt one.

years been a hackneyed subject with crude writers and
maudlin sentimentalists. We have heard the system de-
nounced as iniquitous, shameful, discreditable ; while, on
the other hand, we have been assured over and over again
that as a source of revenue it is most precarious, and that
it is dangerous for the Indian financier to depend upon it.
Mr. Laing and Sir Charles Trevelyan both went into the
subject, and laboured hard to show that the opium trade
was not a precarious source of revenue, nor immoral in itself.

Opium eating and smoking are practices, or vices when
carried to extremes, to which Englishmen are not in the
least addicted. The cold climate of our more northern
latitude awakens no desire for this peculiar drug, which is
a stimulant at one time, and a narcotic when taken to
excess. And in accordance with the national tendency of
Englishmen to condemn those practices in others to which
they themselves are not addicted, overlooking their own
peccadilloes, or dealing very tenderly with them, we find
thousands who hold in the utmost abhorrence the Oriental
habit of opium-eating. There are no statistics from which
any safe conclusions may be formed, and it must rest
therefore merely on individual opinion, derived from what
I myself and others who have travelled and resided both
in the East and West have seen ; but I have no doubt in
my own mind that if a comparative statement of the mischievous results following the consumption of opium and of
that of spirituous liquors were drawn up, the conclusion
would be very much in favour of the former. Mr. Laing
remarks most truly, in his budget speech of 1862-3, " that
every civilized or semi-civilized race of mankind affects
some peculiar form of nervous stimulant, and as the natives
of Northern Europe take to alcohol, so the Chinese take to
opium. Possibly in each case the craving is for something
to supply an innate want. The Englishman, the Dane, the
German, and the Russian resort to that the specific effect
of which is to raise the spirits and produce temporary
exhilaration. The Chinese, whose greatest deficiency, as

shown by the whole history, religion, and the literature of
the race, is in the imaginative faculties, resorts to that
which stimulates the imagination, and makes his sluggish
brain see visions and dream dreams.

" Be this as it may, the fact is certain that under all circumstances and in all climates, as the Englishman is a
drinker of beer, so is the Chinaman a smoker of opium.

" We have therefore at the bottom of our opium revenue
one of those great natural instincts of a large population,
upon which the English Chancellors of the Exchequer
confidently rely for half their revenue.

" It is of course theoretically possible in the case of gin,
whisky, rum, and tobacco, that the exhortations of the
temperance advocates in the former case, and of the ladies
in the latter, might at any moment so far prevail as to
induce the population generally to abstain from habits
which are in many cases pernicious and in many more
wasteful and disagreeable.

" Should they so prevail, the finances of England, and
indeed of almost every country of the civilized world, would
collapse far more suddenly and hopelessly than ours would
in India by the failure of opium.

" But, as I have said, an English Chancellor of the
Exchequer goes on with equanimity, relying on a taxation
of 400 or 500 per cent. *ad valorem* on spirits and tobacco
for 20,000,000*l.* of his revenue ; and while this is the case
I can see nothing in any general consideration as to opium
to prevent us from doing the same."

Without following Mr. Laing in his flight towards the
region of metaphysics, where he seems to hint at conclusions many will be inclined to dispute, and confining
ourselves for the present to a question of facts and figures,
the reader will at once perceive that Mr. Laing is right in
his general conclusions, but incorrect in his method of
stating them. There is no reason for supposing that the
Chinese will suddenly leave off eating and smoking opium,
any more than for anticipating an analogous change of

habit among Englishmen, Irishmen, and Scotchmen, as regards brandy, beer, and whisky. But there is this great difference between the relative position of opium and spirits as regards the revenue, viz. that our revenue from opium is derived not so much from a tax upon it as from the sale of it. The Indian opium holds somewhat the same position in the China market that American cotton did in the European market. Supposing the American Government had had a monopoly of the cotton trade, and carried to the credit side of their revenue all the receipts on account of the sale of cotton, they might have regarded the item as a precarious source of revenue, just as we regard opium. The moment a cheaper or a better article came into competition the sale would fall off. So far there is a great difference between a revenue derived from the sale of a drug which depends upon the superior quality of the Indian product, and the revenue derived from the excise upon spirits. There is, it is true, no reasonable ground for anticipating that the use of spirituous liquors will be abandoned in England any more than that the use of opium will be abandoned in China. But it is obvious that, if the Chinese could get their opium cheaper and better elsewhere than from India, they would do so ; and in that case the Indian revenue might be the loser to the extent of about seven or eight millions per annum.

Sir Charles Trevelyan remarks on this subject, " that we have gone on calling the opium revenue precarious long after the contrary has been demonstrated by actual experience. It is anomalous, but it is not precarious. It rests upon precisely the same basis as the excise upon spirits in England—with this difference, that the spirits are consumed by her Majesty's subjects, while the opium is consumed by the subjects of the Emperor of China ; but the Chinese will no more go without opium than, it is feared, certain classes of our fellow-subjects will forego the use of spirits." Here we find Sir Charles Trevelyan making the same mistake as his predecessor. The opium revenue does *not*

rest upon the same basis as the excise upon spirits in
England at all. There is an affinity between the two
inasmuch as they both depend upon the habit of consuming intoxicating and stimulating articles, which, as Mr.
Laing says, all races have in one form or another; but
the one is a revenue derived from a tax upon, and the
other a profit that accrues from the sale of, an article of
general consumption.

Sir Charles Trevelyan, however, goes on to remark:
"The idea of the Chinese becoming independent of us by
growing their own opium is a mere chimera. The cultivation has been permitted in China for several years, with
the result that the demand upon India for opium has been
continually increasing. India has been bountifully dealt
with in the great division of labour established by nature.
She has an advantage over all the world in producing
indigo, saltpetre, opium, and some other things; the
Chinese on their part are more likely to increase their
cultivation of tea and silk than of opium. Even if the
quantity grown in China was largely increased, Bengal
opium is so much better than the native products, that it
could still be sold as an article of luxury like Manilla and
Havanna cigars."[1]

The analogy between the Indian opium trade and the
South American cotton trade seems to me to be complete,
except that the latter was not a Government monopoly. Sir
C. Trevelyan goes on to admit that the cultivation of opium
in China would increase if the market were not supplied with
a sufficient quantity of Indian opium. Of course it would.
And so we found with regard to the South American cotton
trade, which used to supply pretty nearly the whole world
with raw material; but when owing to the war the supply
dropped off, attention in other countries was turned to its
cultivation, and it seems at present doubtful, to say the
least, whether the South American cotton trade would
ever altogether recover the position it formerly held, even

[1] *Vide* Sir C. Trevelyan's Budget Statement for the year 1863-4.

if there were no difficulty in procuring slave labour in the Southern States.

It is difficult, again, to follow Mr. Laing and Sir Charles Trevelyan in their conclusions on what they call the moral justification of the opium revenue. The latter says, " The moral justification of the opium revenue also follows the parallel of the Home Excise upon spirits." Mr. Laing puts it upon other grounds : " This is not the place," he says, "to go into any lengthened arguments as to the moral bearings of the question. I have heard the most contradictory opinions advanced in perfect good faith by respectable men who had been in China ; some denouncing opium as a deliberate poisoning of the Chinese for the sake of filthy lucre, others contending that it had produced a most beneficial effect, by substituting a comparatively tranquil stimulus for the wilder excitement of intoxicating drinks which led to bloodshed and crimes of violence."

There is something almost ludicrous in the application of such arguments to the maintenance of a source of revenue.

All attempts to obscure the darker shades of the picture by laying on light colours fail most significantly. There is no analogy between the revenue derived from the growth, manufacture, and sale of opium, as a Government monopoly, and the revenue derived from the excise upon spirits ; for the one is an open, avowed, and direct encouragement of the consumption, and the other is just the opposite, unless indeed it be contended that people consume spirituous liquors in proportion to the duty levied on them. The one promotes, the other is manifestly calculated if anything to suppress the consumption. When Mr. Laing goes on to say, as he does in his budget statement for 1862-3, that "opium is neither very much better nor very much worse than gin," he is much nearer the truth. Whether it is, or is not, as injurious as gin, is a mere matter of opinion. What is certain is, that the English exchequer does not derive a revenue from the manufacture and sale of gin, while the Indian does from the manufacture and sale of opium.

So long as the East India Company held the country, there was, in theory at any rate, enough of the commercial element in their tenure left to justify, perhaps, the continuance of the opium trade as a source of revenue. But now that the Government of India is an Imperial Government, there is something truly anomalous, as Sir Charles Trevelyan says, in the condition of this traffic. I do not mean to imply that the anomaly is a sufficient reason for abandoning it, but it may be fairly taken into consideration whether the opium trade might not be thrown altogether over to private enterprise, and the Government be content to lay a tolerably heavy duty upon it. There would be a loss, of course, but it would be a much more legitimate mode of extracting a revenue from opium; and it is by no means impossible, on the other hand, that if all restrictions on its cultivation were withdrawn all over India, the increase of production and consumption would be so great that the export duty might in the course of time almost equal the amount at present realized from the sale.

As regards the objection on the grounds of morality to any steps that may have the effect of increasing the cultivation and sale of opium, we need not have many scruples on this score. Like many other good things, and like all stimulants, opium when used in moderation is, under certain conditions of life, valuable. It has its uses, and it may be abused. Like wine and cigars, it is a luxury; and if one may venture an opinion upon such a subject without practical experience, I should say a great many more people in the world shortened their lives by the habitual use of what is sold and drunk as sherry and port wine, than by the use of good opium.

But all this is beside the question. It may be undignified for an Imperial Government to add to its revenue by the sale of a drug, but there can be nothing criminal in cultivating, or encouraging the cultivation, of one of the most valuable natural products of the soil, or the manufacture of one of the best gifts of nature to the sons of toil, of sorrow, and of pain.

Mr. Laing shows from a table indicating the quantity of Indian opium consumed by the Chinese for ten years from 1852, and the prices paid upon it, that there has been a progressively increasing demand which has not been met with a corresponding increase in the supply. The consequence was, of course, a rise in the price of the Indian opium, and the production of an inferior sort in China to supplement the want of the Indian. Thus, the average price of the drug per chest during the first five of these years was 885 rupees, during the last five, 1,593, or very nearly double ; while the amount realized annually during the latter period from China averaged no less than eleven million pounds.

So that the small section of the Chinese empire with which we are acquainted, and which is within the reach of our trade, is ready to spend from 12,000,000*l.* to 15,000,000*l.* annually on Indian opium. No doubt the interior of this vast continent is supplied by an inferior article grown in the country itself. The opening out of the interior of China to our trade is, however, only a matter of time ; and as there is no reason whatever for supposing that the opium traffic would, if freed from monopoly, not grow in proportion as our trade connexion with the interior advances, there is scarcely any limit to the expansion of this profitable source of income. I would not use this as an argument for increasing the cultivation under the present system, but rather as an argument for Government gradually parting its connexion with it altogether, throwing it into the hands of private enterprise, and contenting itself with export duty. As regards the precarious nature of the opium revenue, it is not precarious so long as India has no rival in the production. If the Chinese could grow opium as good as the Indian, there can be no doubt, as Sir Charles Trevelyan says, they would have done so long ago ; but Nature seems to have given India some special aptitude for the production of the drug, just as she has to China a soil and climate adapted to tea, and to South America cotton.

With reference to the subject of the opium revenue, it must be remembered that there are two systems in vogue in India by which this revenue is obtained. The Bengal opium trade is a direct monopoly of Government, which makes advances to cultivators to grow the poppy, and by its own officers superintends the manufacture of the drug. On the other side of India there is also a large trade in what is called the Malwa opium, but there the poppy is grown by cultivators in native states on their own account ; the drug is prepared by them and transmitted to Bombay for shipment to China — the British Government taking 600 rupees per chest of 120 lbs. as duty.

The latter system, of course, is a legitimate source of revenue as excise. But the value of the trade which can bear so enormous a duty as 60*l.* upon a chest of 120 lbs. is obvious. And this is not all, for a further duty has in some cases to be paid to the sovereigns of independent states.

But to return to the condition of the finance as explained by Mr. Laing's budget of 1861-2. The deficit was 5,868,718*l.* This was met by reductions to the extent of 3,590,750*l.* ; improved revenue chiefly from salt, the income-tax, and stamps, &c. yielded 2,008,864*l.* ; and 500,000*l.* was deducted from the sum originally allotted to public works, and the governments of minor Presidencies were told to raise it as they could by local taxation, and to expend it on local roads and canals.

The cash balances in India on the 1st of May, 1861, were calculated at 12,850,000*l.*, which was higher than was expected, partly because the receipts from opium had been large, and partly because the recent reductions had begun to take effect.

After allowing for the payment of 950,000*l.* for prize money and 500,000*l.* per month for railways, it was estimated that the cash balance on the 1st May, 1862, would be 14,264,302*l.*

It will be obvious that in the whole period from 1859-60 to 1868-9 the greatest financial difficulties had to be encountered in the first two or first three years. Mr. Laing's first budget opened with a deficit of six millions, very nearly the same as that with which Mr. Wilson had to deal. The second budget commenced with a much more favourable condition of affairs—a condition so favourable, indeed, that the announcement of it was received in some quarters with incredulity. Nor was Mr. Laing himself less surprised than the public at the rapid and unexpected disappearance of difficulties. He says:[1] " After finding myself struggling in January with an apparently hopeless deficit, I was able in April, to my own great surprise, and I believe that of every one else, to produce a budget in equilibrium. If," he adds, "the feeling here was one of astonishment, in England it amounted almost to incredulity."

This is how the Finance Minister spoke in April 1862. In January of that year, if we understand him rightly, he contemplated having to provide for an apparently hopeless deficiency.

This rapid change is put down to the elasticity of the Indian resources ; and they are truly called elastic. But the very fact of this elasticity necessarily detracts somewhat from the amount of credit due to the Finance Minister. And exactly in proportion as that credit is deteriorated by the recognition of the elastic nature of these resources, is our wonder increased that former statesmen, who ought to have been aware of this elasticity long before, were nevertheless either ignorant of or indifferent to it, or neglected to avail themselves of it. Elastic the revenues

[1] *Vide* Financial Statement for 1862-3, by Hon. Samuel Laing.

are in both ways. The expenditure could be contracted, and the revenue increased by a government absolutely despotic to any extent it pleased : it was an iron-gloved hand upon an india-rubber ball. There was no House of Commons to be appeased, no force of public opinion to be influenced or cajoled. The minister simply had his estimate of expenditure before him. So much wasteful squandering of public money on useless establishments was to be cut off ; so much revenue to be raised by additional duties upon salt, upon stamps, or by new taxes. If the equilibrium was not restored by this, another squeeze— more useless expenditure curtailed, and more taxes levied. A complacent Viceroy and a subservient Council ratified every measure laid before them, and the thing was done. So that, much as India may be indebted to Mr. Wilson and Mr. Laing, their work was very plain sailing after all.

It may be asked how it was that Mr. Wilson's measures failed to produce the equilibrium which his successor, Mr. Laing, succeeded in obtaining two years later.

Mr. Wilson proposed to meet a deficit of six millions and a half, partly by new taxes, partly by reduction. In reality he did neither. The taxes failed to produce what they were calculated to produce, and the reductions had not had time to take effect when his death deprived the country of his services, and Mr. Laing succeeded him. He of course reaped the results of his predecessor's measures. But there was another item, overlooked in Mr. Wilson's calculation, and that was the home expenditure for debt, railways, and army. The reduction of expenditure was over-estimated by a million and a half, and the increase by new taxes was also over-calculated to the same extent ; no allowance was made for the temporary nature of some of the items to the credit-side, such as the Punjab trade tax and stores. All these items put together made up five millions, and the real result of Mr. Wilson's budget of 1860-61 was a deficit of five millions and a half, after credit-

ing it with a full year's proceeds of all the new taxes, which
produced, as we have seen, much less than was contemplated, and one of which, the licence-tax, was not sanctioned at all till long afterwards.   To meet his expenses
Mr. Wilson drew on the cash balances, which, as has
already been stated, were unusually large.

CHAPTER XXI.

FINANCE (*continued*).

Mr. Laing's policy—Indian political economy—Caste—The Income
Tax a failure—Sir C. Trevelyan's fiscal measures—Mr. Massey's
Licence Tax—The independent member in Council—Principles of
taxation—Want of economy.

THE extinguishment of the great deficit which had so
unnecessarily alarmed the public during the second year
of Mr. Laing's tenure of office, cleared away the main
obstacles to an efficient and enlightened system of Indian
financial administration. For many reasons it is much to
be regretted that Mr. Laing's Indian career terminated so
soon. His ability is too well known to need comment, and
there was a hearty English tone about him that rendered
him popular with the European community, who felt that
their interests were safe in his hands ; while it is clear from
the whole character of his policy, and the tenor of his
speeches, that the interests of the native community would
have been equally protected. He had, perhaps, too little
reverence for that divinity that doth hedge the Indian
Legislative Council and a Secretary of State, to please men
in high office in England. How he maintained his own
opinion against the opposition of Sir Charles Wood is well
known, and the gravity of the Council must have been a
little moved as Mr. Laing's lively imagination pictured to
them the deficit under characters almost as numerous and
diversified as the representations of a showman. First of

all it was a "yawning pit, deep and wide," on the edge of
which "there was no chance of craning, no time to look to
the right or left, for the exhausted cash balances, hungry
and inexorable, were howling in their rear. To stick the
spurs well in and go straight at it was the only plan." [1]
Then his metaphor takes a leap wider even than across the
chasm, and five minutes afterwards the deficit is represented
as a pugilist. "After having fought so many, and I fear
such weary rounds with the huge bully Deficit, we shall
not let him claim a cross, or call it a drawn battle. If so,
in the language of the ring, let us go in and finish."
Another touch of the wand, and in deference to the
audience, who were more accustomed to tiger-shooting
than the "language of the ring," the deficit is a "tremendous tiger," which had given them "such a fright."
"Let us pour a parting shot into his carcase, and so finish
him off effectually." Another wave of the magic wand,
and he is at a game of chess with the yawning chasm, the
big bully, and the tiger; and he asks, "Is it to be a drawn
battle after all, or a stalemate, when we thought the next
move would win the game?" Again the scene changes, and
we have the yawning chasm, the big bully, the tiger, and
the chess-player represented as a dangerous headland
stretching out into the sea, beaten with surging waves, and
the Finance Minister wants but half a million "to weather
it and get into smooth water." And lastly, the changing
Proteus assumes the form of a hobgoblin sitting on the
shoulders of the Council, and the speaker rejoices in having
conjured away "the spectre which rode upon them like the
grim nightmare or hag of the old Norse saga."

Whether however as a yawning chasm, a prize-fighter, a
tiger, a chess-player, a headland, or a spectre, the deficit
had practically ceased to exist when Mr. Laing returned to

---

[1] All quotations and extracts on the subject of Finance have been
made from the "Official Record of the Financial Statements from
the 18th February, 1860, to the 14th March, 1868;" second edition, corrected and revised.

England, thanks to measures of economy principally, and wholesale reduction of wasteful expenditure, and Sir Charles Trevelyan had comparatively an easy task before him ; for it is always more difficult to work up to a certain standard than to maintain it when reached. And after all, the only new principle of taxation introduced was a very questionable one, and one which Sir Charles Trevelyan had from the first consistently opposed.

The Indian revenue increased steadily from 36,000,000*l.* in 1858-9 to 48,250,000*l.* in 1868-9, or twelve millions and a quarter in ten years, and the statesman must be of a very desponding temperament indeed who loses heart in the face of such a cheering condition of affairs. But they who set about the administration of India on principles of political economy recognised in Europe, without any attempt to modify those principles in accordance with the different conditions they find in existence in the former country, will ever be at fault. Yet Indian administrators are perpetually quoting John Stuart Mill, and endeavouring to steer their course in exact accordance with the chart laid down by that great authority. It is as if a mariner were to take a chart mapped out for the navigation of the Pacific to guide him across the Indian Ocean or the Atlantic.

The physical conditions of India and its climate do not differ from those of Europe nearly as much as do the habits, the modes of thought, and the whole social economy of the people from those we meet with in Western countries. In England and America you may always be pretty sure that in dealing with the ordinary principles of trade and commerce certain conditions will be attended with certain results. You may calculate with tolerable accuracy beforehand that such and such causes will be followed by such and such effects. If you look for similar results in India, the chances are you will be disappointed. What is more simple, for instance, than laying a tax on income ? The professional man, the trader, the merchant, will have invested his savings in the funds or some public securities, and you may find out the exact place in the schedule which he ought to fill. But how do you set about taxing the income of a man who has half a million of money which he buries in the ground? You take off your protective duties and institute free trade, feeling confident that the demand will stimulate the supply, because capital is pretty sure to find its way into an open field where profits are secure; and if one man will not take advantage of an opportunity afforded by a great demand, you are sure another will. But in India you are met at every turn by a system which assumes quite as many and as terrible forms as Mr. Laing's deficit, and which is ubiquitous, turning up at every moment to falsify all your preconceived conclusions grounded on the best and most commonly received principles of political economy, and setting at nought all your calculations on the connexion between cause and effect: and this is caste. And as the cramping, crushing nature of this terrible curse to a country is not the least realized in England, and realized very faintly by the most experienced administrators in India, it is always forgotten that caste means combination. A little of the effect of trade combination has been of late years seen in England. Let any one multiply trade combinations till the principle has been carried into every minor detail of commercial and social life, add to it the tremendous force of religious sanction operating upon a superstitious people, and he will gain a slight idea of what caste is doing in India, and has been doing for the last thousand years. One result of this is that we meet constantly with conditions and anomalies so contrary to all our preconceived ideas of commercial principles as to baffle the acutest statesman. In Orissa, in the height of the famine, corn and rice dealers were actually exporting the staple commodity of food.[1] In the autumn (September) of 1868, when wheat was selling at 19 seers the rupee at a place called Allyghur, distant three hours by rail only

[1] *Friend of India.*

from Delhi, the market rate at the latter place was 12.[1]
In Europe and America the prosperity of a people may be
measured by the wealth that trade brings with it. The
money which flows into the hands of capitalists and merchants finds its way through the medium of investments
to a thousand channels, whence it spreads its fertilizing influence over the whole country. In India it is absorbed
and disappears, no one can say where or how. Silver and
gold are melted up into bangles or ornaments, or if retained
in the shape of coin, buried in the ground. Professional
men among the natives, who draw an income of two or three
thousand rupees a month—fully equal to one of eight or
ten thousand pounds a year to an Englishman or an
American in his own country, when the circumstances of
life are taken into consideration—live in the same style, to
all appearance, as the clerk on a monthly salary of six
pounds. Their linen or cotton clothes cost them next to
nothing, and two or three changes suffice. They keep no
carriages or horses, live in houses that are rented for
perhaps 10l. or 20l. a year, and the only display they ever
make of wealth is on the occasion of a marriage festival in
their families, when perhaps they will squander upon dancing
girls and fees to idol temples and priests, three, four, or five
hundred pounds. Traditional ideas handed down through
countless generations have taught them to have no confidence in the stability of government, and they live as
if they were every day contemplating the chance of an
invasion by some Nadir Shah.

If a fact is wanted to illustrate these views, nothing can
more fully substantiate them than the net profits of an
income-tax of four per cent. upon incomes above 50l. a
year on the whole of India, yielding but 1,900,000l. including cost of collection ; and " I have told you frankly," says
Mr. Laing in 1861, " that, financially speaking, I think the

---

[1] The Indian weights and measures are unfamiliar to the English
reader ; but as they are only mentioned for purposes of comparison,
this will not signify.

income-tax has been a failure." Why was it a failure? No one denies the soundness of the principle that income and capital should bear a fair portion of the public burden. And as to the other great tax introduced by late financiers, the licence-tax, Mr. Laing calculated that to raise 600,000*l.* by it, the tax-gatherer would have to be sent to 4,000,000 doors, or, in other words, that it must affect 20,000,000 of the population. Yet on all recognised fiscal principles the licence-tax is as fair an impost as can be levied.

The same rule will be found to apply to almost every other branch of the administration, as well as to systems of finance. Many of our barrister judges, whose experience and reading have been confined to English and American jurisprudence and procedure, have expressed their surprise in no ambiguous terms at what appears to them the very undue weight given in India to documentary evidence over parole. Mr. Justice Phear, of the Calcutta High Court, especially, has on several occasions in public given utterance to very strong views on the subject. They cannot understand why the truth should not be elicited, as it is in other countries, by oral examination, or why an Indian judge should lay more stress upon a single authentic document than upon the verbal testimony of a score of witnesses. Here, again, ordinary principles that are recognised in Europe and America are utterly at fault in India. The practice of a whole country, the firm and deep-rooted belief of a whole people, and customs which have been developed by centuries of growth, do not spring from nothing. We have introduced marvellously little change into India below the mere surface of society; all beyond is much as we found it a century ago, and the practice of giving weight in judicial decisions to authentic documentary evidence has arisen from a well-founded conviction, not confined to the English official, but firmly rooted in the native mind, that oral evidence is comparatively worthless. So it would be in England if it were not for the practice of cross-examination, and that with a few exceptions is in India practically unknown.

These deep-rooted convictions, these ideas and notions and habits of thought which are the growth of centuries, it is the custom of our rulers a great deal too much to ignore. If India is always to be treated as a conquered country, to be kept in subjection by an armed force, we may be prepared indeed to retain it, and our tenure of it may be all the stronger from our never relaxing our hold on the *ultima ratio* of all diplomacy, physical force. But if our administrators are as desirous as they profess to be of giving the country a position among the foremost in progress and general advancement, their attention must be paid to these deep-rooted convictions, these long-established habits, and the stereotyped principles of the political economist must be moulded and modified to meet conditions never contemplated by the writers who enunciated those principles. In other words, and adopting Mr. Laing's expression, "we must give India what it has never yet had, political life."[1]

There were no very important principles ventilated during Sir Charles Trevelyan's administration, which lasted from 1863 to 1866, until the last of his budgets, which may be said to have been thrown after him with contempt as he sailed down the Hooghly, and was returned by the Secretary of State as disapproved. The measure of Sir

[1] The whole passage is so true, and so illustrative of Mr. Laing's enthusiastic views with regard to India, that I give the entire passage from his budget speech of 1861 :—

" I have a vision of an India—when the science of the West has removed impediments to communication ; when the consequent increase of trade has diffused material prosperity ; when English energy and capital stimulate inprovement in every district, and when the native population with expanding ideas and improving intelligence are taught by education of schools and of events, and of books and of railways, to know us, and to know one another ; and are gradually trained in the management of their own local affairs for those of a wider area ; so that India may at length have what it has never yet had, a political life, and at length be, what it has never yet been—a nation."

Charles Trevelyan's offending was that he touched the interests of a class powerful enough to be formidable to any Secretary of State, the Manchester and Liverpool merchants. So long as an act of policy was disapproved of by the Calcutta European community alone, the heathen might rage as furiously as they pleased, but the Government took no notice. But when the injury complained of was of such a nature that it reached the Manchester and Liverpool merchants through their corresponding firms in India, then there was a check at once applied. The Calcutta people raged furiously at the licence-tax, but the sound of their voice awakened no echo in Liverpool, Manchester, or London, for the impost did not in the least affect their corresponding firms, and the licence-tax became law in spite of them. But Sir Charles Trevelyan ventured on a measure which struck a sympathetic chord in Calcutta and Manchester, and he might have been recalled if he had not meantime retired. His offence was taxing exports; and as his policy has on this point been loudly condemned, it will be but fair to let him speak for himself.

"The old policy of the East India Company," he says, starting with an unhappy illustration, "was to levy low rates of duty upon exports and imports. However contrary the practice may have been to some received maxims of political economy, it was suited to the circumstances of the country ; for, owing partly to the abundance and richness of the productions of India, and partly to the simple habits of the people, the exports of merchandise have always greatly exceeded the imports, and our Indian exports have in general such a hold upon foreign markets that they can bear some duty without being seriously checked.

"This policy has of late years been departed from to a certain extent. Under the financial pressure caused by the Mutiny, the 5 per cent. import duties were raised to 10 per cent., and in some cases to 20 per cent., but they were last year reduced to 7½ per cent., while the year before the duty upon iron was nearly nominal. On the other hand, the duty upon several staples of the export trade was entirely omitted in 1860 with the exception of the duty upon saltpetre, which was raised to a rate inconsistent with the prosperity of the trade, and it has lately been reduced by one-half.

" So far as India possesses the monopoly of the foreign market, or a decided superiority over all other countries taken together, our export duty must be paid by the consumer. So far as exported articles are met by an effectual competition in the foreign market, the duty must be paid by the producer. But there never was a time when Indian producers were so well able to bear a moderate charge. While the assessment of the land revenue has been diminished, the price of agricultural produce has risen, and persons of every class connected with the cultivation of the land enjoy unusual prosperity. It must also be borne in mind that the heaviest expenditure in public works is for the construction of roads to facilitate the conveyance of exportable commodities to the coast."[1]

He proposed on the principle thus enunciated to lay a duty of 3 per cent. on the export of jute, wool, tea and coffee; 2 per cent. on hides, sugar, and milk; an extra three-halfpence a maund (80 lbs.) on rice and other grain; and, on the other hand, to reduce the import duty on hops from 7½ to 1 per cent., to encourage the Indian brewer. The Indian tea, coffee, and salt trade, especially the first and last, were just beginning to sprout, and needed all the fostering aid that could be given them. The export duty upon these articles, even on the ground that the public revenue was indented upon to construct roads to enable the producers to carry their stock to the sea-coast, seems hardly consistent with a desire to encourage new branches of industry.

His second great measure, borrowing to carry out public works of permanent benefit, has long since been admitted

[1] Sir Charles Trevelyan's Speech on the Budget, 1st April, 1865.

to be sound. At the time, however, Sir Charles Trevelyan was much blamed for this, his detractors and the
press generally in India exclaiming against him for putting
aside the income-tax with one hand while he stretched
out the other for a loan.

We have seen that Sir Charles Trevelyan laid aside the
income-tax, as he expressed it, "on the shelf, complete in
all its gear, ready to be re-imposed in case of any new emergency." It was not re-imposed by Mr. Massey, but he substituted for it the licence-tax, which was passed into law,
as related in a previous chapter, with such unprecedented
rapidity as to call forth the indignation of the public. As
it first stood, it had much that was objectionable : a distasteful impost under any circumstances, but, passed as it
was, with inconsiderate and indecent haste, it could be
nothing but a crude and unsatisfactory measure. The
second year it was much modified, and, as if ashamed of
their hurry and precipitation on the previous occasion, the
Council now gave the Bill the thought and discussion it
deserved. This debate was famous for advancing the
development of the constitution of the Legislative Council
of India, another step towards perfection. In that august
body, as is well known, the unhappy non-official member
is in such a minority always, that it must really require no
little moral courage to set himself up as a target for every
other member of the Council to aim at. Indeed, under
the recent development of the constitution of the Council,
it is difficult to see of what use the non-official members
are at all. On this occasion, owing to the opposition of
one of the independent members, the Hon. Mr. Skinner—
who said he could not see the necessity for any licence-
tax at all, and proposed to throw out the Bill then before
the Council, and repeal that still in force—the following
principles were laid down, determining the relative position
of the members to the Government. First, that no official
member could oppose any Bill brought forward by Government ; he might advise, but was on no account to do more :

and secondly, that no non-official member could move an amendment to a bill brought forward by Government. As if these two principles were not enough to fetter all real discussion, Mr. Massey took the unprecedented step of endeavouring to silence Mr. Skinner at the outset of the discussion by threatening that, if his budget and his Bill were not passed, he would resign at once : he would not be a party to the construction of a new budget. To this Mr. Skinner replied at the next meeting, with well-pointed irony, that, "if every other argument against him failed, it could hardly have been expected that he should successfully contend against the threat which the Right Hon. Mr. Massey had thought it right to hold out of the consequences that would follow from the adoption of his (Mr. Skinner's) views—a threat in which he must assume to consist the principal defence on which the measure rested."

To an independent thinker, Mr. Skinner's argument against this Bill appears fair and reasonable enough. All he said was, if Government were resolved to impose a burden of this sort on the country, upon what principle was it that particular classes were singled out and fastened upon to bear that burden ? Why levy a tax upon enterprise, and leave property untouched ? Why should the landed and funded interests be exempted from contributions to an impost from the application of which they derived at least equal benefit. In a conclave of rational men, met together to make laws and regulations for a large empire, we might have expected that arguments as reasonable as these would have been answered in some other way than by a threat of Mr. Massey's resignation if opposition was successful. The incident serves to illustrate well the constitution of the Indian Government, and the temper of the official towards the independent classes in public matters. The wonder is that any independent man should sacrifice valuable time to sit in a council where he is made to feel that his position is that of a "dummy."

It has been my object throughout to avoid as much

as possible offering "suggestions on Indian administration," with which the public have been supplied by successive authors *usque ad nauseam.* Every *dilettante* writer on Indian affairs deems himself capable of conducting the government of that country much better than those to whom the onerous duty has been entrusted by the State. In so far as I have been tempted occasionally, from the nature of the subject, to offer suggestions, I have strayed from the legitimate purpose of this work, and must crave my readers' pardon. It has been my object to give a history of the period, and, by exposure of errors where they are palpable, of shortcomings and defects, to imply the necessity rather than to. suggest 'the method of amendment. The question of taxation is one upon which every man living thinks himself much better informed than his neighbour, though it is not often that his neighbour makes the concession to his judgment which Mr. Massey did to Mr. Skinner, when, instead of confuting his arguments, he endeavoured to silence him with a threat. While this discussion, or rather the torturing of·the independent member, was going on in Council, of course the matter was debated out of doors, and the Calcutta Chamber of Commerce addressed the Council, representing their views and suggesting three methods of raising money by taxation which they considered better adapted to the state of the country than the licence-tax. Mr. Massey, in his introductory speech upon the budget, briefly replied to these representations, and stated the points wherein he differed from the authors of the memorial. It is worth while to refer to them, because it may be taken for granted that the Chamber of Commerce would represent the opinion of the independent European community in Calcutta at any rate ; and if there had been any measures capable of being suggested better than the present one, it was probable that it would not have escaped their notice. They suggested three courses, either of which they said was preferable to the present one : 1st, an addition to the salt-tax ;

2d, a succession-tax ; 3d, a tobacco-tax. Space will not allow of a discussion of the merits of these three measures, which would occupy a volume. Suffice it to say that they were rejected : the salt-tax on the ground that that indispensable commodity is already so heavily taxed in India ; the tobacco-tax because the poorer classes, who would be the most affected by it, already paid their share of the public burden in the shape of a salt-tax, and it would be so extremely difficult of collection ; the succession-tax mainly because it was a tax on capital and not on income.

With two remarks, I shall dismiss this subject. One is, that there must be some defect in principle, when an impost like a licence-tax, which is professedly designed to tax income and not capital, only realizes half a million from the whole of India, and when an income of 2,500*l.* per annum pays 40*l.* And the second is, that no fiscal measures in any country can be successful unless designed upon principles of political economy that have been modified and adapted to conditions that are peculiar to that country and not to be met with elsewhere. In other words, the principles which are safe guides in Europe and America are not so in Asia. The Chamber of Commerce and the Legislative Council, in order to devise schemes of taxation for India, studied the history of modern Europe instead of the existing condition of India ; they applied principles they found in vogue in Europe and the West to conditions totally distinct from any they could discover there, or they expected by the force of a legal enactment to modify the character, and change the habits of thought and action, and remodel the social system of a hundred millions of the most conservative races in the world.

While there is every reason to congratulate ourselves upon the condition of the finances of India, whose revenue has increased twelve millions in ten years, with an income as large as that of Austria, far larger than that of Prussia, and not much inferior to Russia,[1] it is patent to every one

[1] Mr. Massey's speech on the budget of 1868-9.

outside the pale of the official world that the most wanton extravagance exists in many Government departments. This, of course, is strenuously denied by the officers of the departments within which the extravagance goes on, and it is to them the Government apply for information if ever they take notice of the allegation. Every independent member of the European community in India who has lived in the country ten years, and been in a position where he could obtain information, believes that in the department of public works alone there is a useless waste of about twenty-five per cent. of the money spent. How the money is spent, the subordinate officers of the department know well enough ; and there are officials in the higher ranks of this branch of the service, who, having made the matter a study, could if they chose point out the exact places where these leaks in the treasure-chest are to be found. Extravagant expenditure prevails, from the smallest item in barrack charges to the largest account for the construction of buildings that cost lacs. If a single nail is hammered into a soldier's cot, ten annas, or one shilling and threepence, is paid for it, because it must be done on a certain system, and must be entered under a certain head in the schedule of petty repairs. And every man who has ever built a house in India—and in the old days it was rare to meet an officer of the Indian army who had not—knows that Government pays for building material from ten to twenty per cent. above the market rate.

The old pagoda-tree, indigenous in the East, is popularly believed to flourish there still. Large profits are to be realized by public contracts, and where there is profit on one side there must be loss on the other.[1] There are many things which are matters of public notoriety in India, which

---

[1] There was a contract for sleepers. The rate the railway company paid was five rupees or ten shillings per sleeper. The contract was underlet again and again, till the supplier paid one rupee and a half, or three shillings. I fail to trace it further, and the sleepers probably cost from twelve annas to a rupee—eighteenpence to two shillings.

in England would be investigated, or thoroughly ventilated in Parliament or by the press. But public opinion is resultless in India, because there is no power, as there is in England, to support it. The ganglionic system of official life totally prevents the Executive from acting under any impulse communicated from the outside world, and, as the feelers of a sea-anemone all contract simultaneously and co-operate to resist the aggressor when you touch any one part of it with your finger, so the different departments of the Indian Government, when any one of them is attacked, all combine to silence or to crush the assailant. The most flagrant abuses flourish under the very eyes of those whose duty it ought to be to check them; and, if brought to the notice of Government, the very officials themselves who, if the allegations are true, are the persons to blame, are deputed to make inquiry. If there were two or three Joseph Humes in India, with an executive power to back them up, a saving of twenty-five per cent. in one at least of the public departments might be effected, and in others proportionately. But in India, the interests of the public are not represented anywhere, and human nature must be other than what we know it to be, if under such a system there was not ample room for reform.

CHAPTER XXII.

State of the army in 1858—Feeling of the officers—The Henley clause — Royal warrants and despatches — Measures of amalgamation—The local and staff corps—Addiscombe abolished—Cadets—Present system—Innumerable references—The birth of grievances—Redress refused—Lord Cranworth's commission—Classification of grievances—Inconsistency of the commission—Complaints remedied—Despatch No. 194, and Royal Warrant 15th June, 1864—Sir Charles Wood's averages—Another royal commission—Their recommendations—Lord Cranborne's despatch —Measures of redress—The Bonus despatch—General results—Total failure—Effects on the army itself—The Indian medical service.

CONSEQUENT on the mutiny of the Bengal army and the subsequent transfer of India to the Crown, it became necessary to take early measures to provide for the future military tenure of the country, and also to dispose of the numerous body of officers whose regiments had either mutinied or been subsequently disbanded.

During the Mutiny seventy-two Bengal native regiments had disappeared ; in Madras twelve, and in Bombay three native regiments were reduced, making a total of eighty-seven regiments officered on the old plan. The officers of these regiments were for the most part thrown out of employment ; no one of these for a moment thought that he should find his position in every way unaltered by the impending changes, nor did any question the right of Government to act as it might think fit ; their homage to the Company was about to be transferred to the Crown direct, and they doubted not it would be the wish and intention of her Majesty's Government to act in the same liberal spirit towards them as the Company would have acted. When, however, persons of the highest authority in England began to talk of such sweeping and wholesale changes as putting the whole of the officers of the mutinied and reduced regiments on half-pay, in accordance with the system in the British army, they naturally became rather anxious about their future fate, and not having the same knowledge of the temper of their new masters as they had of the Company, they thought it advisable to be provided with some basis on which they, on the one part, might take their stand, and from which Government, on the other, should not have power to remove them. Such a standing-point was given to the Indian army by Parliament in the clause inserted on the motion of Mr. Henley, the member for Oxfordshire, in Act XXI. and XXII. Vict. cap. 106, and XXIII. and XXIV. Vict. cap. 100, passed on the 2d August, 1858, entitled "An Act for the better Government of India." This just concession, frequently cavilled at and an eyesore at the India Office, has stood the test of some years now, and should remain the palladium of justice to the last Indian officer.

To give a full and succinct enumeration of the contents of the despatches and orders to which the measures for the amalgamation of the Indian and Royal armies gave birth, would occupy too much time and space, extending as they do from 1858, the year of the transfer to the Crown, up to the present time. The royal warrants are for the most part short and concise : not so the despatches from the India Office, especially those penned by Sir Charles Wood, who had not the faculty of simply announcing the measures he had decided to adopt for redressing grievances, and restricting his official remarks to the words requisite to give them practical effect. His measures, if they were in truth his, appear to require an unusual amount of gilding to make them palatable; certainly his tone and language were so pleasantly chosen, even when perpetrating a fresh grievance, that his very victim reading the despatch was half persuaded that his wrong had little in it to be remedied, and that the grievances of others were altogether mythical. In fact civilians generally, and all who would not be at the pains of mastering a difficult and complex subject, took the view that the officers of the old Indian army had no real cause of complaint, and ought to consider themselves fortunate in not all being put on half-pay.

It is purposed to give, firstly, a sketch of the various measures adopted to effect the amalgamation ; to notice, secondly, the grievances that spring therefrom ; thirdly, the mode of their redress ; and fourthly, the results to Government and the Indian army generally.

The report of the Royal Commission appointed in 1859–60 to inquire into the organization of the Indian army, and the experience gained by the recent Mutiny, showed the danger of maintaining an overgrown native force, so the Government of India in 1859[1] struck off the strength of the Bengal establishment ten native cavalry, and fifty-nine native infantry regiments. It was also determined to do away with a separate European local force. During 1859 a large portion of the local European army had mutinously claimed a bounty or their discharge, on the ground that they had been transferred without their consent from the service of the Company to that of the Crown. Government allowed those who wished it to take their discharge,[2] except the 5th European regiment of infantry, whose conduct was under inquiry ;[3] those who eventually did not take their discharge under the order above, were granted the boon of two years' service to count towards their time for future discharge.[4]

It was determined to re-organize the whole native army on the irregular system.

[1] G.G.O. No. 1,277 of 1859.   [2] See above, Chap. III.
[3] G.G.O. No. 883 of 1859.   [4] G.G.O. No. 884 of 1859.

The formation of a Staff corps was also determined upon. This measure had frequently been mooted in former years, when the evils attending the absence of so many officers from their regiments on staff employ made themselves particularly prominent.

It was also determined to do away, as far as possible, with all distinctions between the officers of her Majesty's British service and the Indian army, and to form them into one united body, retaining for the Indian officers such advantages as were peculiar to their service. To effect these measures her Majesty's Warrant for the formation of a Staff corps in each Presidency, together with Despatches Nos. 27 to 31 from the Secretary of State for India (Sir C. Wood), announcing her Majesty's gracious intentions regarding the officers and men of her Indian forces, were published for general information. By these the option of volunteering for general service was given to native cavalry officers and men of the artillery, cavalry, and infantry of the three Presidencies, with a bounty on certain conditions and rates; and they were allowed to choose whether their pensions should be reckoned according to the regulations of the British service, or according to those of the Indian army.

Those of the artillery who volunteered (and they did so almost *en masse*) were formed into new troops and batteries, forming fourteen brigades under the same conditions as those of the Royal Artillery; the remainder were formed into a local company, for duty in Fort William. Those of the cavalry were formed into the 19th, 20th, and 21st Hussars. The three oldest Bengal European regiments, three Madras, and three Bombay were brought on the strength of the British army and numbered 101 to 109; the designation of Royal being conferred on the "101st Royal Bengal Fusiliers," "102d Royal Madras Fusiliers," "103d Royal Bombay Fusiliers." As in the case of the artillery and cavalry, the men of the infantry volunteered

[1] Staff Corps Warrant, 16 Jan. 1861.

almost to a man; they found themselves in the same regiment, retaining their rank and standing, only the name and
condition of the regiment was altered : the men of the 4th
and 6th European Bengal regiments volunteered into the
three new line regiments of their Presidency ; those of the
infantry who did not volunteer for general service were
formed into a local company, the annals of which, none of
the brightest, are chronicled in the Fort Adjutant's office
in Fort William.

Further to carry out the amalgamation, every officer of
H. M. Indian forces was to receive a royal commission
under the sign manual, conferring rank and command in
her Majesty's army in any part of the world. Artillery
officers holding certain staff appointments were seconded,
and promotions made in their places. Under the Royal
Artillery organization colonels' allowance is drawn by
colonels commandant, and their number was reduced
under the new organization from 12 to 7 in Bengal, 7 to 4
in Madras, 5 to 3 in Bombay. Paragraphs 33 to 35 of G.G.O.
No. 332 of 1861 point out the mode in which the Indian
Artillery is gradually to be absorbed into the Royal
Artillery : in the same manner, pars. 36 to 45 of the same
Order point out the manner in which officers of the Indian
Engineers who elect for general service are to be dealt with
until all are absorbed into the Royal Engineers.

As the officers of the European cavalry, infantry, and
artillery had their regiments to go to when they elected for
general service, and the Engineers had their appointments,
whether they remained local or entered the British service,
the question of how far the amalgamation affected their
interests and future prospects need not be discussed.
There were a few artillery officers who never volunteered,
and their services were transferred against their will from
the Company to the Crown ; and in the case of several of
the officers who went into the twelve new line regiments,
the option was, owing to peculiar circumstances in each
case, in reality no option at all, but the step was practically

as much forced upon them as if they had been transferred
by an order from the Commander-in-chief. But it is
totally impossible in a work of this kind to state the circumstances attending the case of each individual officer
whose prospects have been injuriously affected by the so-
called amalgamation measures. There can be no question
that, in many of these instances, rights have been summarily overridden, for which, had the victims of arbitrary
power the means to seek redress in a court of law, there
is little doubt about the issue.[1]

Leaving these cases, we come to those paragraphs of
G.G.O. No. 332 of 1861 which concern the officers of the
native regiments, and the general and field officers of the
Indian army. By paragraph 46, the "gradation lists of
general and other officers of the three Presidencies, and their
promotions thereon, were to remain exactly as at present :
the promotion of field-officers of cavalry and infantry to go
on as usual in separate regimental gradation lists of major,
lieutenant-colonel, and colonel ; but a gradual reduction to
be made of those of the last grade entitled to colonels'
allowance, by filling only three for every four vacancies.
Regimental promotion to major to continue in cadres.
All the officers of cavalry and infantry to be placed on two
general lists respectively for each Presidency, those below
lieutenant-colonel being retained on the cadres for promotion as above ; from these two general lists officers will
be invited to volunteer for general service to the number
required for the new line regiments. The names of all
officers who volunteer for general service, or elect for the
Staff corps, shall continue to be borne, in italics, on the
cadres of their former regiments, in order to regulate the
promotion of those remaining local ; but the name of a
Staff corps officer borne on the cadre of an Indian regiment,
exchanging from the Staff corps with an officer of a British
regiment other than the twelve new line regiments, to give
an effective step in the cadre of his former regiment. In

---

[1] G.G.O. No. 332 of 1861, par. 89.

the regimental gradation lists of field-officers, the names of officers of the Staff corps or new line regiments, as they are promoted in their cadres, to be placed in italics, in the same position they would have held had they not joined the Staff corps, or volunteered for general service.

" The whole of the native cavalry and infantry regiments of the three Presidencies to be officered on the irregular system, with a complement of six European officers besides the doctor : these officers will eventually be drawn from the Staff corps.

" The present and prospective advantages which officers now in the service derive from the military and orphan funds to be secured to them ; and the retiring pensions under the Indian regulations will be scrupulously preserved."

The Staff Corps Warrant and Despatch No. 27 appended to this General Order (No. 332 of 1861) details the organization and regulations of the Staff corps to be formed in each Presidency. " Officers of the British and Indian armies *now* on staff employ in India, not having the substantive rank of colonel, are eligible for admission. Officers of either service under the rank of field-officer not now on the staff, may now or hereafter become candidates. Officers who may within the *last three years* have been on any *permanent* staff employ, and make application within the next six months, will be considered eligible to join the Staff corps : those whose tenure of appointments at the time of transfer to the Staff corps shall have exceeded one year will not be subjected to probation or any test. The option of joining the Staff corps will be open to those officers only *who may be considered* by the Government to be in all respects fit for the Staff corps. Officers of the *British* army, when transferred to the Staff corps, *will be removed* from the strength of the regiment to which they belonged ; the .promotion of Staff corps officers to be as under, viz. : 12 years' service, including 4 years in Staff corps, to captain ; 20 years' service, including 6 in Staff corps, to major; 26 years' service, including 8 in Staff corps, to lieutenant-colonel; 5 years in the Staff corps as lieutenant-colonel, to brevet-colonel.

"Officers *now* in staff employ will be allowed to count, to the extent laid down in the preceding paragraph, their past service towards promotion as if it had been performed in the Staff corps. One step of rank will be given to every officer whose period of service would qualify him for it according to the above rules: an interval of two years must intervene between each succeeding step. Officers not now on the staff will also be allowed this privilege, should they *be permitted to join the Staff corps.* The officers of the Staff corps will be under the new furlough rules of 1854; a certain proportion of the senior officers of the Staff corps will receive colonels' allowance; eventually the number will be fixed in the proportion of one for every thirty officers on the Staff corps: the necessity for a qualifying term of service (twelve years a substantive lieutenant-colonel) to cease when the proposed establishment, one in thirty, is completed; officers then to succeed by seniority as vacancies occur."

There are altogether 106 paragraphs in G.G.O. No. 332, and 99 paragraphs in Sir C. Wood's five despatches which accompanied it: enough has been extracted to show the working of the Order.

Further, to obliterate as much as possible the distinctions between officers of H.M. British service and Indian forces, officers of the latter who preferred the conditions of general service are given an opportunity by G.G.O. No. 558 of 1861 of obtaining a position in the British army; for every vacancy caused in a line regiment by the transfer of an officer to the Staff corps, a transfer of an officer of the Indian army of corresponding rank may be made to the regiment in which the vacancy takes place. These transfers are not to be made in India even provisionally; the Commander-in-chief in India will submit for the consideration of the Horse Guards the name, rank, date of commissions, and previous services of the officer whom the Commander-in-chief may recommend for each vacancy. Officers so transferred will enter H.M. line regiments as juniors of their rank, and be in all respects on the same footing as officers of H.M. British regiments.

In order to get rid of the burden of surplus of officers which was already beginning to be felt, a bonus pension of £50 a year in addition to the pension of their rank was offered to those who should retire on or before the 1st Oct. 1861; and again, Despatch No. 320 of 1861, acknowledging the receipt of the third report of the Calcutta commission, and the proposal contained therein for inducing a large number of the senior officers of the Indian army to retire, offers to the regimental field-officers of the three Presidencies annuities graduated from £550 to £150, in addition to any pension they may be entitled to, such retirements to date from 31st Dec. 1861. A certain number of captains of 25 years' service and upwards were also offered additional pensions of £120, should all the field-officers to the number of 300 not accept the pension. Some 35 captains availed themselves of this offer. But in consideration of the very liberal terms offered to these officers to retire, "the names of all the lieutenant-colonels so retiring *will be retained in italics upon the list of lieutenant-colonels* to regulate the succession to colonel and colonels' allowances. Promotion in succession to these lieutenant-colonels who retire shall be made in the proportion of one to two of such retirements, so that one colonel's allowance will eventually be struck off for each retired lieutenant-colonel who would have attained it had he remained on the effective list." This despatch winds up by declining to admit any claim, although very strongly recommended by the Calcutta commission, on account of compensation for the extinction of the old "regimental retiring bonus."

Despatch No. 467 of 1861 gives Sir C. Wood's definite orders with regard to the succession to colonels' allowance. The substance of the first seven paragraphs has already appeared. Par. 8 lays down the law that Staff corps officers succeeding to colonels' allowances must vacate their appointments—being, however, eligible for re-appointment, if they have interest enough. The next paragraph shows the anomalous position a Staff corps officer may hold, viz. that of a captain in the Staff corps and major-general in the army. But, however favoured by fortune, whether for his actions in the field or by a little favour at Court, Sir C. Wood brings him up with a round turn in this despatch ; the captain must count six years' actual service as field-officer to entitle himself to the unemployed pay of a major-general. A little balm is added, however, the above six years being inclusive of any time (how long ?) he shall have been obliged to pass upon half-pay in consequence of ill-health contracted in the service, or of wounds received in action.

The Royal Warrant 1st Jan. 1862, prescribes the mode in which the amalgamation of the general and field officers of the Indian and British armies, and the promotion of the officers to higher rank, shall be carried into effect. This warrant is too long for insertion here ; it is only necessary to state that the provisions of it gave great dissatisfaction, and it was cancelled in 1864, except clauses 9 and 10, which provide that on the transfer of the twelve new line regiments to the British service, a like number of general officers shall be taken off the Indian establishment, and be transferred to the list of general officers (British service)— three more being added to make up the proportion (fifteen) due to the number of officers of the transferred regiments.

Sir C. Wood's despatch, No. 494 of 1861, confirms the view he took in a former despatch, No. 296 of 1861, that the benefit of retiring under the rules of 1796, on pension of rank, is not to apply to Staff corps officers, the 9th paragraph of the Staff Corps Warrant notwithstanding, which states, " Officers of H.M. Indian forces joining the Staff corps will be entitled to pensions under the regulations of the Indian service." This wordy despatch allows those who joined the Staff corps under the wrong impression that they were to get a step or two of substantive rank by so doing and then retiring on the pension of that rank, to reconsider their decision. Some twenty officers of standing availed themselves of this option, and withdrew from the Staff corps.

To chronicle further changes, Indian allowances to colonels who may hereafter attain colonels' allowances, and who are not required to reside in India, will be discontinued;[1] such officers will receive, in addition to colonels' allowances, the full rate of regimental pay only as long as they may be unemployed, wherever they may be permitted to reside : Indian allowances will, however, be passed to them for six months from date of promotion to colonels' allowances, or for any *shorter period* during which they may be resident in India. An unemployed major-general of the Staff corps, not having succeeded to colonels' allowances, is permitted to remain in England on twenty-five shillings a day !

Again, it having been represented to the Secretary of State by the Government in India that none of the lieutenant-colonels who retired in 1861 on the enhanced pensions could by any possibility give a step to their juniors unless by their death, their names *being retained on the list*, Sir C. Wood enters into a prolix defence for retaining the names, and finishes the despatch by allowing colonels' allowances to all lieutenant-colonels of date prior to 1st January, 1862, when they have served twelve years in the grade of lieutenant-colonel : this was another in the long list of grievances to be redressed hereafter.

Among the many measures, and the last that need be mentioned, involving a total change in the future of the Indian army, was the abolition of Addiscombe and the cessation of the long line of Indian cadets. As far back as December 1858, the India Office, in anticipation of coming events, had decided that all future appointments

[1] G.G.O. No. 663 of 1862.

of cadets should be subject to any alteration that might be decided on; so those appointed after that date have nothing to complain of. The last cadet's appointment bears date 4th March, 1862. As, perhaps, many fathers of families, on the look-out for a provision for their sons, have not the means of a ready reference to General Orders, the following memorandum may be of service :—

NOTICE.

" INDIA OFFICE, 5th June, 1862.

"Cadetships having ceased, a limited number of commissions shall be given annually to persons selected by her Majesty's Secretary of State from among the sons of civil and military officers who have served in India. These cadets will be required to pass through Sandhurst; the expense of the education, board, washing, and medical attendance will be borne by the Secretary of State for India in Council : the number of such cadets allowed to be borne on the establishment of the college is twenty.

"Persons entitled to apply for these appointments should address the Under-Secretary of State, India Office." ·

And now, after so many despatches reflecting but little credit on the sense of justice of those from whom they emanated, the following abrupt communication comes upon us with startling effect :—" The contingency specified in the deeds constituting Lord Clive's Fund, that the sum of sicca rupees five lacs should be returned to the heirs of Lord Clive, having occurred by the passing of Acts XXI. and XXII. Vict. cap. 106, you are in future to admit all persons who would have been entitled to pension from that fund to an equivalent rate of pension, without reference to the name of Lord Clive."[1]

An immense amount of questions and references followed the general order (332 of 1861), and the despatches just noticed. They poured into the Military Department,

[1] Despatch No. 218 of 1863 : Lord Clive's Fund.

and were published afterwards in the official Gazette, the columns of which were filled with them, for general information. But they had to be referred to Sir C. Wood for confirmation, and consequently there was much delay, and not unfrequently a good deal of confusion, for the answers given by the Government of India were not always confirmed by the Secretary of State, or were so much modified as to beget doubt and uncertainty where all ought to have been precision and exactitude; as, for instance, in the following Question 96, G.G.O. No. 125 of 1862 :—

Q. "An officer leaves England in consequence of the Mutiny, having ten months of his leave unexpired; can he, if he joins the Staff corps, take this balance of furlough without losing his appointment?"

Ans. by Government of India. "Yes, he would be allowed the balance of his furlough, *retaining his appointment.*"

Ans. by Sir C. Wood. "Approved, but add the words, *to the Staff corps !*"

Once having joined the Staff corps, where was the poor wight to go? how could he but *retain his appointment to the Staff corps?* the Staff corps being nevertheless no appointment, but his only regiment.

By the foregoing measures, these changes were effected :

1. The transfer of *nearly* all the officers and men of the European cavalry and infantry of the Indian army, with their own consent, to her Majesty's general service.

2. The assimilation of the Indian Artillery and Engineers with that of the Royal Artillery and Engineers.

3. The re-organization of the reduced Native army as irregulars.

4. The formation of the three Staff corps of Bengal, Madras, and Bombay.

By the General Order No. 332 of 1861, the option was given to all officers, first, of joining the Staff corps; secondly, of electing for general service; thirdly, of remaining in the locals. Three optional courses appeared to be

open to all officers at a first glance ; but an officer to be
eligible for the Staff corps must be under the rank of
substantive colonel, must have been on permanent staff
employment within three years of the date of this order,
and must be considered by Government to be in all
respects fit for the Staff corps : *i. e.* the same amount of
interest that was previously required to obtain a staff
appointment was now required to get entrance into the
Staff corps. To elect for general service was out of the
question to officers of many years' standing, or those with
families, most of whom probably also had the option of
joining the British army when they first contemplated a
military career ; for such men to start afresh in a British
regiment, to learn all the innumerable details and internal
economy and working of the British service, and eventually
to take a turn of home service on English pay in their
old age, was simply impossible. So that the great body
of officers were virtually excluded from this alternative also,
and there remained for them nothing but to choose the
"locals," and take their chance ; no hardship, one might
think, with the parliamentary guarantee, and the promise
of Government, that all their rights should remain intact.
But the working of Sir C. Wood's measures, and his
subsequent policy in refusing any redress until wrung from
him by the reports of the Royal Commissioners, point
out pretty clearly what would have been the fate of the
"locals" if there had been no parliamentary guarantee in
the first instance.

These extensive changes could not be effected without
altering in some measure the position of every officer in the
Indian army, and no officer for a moment expected otherwise ; but it behoved the India Office that instituted these
changes to take special care, keeping the parliamentary
guarantee in view, that the position of any officer should
not be altered for the worse. The question was not
unattended with difficulty, but it was assuredly not in
London that a series of measures requiring so much special

knowledge and such careful handling was likely to be
efficiently decided.   Sir Charles Wood thought otherwise ;
and he and the other officials who must be held responsible
for the deplorable failure of the amalgamation and the
ruinous expense in which it has involved the country,
instead of empowering the Indian local government carefully to draw out a scheme from the materials at their
disposal, by the advice of the able and experienced
officers whom they might have summoned to their assistance, placed themselves under the guidance principally of
one officer who had risen rapidly to one of the highest
military staff appointments in India.   He was remarkable
for possessing a most wonderful memory.   He could quote
chapter and verse for every order that had issued from the
Adjutant-General's office for the last twenty years or more ;
and, as an office-man, of course was invaluable to the commander-in-chief of an army like that of British India.   But
the gift of a wonderfully retentive memory is not by any
means necessarily accompanied by the faculty of organization, and to arrange the innumerable differences that were
inseparable from an amalgamation of the Royal and the
Company's services required the power of organization in
the very highest degree.   Here the framers of the amalgamation scheme totally failed, and one result of their
first measures was that in 1863 almost every officer had a
grievance of some sort; and though but a section of these
sent in petitions, a Royal Commission was appointed under
the Presidency of Lord Cranworth, consisting of the Earl
of Ellenborough, Lord Hotham, Mr. Henley, Sir C. Yorke,
General Clarke, Sir P. Melvill, "to inquire into the complaints made in certain memorials from officers of the late
Indian armies."   The composition of this court did not
altogether please the memorialists: whilst retaining grateful
recollections of Lord Ellenborough and Mr. Henley, they
were afraid of the preponderance of the legal element.
This commission, with a mass of oral and written evidence
before them, yet exhibited in their decisions on various

points connected with the military system of India the utmost ignorance of details. The Commissioners classed the grievances under the following heads ; those negatived we shall take first in order :—

1. Retention of the names of officers who joined the Staff corps, on the cadres of their regiments.

2. Retention of names upon their old cadres of officers who joined the new line regiments from the European regiments.

3. Retardation of promotion by Staff corps officers whose names are still borne on the cadres, they being engaged in service attended with less risk.

4. Retardation of promotion by new line officers whose names are still borne on the cadres, they being employed many of them in England.

5. Arrangements for regulating future colonels' allowances in the Ordnance corps.

6. The effect produced by the late measures in preventing the purchasing out of senior regimental officers.

7. Officers in receipt of colonels' allowances, precluded from receiving Indian allowances while residing unemployed in India.

8. The G.G.O. No. 1,070, 23d July, 1859, revoking so much of the G.G.O. No. 1,238 of 1858 as related to the antedating the commissions of certain lieutenant-colonels of artillery and engineers.

The Commissioners decided that all the above eight complaints were not infringements of the parliamentary guarantee, and they dismissed them accordingly.

The three following subjects of complaint the Commissioners considered to be well founded :—

1. Supersession of locals in army rank by Staff corps officers under the promotion rules of the Staff corps.

2. Retention of names on the native cadres, of officers who joined the new line regiments from those cadres.

3. Arrangements in the Royal Warrant 1st January, 1862, for the future promotion of officers of the Indian

army of date subsequent to the 17th February, 1861, to the rank of general officer, as far as they affect officers of cavalry and infantry.

With regard to these two following they express a doubt, namely :—

1. The arrangements for regulating future colonels' allowances in cavalry and infantry. On this head the Commissioners stated : " The new rule is, however, not to affect lieutenant-colonels who attained that rank before the date of the new system, and so the question whether twelve years is a fair average for the future, for the three Presidencies, will, be tested by the time at which these lieutenant-colonels will succeed to the allowances in question. If it should be found that they attain them generally in less than twelve years, we consider that, unless the shorter average period be adopted, the guarantee will not have been strictly adhered to."

2. Reducing the number of regimental lieutenant-colonels by filling up only half the vacancies of those lieutenant-colonels who took the special annuity in 1861. On this point the Commissioners stated : " We are unable to calculate the loss or the advantages, varying as they do, which may have fallen to the lot of the different regiments; but we think that where loss can be ascertained to have taken place, there the guarantee has not been adhered to."

Before noticing Sir C. Wood's measures for the redress of the three subjects of complaint considered by the Commissioners as well founded, it would be well to ask, why the Commissioners did not give the Indian army, instead of Sir C. Wood, the benefit of the doubt on the two last questions ? Of the twelve years' period of service for colonels' allowances (first doubtful point) the Commissioners also stated : " It appears by information which we have received from the India Office that the average in Bengal is 10.2 years, in Madras 11.8, and in Bombay 10.9 ; so that twelve years is just more than a year beyond what has been the average for the three Presidencies ; but it is

very nearly two years above the average in Bengal, of
which the army constituted nearly one-half of the whole
army of India." If there is a doubt, it is as much as two to
one in favour of the Indian army. Again, on what principle did the Commission find the guarantee infringed by
retaining on the *native* cadres the names of officers transferred to the new line regiments? And why did not the
same principle hold good in the case of officers transferred
from the *European* cadres, and of Staff corps officers whose
names were still retained on their old regimental cadres?
If the guarantee was infringed in one case, it was
infringed in all three. A writer in the *Examiner*, whose
review of a later commission is particularly concise and
clear, states with regard to the retention of Staff corps
officers' names on the cadres: "Lord Cranworth's commission was not only singularly weak in its composition,
but was most unfairly prevented from receiving evidence
which Captain Jervis offered to produce through witnesses
whose names he gave. Still there was one member, an
officer of the Indian army, serving on the Commission,
who ought to have prevented his colleagues from falling
into error, as to the removal of Staff corps officers' names
from regiments necessarily occasioning an undue extent
of promotion. That officer was Major-General Sir P.
Melvill, who had long been secretary in the Military
Department at Bombay: he, having served on Lord
Hotham's commission, ought to have been fully aware
of the groundless nature of the plea thus urged for withholding from the officers that justice which they had a
right by military usage (and the parliamentary guarantee)
to expect."

Sir C. Wood, by his Despatch No. 194 of 1864, proceeded to meet and rectify the evils complained of in
the three grievances which the Commissioners thought
were infringements of the guarantee, in the following
manner. "Although," he writes, "the views of her
Majesty's Government may not be changed, they are,

nevertheless, prepared to accept the opinion of the Commissioners."

1st point: the supersession in army rank of regimental officers by the promotion of their brother officers under the Staff corps rules, he rectifies by a scheme of *brevet* promotion—giving, in fact, to all local officers brevet rank as an equivalent for the substantive or regimental rank of their brother officers in the Staff corps: after twelve years' service, to brevet captain; twenty years' service, to brevet major; twenty-six years' service, to brevet lieutenant-colonel. "Instead of striking out the names of officers who have joined the several Staff corps and new line regiments from their former cadres, Government have determined to strike out the names of all such officers upon their coming on the list of regimental lieutenant-colonels, promotion being made in their places up to the establishment laid down in a succeeding paragraph."

2d point: the retention on the cadres of native regiments of the names of officers transferred to the new line regiments. This was rectified by the removal from the cadres of native regiments, the 4th and 5th European cavalry, and the 4th, 5th, and 6th European infantry cadres, of all officers appointed from them to the new line regiments, and by making promotions in their places; the promotions to date from 18th February, 1861.

3d point: the arrangements laid down in the Royal Warrant 1st January, 1862, as far as they affect the officers of cavalry and infantry of the Indian army, for regulating the promotion of colonels of date subsequent to the 17th February, 1861, to the rank of general officer. This point the despatch rectifies thus: "No promotions have yet been made under that Warrant, and there is no difficulty in altering the arrangement; the Royal Warrant 1st January, 1862, is cancelled except clauses 9 and 10 (previously noticed) by Royal Warrant 15th June, 1864, which accompanies this despatch." This sets forth that the whole of the officers of cavalry and infantry of H.M.

Indian army shall remain on the Indian general list as before the Warrant of 1862, and shall rise in that list to the rank of general officer; the establishment of general officers of the Indian army being from time to time reduced as provided for in the Warrant. Each branch of the Ordnance corps in India is provided with a separate establishment of general officers calculated in the same proportion as that of the Royal Ordnance corps: all colonels of these corps of date prior to 18th February, 1861, will continue to rise on the general list of the Indian army: the absorption of the Indian Ordnance corps into the Royal corps is provided for. The field-officers of the Staff corps to be brought hereafter on to the general list of the British army; their promotion then, and the mode in which the whole of the officers of the several Staff corps shall be transferred to the list of the British army, is also shown; as also the manner in which the establishment of general officers of the Indian army shall be gradually reduced.

The question of the twelve years' period of service as lieutenant-colonel for the colonel's allowances, is one on which the Commission, although doubtful, expressed a very decided opinion in favour of the Indian army under certain contingencies. Sir C. Wood, taking the benefit of the doubt to himself, quietly ignored any cause of complaint on this head, and took no measures in his despatch to remedy it; stating in so many words "that by his measures officers will attain colonels' allowances in a shorter time than was ever before known," although the memorandum furnished from his own office says on this matter: "The period of twelve years was taken as a fair average, being somewhat *more* than the time recently taken to pass through the colonel's grade in *Bengal and Bombay*, but less than that in Madras. It is possible that the promotion of some of the older lieutenant-colonels, in the year 1862, in the two former Presidencies may be *slightly retarded*, but such retardation cannot be material. It is obvious, moreover, that some such retardation must have followed any

reduction, however effected, in the number of colonels."
Sir C. Wood's dictum, that an officer *may* attain his
colonel's allowance in a shorter time than heretofore, from
his first entrance into the service, cannot affect the question
of twelve years in the grade of lieutenant-colonel not being
too long, an officer's promotion up to lieutenant-colonel
being uncertain and dependent on his luck in his individual
regiment. As to Sir C. Wood's idea of average, it must be
remembered that Bengal and Bombay together represent
$\frac{7}{10}$ths of the whole Indian army.

The second point considered doubtful by the Commission
was the reduction of the number of regimental lieutenant-
colonels by filling up only half the vacancies caused by
those who retired in 1861. The Commissioners' remarks
already quoted on this grievance, and their further arguments in pars. 54, 55 of their report, show them to have
totally misunderstood the cause of complaint, which was,
not whether the Government could or could not reduce so
many regiments, but simply whether it was not contrary
to the rules of the service, and an infringement of the
guarantee, not to make promotions in the room of all
officers who retired, however such retirements might have
been brought about. Sir C. Wood orders additional promotions to be made from *the date of receipt of his despatch*
(16th July, 1864), namely, for Madras five lieutenant-
colonels, and three for Bombay; but he entirely loses
sight of the real cause of grievance, and dilates on the
prerogative of Government to make reductions—which no
one questioned—and attempts to justify his plan of reduction by only filling up half the vacancies; ending this
memorable despatch by asserting, "With these measures
the arrangements as regards the officers of the Indian
armies will be closed;"—rather a rash assertion for a man
who might at any moment by a change of Ministry have
given place to a more liberal successor.

Captain Jervis' motion for a commission to inquire into
the grievances of the officers of the Indian army was

carried on the 2d May, 1865, by a majority of the House
of Commons, in spite of the opposition and vote of Sir C.
Wood; and in June 1865 a Royal Commission, consisting
of Sir T. Aitchison, Sir R. Napier, Sir Sydney Cotton,
General Eyre, General C. A. Brown, General Russel, and
Sir W. Coghlan, was ordered to assemble to inquire and
report "whether the measures adopted to remove the
grievances which Lord Cranworth's commission had reported
well founded, had been effectual and sufficient."

The Commissioners arranged the points for their consideration in the following order :—

First, the retention on the cadres of native regiments of
the names of officers transferred to the new line regiments.
They reported that the measure adopted upon this point
had been effectual and sufficient.

Second, arrangements for promotion to general officer.
The warrant of 1862 had been modified, and a revised
warrant substituted : this measure reported effectual and
sufficient.

Third, the filling up of only half the vacancies of the
lieutenant-colonels who retired in 1861. Upon this point
the Commissioners were of opinion that if certain promotions to lieutenant-colonel were made *from 1st January*,
1862, to complete the reduced establishment, no loss will
have been sustained either by regiments or by officers, and
no grievance will remain under this head.

Fourth, the rule fixing twelve years' service as
lieutenant-colonel for colonel's allowances. The Commissioners reported that, "in regard to lieutenant-colonels of
rank prior to 1st January, 1862, the term of twelve years
was two years in excess of a fair period; as regards lieutenant-colonels promoted after 1st January, 1862, the
twelve years' rule may not be in excess : but we may here
observe, that the periods of service of officers in the grades
of major and captain are in numerous instances much
longer than is generally supposed, so that with all the
advantage of accelerated promotion, they will for the

greater part reach to forty or more years' service before promotion to regimental colonel. There are, for example, many officers, now regimental captains, who have already completed more than twenty-five years' service. We therefore submit that it might be for the advantage of the public service to provide a means of relieving the Indian army from old and worn-out officers ; such a means might perhaps be afforded by an extension of the existing Indian regulations (of 1837), under which graduated pensions are granted for length of service, irrespective of rank."

Fifth, the supersession of regimental officers by officers of the Staff corps. The Commissioners on this point reported that the brevet adopted in Sir C. Wood's despatch to remedy the above grievance "not only failed fully to do so, but created a new and continually increasing class of grievances, thus aggravating instead of removing the original cause of complaint. We have given our most earnest and anxious consideration to this very difficult and complicated question, and we consider that we should not fulfil the duty imposed on us if we fail to submit our opinion that the measure adopted by your Majesty's Government upon this point has not been effectual and sufficient to remove the grievance originally complained of : the main ground of that grievance we consider to be—the regimental connexion between the local line and the Staff corps, by the retention of the names of Staff corps officers on the cadres of regiments, and also by the retention on the old European regimental cadres of the names of those officers who have been transferred to the new line regiments. The measure adopted by your Majesty's Government therefore falls short of what is required, inasmuch as it has not removed the cause of grievance, whilst the grievance itself has been aggravated by the disturbing effect of the brevet. The removal of Staff corps officers from regimental cadres might not prevent supersession either of the local line officers by those of the Staff corps, or of

Staff corps officers by those of the local line ; but belonging, as they would then do, to entirely distinct cadres, each body having its own distinct terms of service, such individual supersession would constitute no invasion of principle." And the Commissioners concluded their report by saying, " It appears to us perfectly practicable to remove all just ground for complaint of the infraction of any real and established right in connexion with the particular points referred to us for report."[1]

With this strong recommendation as to the best method of removing all cause of complaint under this head, the India Office, it would be imagined, would have readily complied, and removed Staff corps officers from the cadres ; but such a plan would have been directly opposed to the principles of those who originally devised the great amalgamation muddle, and in February 1866, when this recommendation of the Commission found its way to Calcutta, it was at once affirmed in military circles that it would never be carried out.

On the accession of Lord Derby's government in 1864, Lord Cranborne became Secretary of State for India. A new man, and not bound in any way to recognise the faulty one-sided views of the India Office as carried out by Sir C. Wood, it was expected that he would have been guided by the recommendations of the Commission of experienced officers then before him. But Lord Cranborne, in his despatch No. 159 of August 1866, showed very clearly that he was not able to escape the pitfall into which his predecessor had been precipitated. Fifteen paragraphs of this despatch are devoted to a review of the report of Lord Cranworth's commission, and the measures adopted by Sir Charles Wood thereon. Lord Cranborne enters into an elaborate commendation of the views taken by that Commission, although those views and the measures adopted by Sir C. Wood had been judged, and to a great extent found wanting, by a later Royal Commission ordered to assemble

[1] Report, dated 14th Sept. 1865.

for the express purpose of passing sentence on the Cranworth commission ; yet Lord Cranborne, ignoring the
object with which Sir T. Aitchison's commission had been
ordered to assemble, says, " He has determined to adopt, as
far as practicable, those recommendations of Sir T. Aitchison's commission which *are not inconsistent with the opinions
expressed by the former commission."*

The third, fourth, and fifth points which Sir T. Aitchison's commission considered remained still to be remedied,
were disposed of by Lord Cranborne in the following
manner :—

Third point: the filling up of only half the vacancies
occasioned by the retirement of lieutenant-colonels in
1861, which the Commission thought would be remedied by
making some few promotions, *dating them from 1st Jan.*
1862.—Lord Cranborne orders that "without delay, the
promotions in Madras and Bombay, made under paragraphs
52 and 80 of Sir C. Wood's despatch, No. 194 of 1864, and
those in succession to them, should have retrospective
effect from the 1st January, 1862." Lord Cranborne is
quick enough—*vide* his despatch, paragraphs 20 to 23—in
retorting on the Commission for its oversight in recommend-
ing the promotion of two lieutenant-colonels short of the
number who had already been promoted by Sir C. Wood's
despatch—an unaccountable oversight certainly ; but why
lay so much stress on a simple oversight, which even the
India Office could not take advantage of, when the real
question was the antedating these promotions some two
and a half years ? Was it that the persistent opposition of
Sir C. Wood to the interests of the Indian army had
descended, together with his office, on Lord Cranborne ?
The tenor of this despatch looked very much like it.

Fourth point: the rule fixing twelve years' service as
lieutenant-colonel for colonel's allowances. Lord Cranborne adopted the views of the Commission, and ordered
that " all officers of cavalry and infantry of the Indian
army who attained the rank of lieutenant-colonel (regi-

mental) prior to 1st January, 1862, and all officers of the several Staff corps who had attained the rank of regimental lieutenant-colonel prior to the formation of those corps (18th February, 1861), shall hereafter, upon the completion of ten years in that grade, be placed in receipt of the colonel's allowances, in the event of their not having already attained to that allowance in ordinary succession under the operation of the system laid down in Sir C. Wood's despatch, No. 340, dated 10th August, 1861, paragraph 18. Under this point also the military retiring regulations of 1837 will be extended by the addition of the two following rates of pension : after thirty-five years' service, 600*l*. per annum ; after thirty-eight years' service, 750*l*. per annum. All officers now in the several Staff corps, and all who may join them under the terms of this despatch, will be entitled to the colonel's allowances after twelve years' service in the grade of substantive lieutenant-colonel, without reference to any fixed establishment of colonels with colonels' allowances ; the brevet rank of lieutenant-colonel attained to under the regulations published in general order by your Government, No. 632 of 4th August, 1864, being however considered a substantive rank for this purpose, and being allowed to count towards the above period."

Lord Cranborne says : " It will be seen that the Commission appointed by her Majesty, on this occasion have not confined themselves strictly to the questions submitted for their consideration. They have suggested in one instance a measure—viz. the introduction of additional rates of retiring pension—which has no reference to the complaints brought under the consideration of Lord Cranworth's commission." This is rather hard on the Commission, who in good faith, and for the advantage of the public service, made this suggestion to Government as a means, perhaps, of getting rid of old and worn-out officers. Lord Cranborne, however, jumps at the suggestion ; it would be regarded as an additional boon by the public in

England; but how many officers have availed themselves of it up to the present time?

Fifth point: the supersession of regimental officers by officers in the Staff corps. On this last point Lord Cranborne says: "The Commission have recorded their opinion against an important feature in the scheme for the re-organization of the Indian army, which the former Commission had pronounced to be no breach of the parliamentary guarantee, and which therefore did not come within the scope of their inquiry. I allude to the retention of the names of officers of the Staff corps on the cadres of their former regiments." It is only necessary to refer to the report of the Commission [1] on this point, and their opinion that Sir C. Wood's general "brevet" increased instead of remedying the grievance, which was of course caused by retaining Staff corps officers on cadres of regiments to which they no longer belonged. [Sir C. Wood said emphatically to Staff corps officers that the Staff corps was their only regiment.] These were not two separate grievances, but cause and effect; the cause was retaining the names on the local cadres, the effect was supersession of the local officers thereby. It was undoubtedly within the scope of inquiry of Sir T. Aitchison's commission to ascertain the direct *cause* of any grievance which the former Commission had allowed to be a breach of the guarantee. If Lord Cranworth's commission purposely or ignorantly ranged *the cause* into a separate grievance, and so disposed of it in the interest of the India Office, it was all the more incumbent on Sir T. Aitchison's commission to repair the error or expose the trick, and they did so, suggesting the only remedy; but Lord Cranborne, preferring a course of his own, the result of which will be shown hereafter, directs that "From and after the receipt of this despatch, the qualifying period of service in the Staff corps, laid down in second paragraph of the Royal Warrant, 16th January, 1861, will be dispensed with, so far as concerns officers now in

[1] *Vide* infra.

the Staff corps and those of the Indian army who may join any one of those corps under the terms of this despatch. Officers of the Staff corps who may be entitled to promotion to a higher substantive rank under the modification of the existing rule, will receive such promotion from the date of receipt of this despatch. All officers of the cavalry and infantry of .the Indian army, with the exception of those who entered upon the new conditions of service and are borne upon a general list, will be allowed to enter the Staff corps of their respective Presidencies upon the conditions above laid down, from the date of receipt of this despatch, without being subjected to previous examination."

This despatch appeared to be a throwing open of the Staff corps under the terms of its first constitution to all officers of the Indian army who were qualified. No class would be more likely to jump at the redress thus held within their reach than the officers of the twelve new line regiments and artillery, who had been transferred under a system called voluntary, but which was in reality not so, to the Royal service. They were, however, informed that they came under the somewhat ambiguous reservation "of those who had entered upon the new conditions of service," and being no longer officers of the Indian army, were not entitled to the benefit of measures designed to remedy the prospects of that body.

Lord Cranborne's despatch No. 160, 8th August, 1866, called "the Bonus despatch," needs little comment.

The East India Company permitted officers to buy out their regimental seniors, and rather encouraged this mode of getting rid of old officers, and it was very good policy on their part : the measures adopted since 1860 broke up regimental promotion, and the system of buying-out majors and senior captains went with it. The usual bonus for a major's step was 3,000l., for senior captain 1,800l. to 2,500l. from the officers below them, each paying his quota : the money value of the step decreased by every

step the major got towards his lieutenant-colonelcy. The
loss of the opportunity, through the measures of the
India Office, of getting from 1,800*l.* to 3,000*l.* on retirement, was not considered by Lord Cranworth's commission
a legal cause of complaint; all they could say was, "that
the Crown would observe the same passive state which
had existed on the part of the Company, in the matter:"
but what analogy can there be between the Crown or
India Office, which broke up the whole system, and the
late Honourable Company who fostered it ? Will the pas-
siveness of the Crown give officers the bonus on retirement which they had always calculated upon receiving, and
which a great number of officers had borrowed largely to
ensure? However rapid, according to the India Office,
an officer's promotion may have become in consequence
of the new order of things, and his prospects in every
way brightened, this fact remains, and no amount of
arguments from Sir C. Wood, or any other India Office
official, can gainsay it, that the comfortable little sum
of 3,000*l.* is lost to every Indian major and his heirs for
ever.

Lord Cranborne's intentions, as displayed in the preamble of this despatch, are much to be commended;
but the amount of restrictions in the details imposed by
the India Office render the whole despatch little better
than a dead letter.

The result of the before-noticed measures, both to
Government and to the Indian army, obtrudes itself in
certain hard facts which may be gleaned from the Indian
army list. Taking the Bengal army list, corrected to 1st
October, 1868, it will be found that the Staff corps of
that Presidency consisted on that date of the following
officers :—Lieutenant-colonels 226, majors 263, captains 331,
lieutenants 229; total, 1,049 officers. Calculating the promotion of these officers by the rules laid down, the
following tabular statement will show the result five
years hence, and on the 1st October of each year.

Rank.	No. 1869.	No. 1870.	No. 1871.	No. 1872.	No. 1873.
Lieutenant-Colonels. .	273	313	375	416	451
Majors	258	258	237	230	219
Captains	357	376	385	370	367
Lieutenants	161	102	52	33	12
Totals.	1049	1049	1049	1049	1049

There are at present (Oct. 1868) 73 probationers to be added ; but as these have accrued since 1866, it gives a yearly average of only twenty-four admissions to the Staff corps : this, it will be seen, does not keep pace with the promotions, and as there are no retirements, only time is required to render the corps like some huge tadpole—all head and very little tail—a regiment of field-officers.

The amount which will have to be paid for colonels' allowances will in a few years be so large that the Indian tax-payers, if they had any voice in the matter, might be only too glad to make some present composition with their future creditors. To ascertain the amount of colonels' allowances for any one year, take the number of lieutenant-colonels in any column of the tabular statement ; to these add 7 local cavalry and 59 local infantry lieutenant-colonels, and multiply that amount by 1000, the product will give the amount of colonels' allowances in pounds sterling ; to the year at the top of the column add 12, which will show the year from which that amount will be payable. Take the year 1872+12=1884 ; in that year the sum will amount for Bengal alone to—

Lieutenant-Colonels 416
Local Infantry Lieut.-Colonels . . 59
Local Cavalry Lieut.-Colonels . . 7
_____
Total Lieut.-Colonels . 482
1,000£.
_____
Total per Annum . £482,000

No casualties except those by death are likely to occur, for no inducement to retire is held out by Government: the loss of the 3,000*l.* on retirement as major is producing its speedy result ; so also, in a measure, is the disallowing the rule of 1796, by which officers could retire on the pension of their rank. No allowance has been made for casualties by death in the tabular statement ; let any one do so, taking off ten, twenty, or even fifty per cent. according to his calculation,—even then there remains an enormous yearly expenditure on this head : to which must be added that for Madras and Bombay, and the officers of the present pension and retired lists who may be living fifteen years hence. Several schemes for pensioning off the older officers have been proposed, but the Secretary of State has stated in the House that he does not intend to take any steps in that direction.

Another mistake, which may be classed under this head, is beginning to tell seriously against the Government. It arose out of Lord Cranborne's hasty endeavour to patch up and amend the admission to the Staff corps, by allowing all cavalry and infantry officers on the cadres of regiments in 1866 to enter the Staff corps, instead of taking the advice of such experienced officers as those on Sir T. Aitchison's commission, and removing the Staff corps officers from the cadres ; but this latter mode would have been contrary to the views of Sir C. Wood and the advisers by whom he was led.

This, however, is the result. Although most of the locals availed themselves of Lord Cranborne's order, still a number did not. The Bengal army list for October 1868 shows there are still : Local majors — cavalry, 6 ; infantry, 3. Local captains—cavalry, 38 ; infantry, 51. Local lieutenants—cavalry, 3 ; infantry, 31. Total, 132.

On the infantry regimental majors' list of 80 majors, all but three are Staff corps officers, who by the rules are struck off on promotion to lieutenant-colonel and promotions made in their places, so that three casualties among the general officers or local lieutenant-colonels will give eighty line steps to the cadres. One local has already become a substantive lieutenant-colonel, after seventeen years' total service, so that by the twelve years' rule he will be entitled to colonel's allowances in twenty-nine instead of thirty-eight years' total service. Major Chalmers will be entitled to his after only twenty-eight years' service, and there are several captains of ten, eleven, and twelve years' service who must almost immediately become majors, and a month or two afterwards lieutenant-colonels. No one can seriously suppose that Government contemplated paying colonels' allowances to a host of young men ; such, however, is one of the results of Lord Cranborne's despatch : Madras and Bombay will also contribute their quotas to this phalanx of youthful veterans. By a system of double shuffling, resulting from the measures of the trio before-mentioned, and Lord Cranborne's amendments, the "locals" have now left the Staff corps behind in substantive promotion.

Letting all officers enter the Staff corps in 1866, besides being a mistake, was a slight on those officers who had taken the trouble of qualifying themselves for the Staff corps by passing in the languages. Those who had not passed had no claim whatever to seek admission ; they could not hold appointments and draw the pay, however great their interest might be ; and while the option of another election was given to all local officers, the same option of re-election ought to have been extended to those officers of the Staff corps who wished to withdraw from it.

"Doing general duty" is an order which, like the "Exalted Star of India," has sprung from the exigencies of the times ; it is the last—though not the least— blunder which need be mentioned as having sprung from the incongruous measures hatched under the name of the Amalgamation. In considering the enormous prospective liability of the Indian tax-payers in the matter of colonels' allowances, it was said that, if they had any voice in the matter, their common sense might suggest a present composition with those future creditors. Another glance at last October's Army List (Bengal) will show that, in thus taking thought for the morrow, the tax-payers would be receiving a double return for their present outlay. Let the Army List speak for itself. On the 1st October, 1868, the following officers in the Bengal Presidency were in excess of the requirements of the service, unemployed, "doing general duty," in fact :—

	No.	Per Month.			Total.		
		Rs.	a.	p.	Rs.	a.	p.
Staff Corps Lieut.-Colonels .	27	827	14	0	22,352	10	0
,, Majors . . .	24	640	14	0	15,381	0	0
Local Lieut.-Colonels . .	21	1,032	4	0	21,677	4	0
Cavalry Lieut.-Colonels . .	3	1,157	0	0	3,471	0	0
,, Majors	4	929	6	4	3,717	9	4
,, Brevet Majors .	1	563	0	4	563	0	4
Infantry Brevet Majors . .	3	415	6	0	1,246	2	0
Total Officers . .	83	Total Monthly			68,408	9	8

Or, in English money, 6,840*l.* 17*s.* 2½*d.* a month : multiply by 12, and the product will show the very comfortable yearly expenditure of 82,090*l.* 6*s.* 6*d.* Madras and Bombay have also their number of unemployed field-officers to swell the amount of this heavy liability, which, moreover, increases monthly. So much for this last result of ill-advised measures, taken in a monetary aspect. The cruel injustice of keeping a large number of old officers "doing general duty" in a climate like India, in which the first *sine quâ non* for preserving health and life is action and employment, is not likely to touch the hearts of those who decline taking any measures to further retirement, although such a course would be the annual saving of a large and ever-increasing sum to the State. The number of field-officers is greatly in excess of the requirements of the service. Although 111 field-officers of that corps

from Bengal alone were, on October 1, 1868, on leave
in Europe, there was still the number mentioned on the
last page unemployed ; and every promotion increases
a state of things which even Sir C. Wood wished particularly to guard against.   In his Despatch No. 318 of
1861, he says, " So that the revenues of India may not be
charged for more unemployed officers than is inevitable
under the circumstances of the time." And on the 30th
April, 1863, he says again, " His Royal Highness concurs
in the opinion I have expressed as to the inexpediency of
multiplying the number of unemployed field-officers of the
Staff corps." Has even the echo of such sentiments died
away in the India Office, that nothing is done to remedy an
error which is a sore burden on the resources of India, and
a sorry way of treating a large number of old officers ; the
only excuse being, that the measures adopted for the
amalgamation of the services have thrown them out of
employment ?

It must be apparent, one would think, to every one by
this time, even to those who originally devised the amalgamation scheme, that it has proved a total failure.   And the
result is, that the country is burdened with a huge Frank-
ensteinian monster, in the shape of an army of highly-paid
field-officers for whom no employment can be found.   The
evil, it is true, is not one which will be perpetuated for
ever.   The Local Service will die out in time, and the
excess of expenditure for the Staff corps will, as calculated
by General Hannyngton, culminate in 1896, from which
year a rapid diminution in the number of colonels will
continue till the corps falls into its normal state.

Several propositions for increased pension and bonus, as
an inducement to officers to retire, have recently been laid
before Government, but they have each been rejected for
reasons stated in some detail in a despatch from the Duke
of Argyll, dated March 11, 1869, which, although it deals
with this question from a point of view adopted at a
period subsequent to that which is embraced in these

pages, yet treats of so many points of interest in connexion with the Indian army, that I have thought it best to insert it in the Appendix.

Hitherto I have dwelt, briefly indeed but exclusively, on the mode in which the amalgamation has affected the commissioned ranks of the army. The summary of results would not be complete without a few words upon the state to which the army itself has been reduced by this wretched disregard of the law of cause and effect.

Under the old system that prevailed before the Mutiny, when the Bengal native army was shown to be—what Sir Charles Napier declared it—more dangerous to its friends than its foes, the Bombay and Madras native armies had much to recommend them. Under the present system, all that was good in the systems of Bombay and Madras has been carefully eliminated; and every faulty, vicious principle which the Mutiny brought out in bold relief, has been carefully engrafted on them. The cry before the Mutiny was, that there were too few European officers with native regiments; now the number has been considerably reduced by the introduction of what is called the irregular system—a system, more properly speaking, of selection, which of course loses its essential characteristic directly it is made general, and selection is no longer feasible. The complaint was that, before the Mutiny, officers did not take that interest in their men, or their regiments, that an efficient discharge of duty required. Under the new system, by which officers are perpetually being changed about from one corps to another, it is next to impossible for them to take any interest, almost impossible for them even to know their men. One beneficial reform was introduced, and that was, that much larger powers were entrusted to commanding officers than under the old *régime.* These, however, have been taken away from them by the new Articles of War recently passed. The men are discontented, the officers are dissatisfied; there are no common interests to link them together, there is no *esprit de corps*, no bond of union. The condition in which so many officers are forced to pass their time, month after month, year after year—vegetating at small stations, or living at larger ones at the club, where the only call to duty that ever varies the monotony of their indolent existence is a court-martial perhaps once a month, or a tour of duty as field-officer of the week every ten days—has been attended with its inevitable results, the habit of confirmed idleness. The amalgamation has been not only the professional but the moral ruin of hundreds, who, with their experience of India, might have been made valuable servants of the State. The native infantry regiments are in many cases inefficiently drilled, while the whole continent of India swarms with a semi-drilled, semi-armed police, enlisted from the worst and most turbulent classes, isolated in localities where no supervision can be exercised over them except by their native superiors, and where, should a second rebellion be planned, they have every facility for extending, unchecked, the network of a deadly conspiracy over the whole surface of the country.

Another effect of the amalgamation was to do away with a local European force. The consequence of that is, that the country is put to an enormous expense by incessant reliefs. The men of old local European regiments were inured[1] to the climate, accustomed to the country, and maintained among themselves a sort of traditional system, which every new comer speedily caught up, and in a wonderfully short space of time adapted himself to the exigencies of the climate and the altered circumstances of his condition. A new regiment takes nearly five years, or half its term of service, to learn all these things, and the experience is frequently only pur-

---

[1] I use the expression, "inured to the climate," not as indicating "acclimatization," for there is in reality no such thing, but as signifying a certain hardihood of constitution which old soldiers enjoy, simply from having learnt not to defy, but to guard against, the effects of the climate.

chased at the price we are accustomed to pay for that precious article. In the royal regiments generally, Indian service is so distasteful as almost to counteract the efforts of the recruiting sergeant; and after the first two years scarcely an officer is left with the new corps who has the means to exchange and maintain himself at home; while the officers of the twelve new line regiments, now that their time of home service has actually commenced, are dismayed at the prospect of having to support themselves and their families on English pay. The system of promotion is so cumbrous that a Staff corps officer who has brevet rank has to receive and pay for three commissions for each grade he attains; while the promotions necessarily ensuing upon two vacancies, moving as they do through the whole army, fill five columns of a newspaper the size of the *Times*, in the smallest print; and as these promotions have to be gazetted after confirmation in England, ten large newspaper columns will be occupied by the results of two army steps, while the system of promotion is so extremely complicated that it is doubtful if there is any one who thoroughly understands it.

It remains to add a few words with regard to the Indian medical service, the amalgamation of which with the Royal medical service was, after much consideration and delay, wisely abandoned. The present status of the Indian medical service will be perhaps better understood after a brief reference to its condition under the Honourable East India Company. At that time the service was divided into assistant-surgeons, surgeons, and senior surgeons, with an administrative staff consisting of a liberal number of divisional superintending surgeons, and a controlling board composed of three members. All the administrative appointments had special salaries attached to them, and these were without exception in excess of the pay of their corresponding army rank, and also of the emoluments granted to corresponding grades of the medical service under the *present organization.* Under the Company it was, moreover, the rule to bestow upon all military officers, medical being included in the term, an addition to their pay, under the name of "staff allowance," varying in amount with the responsibilities, or presumed responsibilities, of their charge. In addition to this, those in military employ drew "head money," and also in certain cases "palkee allowance." When military medical officers were made over for duty in the civil department, in addition to the consolidated salary of the appointment, the civil medical officer could always count upon an increase of income from various other sources. Such offices as superintendent of dispensaries, or asylums, registrarships of deeds, and postmasterships, were almost invariably conferred upon the civil surgeon, each carrying with it an augmentation to the monthly salary. At that time also, few medical men, other than those in Government employ, were to be found in India, and hence as a necessary consequence emoluments from private practice were greater than they are now, which in most localities may be represented by a cypher. As regards furlough pay and privileges the army medical staff were placed on exactly the same footing as military officers of corresponding rank![1] The pensions also were essentially computed with reference to army rank.[2] Although the relative rank assigned was admittedly too low, yet, such as it was, it carried with it all privileges of the grade. All these causes combined to render the Indian medical service, and especially the civil branch, exceedingly popular and attractive. Each assistant-surgeoncy was in the gift of a director of the Honourable East India Company. No director was ever without candidates on his list. Such an occurrence, so often known more recently, of an assistant-surgeoncy "going begging,' never happened. Neither can it be stated that the social or professional status of the older men was inferior to

---

[1] Vide old Furlough Rules, par. 32, et seq.
[2] G.O.G.G. No. 122, 14th April, 1844.

that enjoyed by officers who have more recently entered the service under the so-called competition system.

In November 1858 the government of British India was transferred to the Crown, and about this period a Royal Medical Warrant appeared for the Queen's service, in which an official acknowledgment was made that the relative rank assigned to army medical officers was insufficient.[1] Accordingly, the warrant increased the relative rank, with pay and pension, of Queen's officers : but those of the Indian service were not benefited in any way. Two years after, in March 1860,[2] another Royal Medical Warrant was issued for India, being almost a counterpart of the one for the British service of 1858, *excepting as regards pay and pension.* Although the increase of relative rank was given, neither of the vitally important points above mentioned was touched upon ; and the Indian service therefore presented the anomaly of officers ranking relatively as major and lieutenant-colonel, &c., and being expected to subscribe to funds as such, though receiving the pay of the lower grades. In other respects also there was an invidious distinction between the Indian and the British service. In the latter an assistant-surgeon might for distinguished service be promoted *substantively*, in the former by *brevet* only.[3] According to the Queen's British Warrant the rank of surgeon-major[4] (corresponding with that of lieutenant-colonel) was attained after twenty years in the service, all recognised leave included ; while by the Queen's Indian Warrant twenty years' actual service in India were required to attain such rank.

On the 20th June, 1864,[5] a despatch appeared, signed by the Secretary of State, which professed to supply for the Indian service the deficiencies of the Warrant of 1860.

[1] Warrant dated 1st October, 1868. Paragraph referred to, No. 16.
[2] G.O.G.G. No. 353, *Calcutta Gazette*. 30th March, 1860.
[3] *Vide* par. 6 of each Warrant.
[4] *Vide* par. 8 of each Warrant.
[5] *Government Gazette*, 20th June, 1864.

It authorized a readjustment of the numbers of assistant-surgeons and surgeons, and thus to some extent rectified the slowness of promotion which had kept officers for seventeen years in the junior grade. It permitted recognised leave to count as time for the rank of surgeon-major, and it granted to Indian medical officers the Home rates of the pay of their rank, as laid down in the British Medical Warrant of 1858. It also sanctioned a full and half batta scale of pay for India, but *abolished staff and extra allowances*, with one solitary exception, viz. in the case of assistant-surgeons in actual charge of British regiments or brigades of artillery. As, however, neither of these ever were assistant-surgeons' charges, and as the charge of British troops was soon after taken from Indian medical officers, it is difficult to understand the motive inducing the insertion of this clause in the Warrant. And an after order,[1] nullifying paragraph 15 of the despatch, was subsequently published, by which the scale of invaliding pensions granted in 1858 to British medical officers compelled to leave the service from ill-health or wounds, was denied to officers of the Indian service.

But the despatch of 1864 professed only to deal with military charges, and left all civil appointments and non-regimental charges as before. In some cases, owing to the recent increase, the pay of rank was found to be greater than the emoluments of the civil appointment. Under these circumstances many medical officers applied to be permitted to draw the pay of their rank, the pay they were entitled to on leave, but an after order[2] in the Financial department stated, that in the event of any medical officer wishing to draw the military pay of his rank, he must first obtain a certificate from the local government stating that his services could not be dispensed with. If he could not

---

[1] No. 292, dated 23d September, 1864, Secretary of State to Right Hon. the Governor-General.
[2] G.O.G.G. No. 252, 1865.

obtain this certificate, he was still kept at his duty and denied the pay ordered by the Secretary of State.

A document compiled by the Financial department proves that the relative pay and allowances drawn by medical officers in various situations under the old rules, were in very many instances more than those ordered by the Secretary of State's despatch of 16th May, 1864. Members being also obliged to subscribe to the service funds at the rate of the higher relative rank, the actual receipts were still further practically curtailed.

On the 14th December, 1864, a second despatch was received, which in some measure rectified the omissions of the previous one. It granted to assistant-surgeons promotion after a definite period of service. It bestowed additional pensions on inspectors and deputy-inspectors-general, and it slightly increased the rate of retiring pensions for the whole service. It also entirely separated the Indian from the British service, reducing the administrative staff of the former, and increasing that of the latter; consequent on which the charge of European troops ceased to be a duty of Indian medical officers.

Upwards of two years now elapsed, during which period the majority of the members of the Indian medical service were confined to pay of rank irrespective of the appointment held. On the 4th of April, 1867,[2] a third despatch was published, laying down a revised scale of salary for civil appointments. In this the principle of staff allowance is acknowledged. While some few positions, as that of Secretary to the Inspector-General and Principal of the Presidency medical colleges, have fair staff salaries attached, other appointments afford but little increase to the pay of rank, and a third class actually entail reduction. As pointed out at the time,[3] district and

---

[1] *Vide* "A Sketch of the Past and Present Condition of the Bengal Medical Service," p. 18.

[2] No. 370 of 1867.

[3] *Indian Medical Gazette*, June 1, 1867.

Presidency surgeons, the chemical examiner to Government, N. W. P. garrison surgeons, &c. receive, if of fifteen years' standing, only Rs. 24. 4. 7 more, and if surgeon-majors, Rs. 6. 9. 7 to Rs. 43. 2 less, than they are entitled to when unemployed.   The same absurdity is even more striking in the case of second class civil surgeons, comprising nine-tenths of the whole.   A surgeon of ten years' service receives Rs. 49. 3, and one of fifteen years' service Rs. 75. 11. 5, *less* for one of these charges than he would if on leave.   All extra or staff allowances attaching to civil surgeoncies were merged in the consolidated pay laid down in the despatch, excepting for the administrative super-intendency of colleges, jails, and asylums, &c., for which an additional allowance is sanctioned, varying from Rs. 25 to Rs. 150.   The value, therefore, of those civil surgeoncies to which such extra posts attach, is on the average about equal to the charge of a regiment; those without such extra posts less remunerative.   Although the prospects of the Indian medical service have during recent years (particularly as regards the pay of the junior ranks) been certainly improved, there still appears to be just grounds for at least a portion of the dissatisfaction which exists.   Many are disposed to consider the reductions in the administrative ranks, consequent on the transfer of all charge of British troops to the Queen's service, as a breach of faith.   This, however, cannot be admitted.   Rightly or wrongly, it was decided that the Indian medical officer is not " the style of officer contemplated " by the existing organization of the medical department of the British army,[1] and the reduction of the administrative branch followed as a natural and inevitable consequence of much work being given over to a larger body of executive and administrative Queen's officers.   Even Mr. Henley's clause in the Act of Parliament transferring India to the Crown, guaranteeing the rights and privileges of Indian

---

[1] *Vide* pars. 1, 2, 3, of Secretary of State's Despatch, 7th November, 1864.

officers, cannot be fairly twisted into a promise that injury to the prospects of Indian officers should not occur from reduction of establishment. But Mr. Henley's clause most certainly guaranteed to Indian officers of every class that all legal rights and privileges should be observed intact. Of these rights, staff allowance was one. That has been withdrawn from the Indian medical service as a body, though continued to every other class. It has already been demonstrated that the rank and pay of Indian officers was fixed by the Queen's Warrant of 1861, and by the Secretary of State's despatch dated June 1864. Yet the issue of the pay consequent on the increase, or rather the admission, of relative rank, was made the opportunity of the reduction, or rather withdrawal, of staff allowances.

There are two principal causes of complaint of the old Indian medical services : 1. The withdrawal of staff allowances; 2. The non-issue of pay of rank. Whatever may be advanced in defence of the former, the latter is an extraordinary and absurd anomaly. One order lays down the pay of rank to which all are entitled even on leave, another order lays down the pay of nine-tenths of the civil appointments at less than the pay of rank ; so that many medical officers now draw less for doing their duty than they do on leave.

As regards the new Indian medical service, there are grievances peculiar to the class. The regulations under which assistant-surgeons enter, supplied to them by the India Office at home, state without reservation that there are two scales of pay, one of which will be received when the officer is employed and the other when unemployed. This is clear and distinct, and printed in as plain language as pure Anglo-Saxon admits. But when the medical officer arrives in India he finds his pay is not as stated above. First, he is not permitted to draw "employed pay" until he has passed an examination in the languages. Secondly, he is subject to deductions of pay when "acting" in any appointment.

It is not of course intended to underrate the advantages to the medical officer of acquaintance with the vernacular, but it is a decided injustice that a young assistant-surgeon should be told in England that he will receive so many rupees a month in India, and find out when he gets there that he only draws half the amount.

As regards the junior ranks of the Royal medical service, it must be admitted that they are shabbily treated. They get no staff pay for the duties they perform. Their allowance ought to be assimilated to the corresponding grade of the Indian service. But even the British army assistant-surgeons are better off than many Indian surgeons. They at all events receive the pay of their rank, which, as already shown, many Indian surgeons are not permitted to draw.

It must be recollected that medical men enter on public duties after having learned their profession at the cost of much money and time, while other classes acquire their experience after entering the public service ; and the conclusion is unavoidable, that, in comparison with other skilled labour, the medical art is undervalued in the Indian market.

CHAPTER XXIII.

HYGIENE AND SANITATION.

Progress of sanitation — Publications — Camps — Cantonments — Sanitary commission—Conservancy—European colonization of India—Cholera—Cinchona—The Delhi sore—Sanitary arrangements for emigrants—Indian Jails—Leprosy—Malarious fever— Medical schools—The medical service—Meteorology—The rainfall on mountainous ranges—Rural sanitation—Space in barracks, &c. —Salt—Sanitaria—Scurvy—Snake-bites—Condition of European soldiers—Wives and children—Transport service—Vaccination— Vegetables—Venereal disease—Water.

SYSTEMATIC sanitation in India can scarcely be said to have commenced with the decade now closed. It was not, indeed, until after the publication of the voluminous blue books in 1863 of the Royal Commission appointed under the presidency of Lord Herbert, to inquire into the sanitary condition of the Anglo-Indian army, that the urgent necessity of considerable pecuniary outlay on sanitation was admitted. But since that period, whatever may have been former shortcomings, want of attention to sanitary matters can neither be urged against the local government, nor imputed to the Secretary of State. Sir Stafford Northcote himself, in one of his last budget speeches, while admitting that much remains to be done, stated : " We have now established a sanitary department in our office, and are in communication" (on sanitary subjects) " with the Government of India." The share taken by the latter in the good work will, though perhaps imperfectly, be shown in the following pages. Subordinate officials are still to be found, who, unacquainted with the subject, in the pride of youth, health, ignorance, and little brief authority, or with the obstinacy of senility, regard sanitation with contemptuous indifference, and who, as a consequence, do not act according to the spirit of the orders of Government ; but, as a general rule, the reverse is now the case. And although we cannot yet congratulate ourselves on the perfection of a system of State medicine and hygiene, there is sufficient evidence to warrant the conclusion that, making allowance for unalterable differences of climate, what has been effected in other countries will be the eventual result in India. It can never be forgotten, that one hundred years ago the diseases of tropical climates, scurvy, dysentery, and malarious fevers, prevailed in London and throughout England generally, pretty much as they do now in the principal Indian cities. About that period, and during previous years, jail fever occurred epidemically in most of the prisons of Great Britain, often spreading to judge, jury, and witnesses assembled together, or to the inhabitants of the country towns. From maladies similar to those above mentioned, barracks were little better than pest-houses, while ships of the Royal Navy were floating homes of pestilence and disease. All this, however, is now altered. Sanitation has nearly banished scurvy, malarious fevers, dysentery, and allied disease throughout the length and breadth of the United Kingdom. Jail fever is unknown in English jails. The mortality among soldiers in England scarcely exceeds that of classes of the same age among the general public. And the career of a sailor in her Majesty's vessels of war, apart from the accidents and perils of a seafaring life, presents as good a chance of longevity as the great majority of laborious occupations. As an example of both the neglect and application of sanitary measures, we have only to refer to the condition of the Crimean army before and after the necessity of such precautions was acknowledged. In the earlier period of the war our regiments were decimated by preventible maladies. Before the capture of Sebastopol they presented bills of health scarcely inferior to those of battalions serving in the United Kingdom. Again, during the China war, which immediately followed, the sanitary condition of the army was regarded as secondary only to success in the field ; as a consequence, the health of the troops, although passing rapidly from the temperature of a torrid to that of an arctic zone, was more favourable than had ever happened in similar operations. Similarly, the rapid despatch of numerous troops in 1861-2 to the snows of Canada, and the recent Abyssinian campaign, both effected without loss from epidemic disease, may be regarded as furnishing illustration of the value of sanitation. Thus, whether inferences are drawn from military or civil life, from tropical or temperate climates, the power we possess to prevent disease is abundantly manifest.

In order to present a brief but clear view of what has been effected in India during recent years, it will be necessary to remark on a variety of subjects. Their nature being so varied and distinct, an arrangement approximating to the alphabetical is adopted, as better suited than any other to the desired purpose.

BOOKS.

The principal publications during the decade on sanitary subjects, with especial reference to India, are as follow :—

1. The British Soldier in India. By Julius Jeffreys, Esq. Surgeon, Retired List, Bengal Army, 1859.

2. The Sanitary Condition of Indian Jails. By Dr. Joseph Ewart, Professor of Physiology, Calcutta Medical College, 1860.

3. Vital Statistics of the Anglo-Indian Armies. By Dr. Joseph Ewart, Professor of Physiology, Calcutta Medical College, 1860.

4. Hygiene of the Army in India. By Stewart Clarke, Esq. Inspector-General of Jails, North-West Provinces.

5. Health in the Tropics; or, Sanitary Acts applied to Europeans in India. By Dr. W. J. Moore, Surgeon, Rajpootana Political Agency, 1862.

6. Army Hygiene. By Dr. Gordon, Deputy-Inspector-General of Hospitals, Bengal, 1863.

7. On the Condition of Seamen in the Port of Calcutta. By Dr. Chevers, Principal, Calcutta Medical College, 1865.

8. Report of the Royal Sanitary Commission appointed to inquire into the Condition of the Anglo-Indian Army, 1862.

9. Army Statistical Sanitary and Medical Reports, 1859 to 1865.

10. Sanitary Reports of the Commissioners for Bengal, Madras, and Bombay, for the years 1864—1866.

11. Treatises on Vaccination, for distribution among the People. By Dr. Thompson, Madras; Dr. Shortt, Madras; Dr. Plumptree, Bombay; Dr. Moore, Rajpootana; Dr. Pearson, North-West Provinces.

CAMPS.

With the view of securing the health of men in camps, it is now ordered,[1] that trenches for the burial of refuse are to be dug in echelon on the flanks—being so placed that the prevailing winds cannot carry effluvia to the tents. The position of these trenches to be marked by a flag : they are to be thoroughly filled in before the rear-guard leaves the ground. The commanding officer is desired to place himself in communication with native local authorities, and arrange that effectual measures are adopted for cleansing the ground immediately it is vacated. Particular attention is to be directed to the water supply previous to the arrival of the troops. Before leaving the camping ground, and sometimes during the march, soldiers are now invariably supplied with tea or coffee.

[1] *Vide* G.O., 30th January, 1863.

In the neighbourhood of all cantonments, sites are fixed upon for the encampment of the men in case of cholera breaking out.[1] It is also ordered that such sites are to be ploughed up after occupation.[2] Except when unavoidable, cholera-encampments after being ploughed up are not to be occupied within twelve months.[3]

CANTONMENTS.

There is evidence of a desire to institute some amount of sanitary measures in Indian cantonments long before they were considered essential in neighbouring towns and villages. Thus, the necessity of keeping down rank vegetation was early acknowledged and provided for, while cantonment funds under the direction of committees were instituted.[4] The position of bazaars was also regulated,[5] and rules, including sanitary regulations for their management, laid down.[6] Public latrines were generally instituted about the year 1850, but owing to the wet system of conservancy they were very frequently nuisances, and in some places were abandoned. Station burial-grounds,[7] roads,[8] and slaughter-houses,[9] were also subjects of regulation. By the Army Medical Regulations of 1859, the senior medical officer at any station was constituted *ex officio* sanitary officer,[10] while the general sanitary condition was to be carefully inquired into by the Deputy-Inspector-General of the division on his periodical tour of inspection.

In 1864 an Act[11] was passed for the better administration

---

[1] G.O.C.C., dated 7th April, 1862.
[2] G.G.O. No. 554, 1st October, 1867, Bombay.
[3] G.G.O. No. 688, 2d December, 1867.
[4] Code P.W.D., chap. i. sect. 5, par. 15.
[5] Op. cit., chap. v. pars. 6—8.
[6] Bengal Military Regulations, sect. 6.
[7] P.W. Code, chap. xx. sect. 4, par. 4.
[8] Op. cit. chap. v. sect. 3, par 1.   [9] Op. cit.
[10] Par. 22, page 81.   [11] No. 22 of 1864.

of military cantonments, providing for the conduct of civil
and criminal justice; for police, conservancy, sale of liquors,
and general sanitation. A standing sanitary committee
or local board of health has also been established in every
cantonment ;[1] while, by a more recent order, the senior
medical officer of either British or Indian troops is
ex officio sanitary adviser[2] to the commanding officer
regarding all matters affecting the different branches of
the service.[3] Executive medical officers are, moreover,
required to submit through their administrative superiors
monthly sanitary reports, afterwards forwarded through
the Quartermaster-General for the information of the
Commander-in-chief. Standing orders of the Public
Works department still provide for roads and drains.[4]
With regard to the sanitation of cantonments, it may be
stated that if all the rules and regulations laid down by
Government and the military authorities are effectively
carried out, everything will be done to secure the public
health which can at present be attempted.

COMMISSION, SANITARY.

Perhaps the most important sanitary step taken during
the decade was the formation of sanitary commissions for
the three Presidencies, in accordance with the suggestion of the Royal Sanitary Commission appointed in 1859
to inquire into the condition of the army. The Commission for Bengal—consisting of four members, a president,
and secretary—were nominated in February 1864,[5] and
shortly afterwards for the Presidencies of Madras and
Bombay. These commissions were to afford advice and
assistance in all matters relating to the health of the army,

---

[1] Sect. xix. Act XXII. of 1864.   [2] G.G.O. No. 442, 1867.
[3] G.G.O. No. 268 of 1867.   [4] P.W.D. No. 662 of 1895.
[5] G.G.O. No. 87. 2d February, 1864.

and to supervise the gradual introduction of sanitary improvements in barracks, hospitals, and stations, as well as
in towns in proximity to military stations. The president
and secretary were required to devote their whole time to
the work; but the members were to serve in addition to
other duties.

In 1866, however, the constitution of the various sanitary
commissions was modified.[1] The duties have since been
carried on by a commissioner and secretary. But it was
ordered that, when desirable, officers civil, military, or
medical, best acquainted with the subject, should be asso-
ciated with the sanitary commissioner in any part of the
country where it might be deemed necessary to assemble
a committee.

Up to August 1868, three annual reports have been
published by the commissions, or commissioners, of each
of the Presidencies. All contain a vast mass of valuable
information, both regarding military and civil hygiene.
At the present time, plans for military buildings, as barracks and hospitals, are referred before final sanction to the
sanitary commissioner, as also all questions connected with
the condition of jails and with sanitation generally.

CONSERVANCY.

Another of the most important sanitary changes which
have recently been effected is the adoption of the dry
earth, or the so-called "Moule's system" of conservancy.
In 1864,[2] this system was reported upon, after experiment
in the Allipore jail, and the abolition of lime, charcoal, ashes,
or other substances in favour of dry earth, was strongly
recommended. But this dry-earth conservancy can scarcely
be regarded as a novel conception of Mr. Moule. A very
similar method had been introduced into the Punjab jails

---

[1] G.G.O. No. 196, 28th February, 1866.
[2] *Gazette of India*, May 7th, 1864.

years previously, by Dr. Hathaway.[1] In the latter province
the use of water had not only been prohibited, but it had
been pointed out that lime, coming in contact with urine,
results in the formation of uric acid, and the evolution of
offensive ammoniacal gases. The deodorizing powers of
earth have indeed been long recognised.[2] Such properties
have been employed by the Italians for ages.[3] But there
is an immense difference between a deodorizer and a dis-
infectant. There is reason to believe that earth does not
act with any great certainty in the latter capacity. Some
soils, as clay and aluminous earths, retain organic matter
for a lengthened period undecomposed. It is on record that
maladies, such as cholera and small-pox, have appeared immediately on the opening up of earth in which the bodies of
those dying from such diseases had been years since in-
terred.[4] As mentioned below in the remarks on cholera, this
disease, as also typhoid fever, small-pox, and several varieties
of the entozoa affecting man,[5] belong to the group of diseases
affecting, or capable of being preserved in, the ground. And
if this is the case, the wholesale burial of human ordure now
going on, under Moule's system of conservancy, is probably
a storing of epidemic poisons to be turned up hereafter.[6]
The destruction of such material requires exposure to the

---

[1] Reports on Punjab Jails.
[2] Moore's "Health in the Tropics," p. 159.
[3] Medical Times, Jan. 4, 1868.
[4] Cholera appeared among workpeople employed in cutting into an
old cholera graveyard. (Madras Medical Journal, 1862.) Dr. Gibb
refers to an epidemic of small-pox following the opening up of an old
small-pox cemetery at Quebec. (Sanitary Review, No. 2 : vide also an
article on "Sealed-up Poisons," Medical Times, 1868.) The vitality of
epidemic poisons is also proved by the length of time—10 years—
vaccine lymph has been preserved. When it is recollected that seeds
from Pharaoh's pyramids have germinated, and that there are forms
of infusoria preserving vitality in boiling water, the preservation of
poisonous germs in the earth can scarcely be a matter of surprise.
[5] Cobbold "On Human Entozoa."
[6] Vide "Remarks on the Dry System of Conservancy," by Dr.
Moore, Indian Medical Gazette, April 1868.

atmosphere. Animal charcoal, one of the best disinfectants known, acts by condensing putrid vapours within its pores, so as to cause rapid union with oxygen, or slow combustion, or *cremacausis*. To effect this, however, there must be free access of atmospheric air. By burial deep in the earth, the contact of oxygen is reduced to a minimum. Deodorization may take place, but destruction or *cremacausis* is less possible. Could we be certain no diseased fæcal material was ever buried, this would not much signify. But as this cannot be assured, combustion in furnaces rather than burial in the ground appears the better plan.

COLONIZATION.

Nothing has been attempted during recent years towards colonization. It may be indeed regarded as decided that the Indian plains cannot be colonized by Europeans.[1] But with regard to the Hills, the question must be looked upon as still *sub judice*. Even on the elevated regions, *military* colonization by pensioners, as proposed again and again since the time of Sir Thomas Munroe, can scarcely be expected to prove successful. For the labour of a colonist, the young, strong, and healthy are required. Personally, I

[1] The statistical tables of the Royal Sanitary Commission prove that sickness and mortality increase every year with length of residence in India, at a much greater rate than is explainable by age alone. The natives of temperate zones degenerate in the tropics, as the Esquimaux or negroes do when removed to temperate climates. As Henry Marshall long since pointed out, even inferior animals, as cows, dogs, and sheep, deteriorate in the tropics. All authorities agree, that not one pure descendant of the Portuguese is to be found in India. Sir Ranald Martin (Evidence before the Royal Sanitary Commission), Moorhead (Clinical Researches on Diseases of India), Chevers (Indian Annals of Medical Science), Moore (Health in the Tropics), and other writers, all express opinions, more or less decided, against the possibility of colonization of the plains. If Europeans ever inhabit the plains of India, otherwise than as sojourners for a period, they must first pass into the country during centuries, and alter in characteristics as the Hindoos did.

believe colonization even of the Hills would be a failure, but many hold different opinions.[1]   It is therefore desirable the matter were authoritatively decided by a practical experiment. This, however, could only result after generations had passed away, the initiation merely of any such movement being in our hands.

The question whether settlers on the Hills could find sufficient remunerative occupation is one apart from the purely sanitary query. But the prospect of an affirmative answer to the former appears as doubtful as to the latter.

CHOLERA.

A great step in the prevention of this malady has been made during recent years. The communicability of the disease has been admitted, and consequently removal and isolation have been adopted as the means of staying epidemics.   Whether the germs of cholera are in the air, in

---

1 The question whether a healthy and vigorous European stock can be maintained in the mountain climates of India, has certainly never yet received authoritative answer from experience. But the opinions of those best qualified to judge are unfavourable. Sir Ranald Martin, in his answers before the Committee on Indian Colonization (1854), gives the guarded opinion that "it might be the case to a certain extent, not yet determined." Beattie, before the same board, had no doubt a race of persons well off in life would be continued on the Hills, but whether they would deteriorate under the most favourable circumstances was a question nothing but time could solve. Dr. Moore writes: "Whether European progeny would retain their characteristics, if obliged to undergo the exposure and labour consequent on tilling the ground of even hill ranges, can only be determined by time and experiment : with constant infusion of new blood, and due attention to sanitary principles, such might be the result." Dr. Chevers remarks: "To become enterprising colonists on the slopes of the ghauts and of the Himalayas, they must be a robust, vigorous, intelligent race, capable of maintaining our wealth and our empire equally by commercial industry and by force of arms." Reared as exotics on the summit of the mountains, apart from the great world, we can scarcely expect colonists would retain these characteristics : neither could we look for such qualities in a mixed race.

the water, or in food, or in all, it is now sufficiently proved that isolation and removal from the infected locality is the one great means of arresting the disease. This is not the place to review the different theories of cholera, but it may be remarked that the spread and course of the malady, and the means of prevention now adopted, are consonant with the views first promulgated by Pettenkofer[1] and Thiersch,[2] viz. that the cholera germ is contained, like that of typhoid or intestinal fever, in the diseased excretions. This fact has since been more or less fully admitted by many independent observers, as Acland,[3] Snow,[4] Carpenter,[5] Allison,[6] Routh,[7] Sutherland,[8] Bidie,[9] Parkes,[10] Moore,[11] Simon,[12] Budd,[13] the two latter of whom state, " Cholera is one of the group of diseases which affect the ground."

In consequence of the growing belief, based on accumulated facts, of the communicability of cholera, medical men had for some time urged the removal and isolation of troops when attacked by this disease.[14] In 1861, want of action at Meean Meer was followed by lamentable mortality. The Meean Meer catastrophe doubtless hastened the publication of the famous standing order of Sir Hugh Rose, dated April 1862. The fourth paragraph of these regulations states : " As soon as any case of cholera is reported in the station, the troops will be moved into camp, and no unfavourable condition of the weather is to prevent this movement being carried out."

[1] Mode de Propagation du Choléra, 1854.
[2] Infectionsversuche an Thieren, mit dem Inhal des Cholera dermes, 1856.
[3] Memoir of Cholera in Oxford, 1856.
[4] On the Mode of Communication of Cholera.
[5] British Med. and Surg. Association Journal, Oct. 1854.
[6] On Cholera : Edin. Med. Journal, 1854.
[7] On Fermenting Alvine Evacuations : San. Review, No. 6.
[8] Report on Cholera : Blue Book, 1855.
[9] Etiology of Cholera : Madras Med. Journal, No. 1.
[10] Practical Hygiene, p. 431.   [11] Health in the Tropics, p. 178.
[12] The Times, July 17, 1861.   [13] The Lancet, July 23, 1859.
[14] Moore, Health in the Tropics, p. 183.

Since that period to the present time, the practice has been pursued whenever epidemic cholera appeared. The results, as regards the Upper Provinces, have been latterly reported by Inspector-General Dr. Murray,[1] than whom no man in India is, either in experience or attention to the subject, better qualified to speak authoritatively. In seven epidemics coming under Dr. Murray's observation or direction, removal of the affected was adopted with good results. During 1867 alone there were eighty removals of European and native troops, or prisoners, in the North-West. In thirty-four of these, no fresh cases appeared after removal. In eleven, cholera returned only on the first and second day. In thirty-five instances, it appeared after the second day. And in addition to the benefit conferred on those removed, all left behind in cantonments were freed from an imminent source of danger. The objections to removal and encampment of troops are three; the probability of suffering from sun-stroke, or from fever, and the expense. Dr. Murray points out that in many instances the health of the men actually improved under canvas, showing a smaller sick list than from those left behind. "When a regiment arrives at the encamping ground before tents have been prepared, in the hot season, or is pitched in low marshy ground, in the rains, makes too long marches, or commits excess, extraordinary sickness may be expected to ensue. To infer that an increase of sickness was solely owing to the removal, is to ignore these facts and the after-effects of cholera." A comparison of the loss of life before and after the system of removal came into operation shows that the mortality is now diminished one-half, the saving of life in a pecuniary point of view amply compensating for the outlay. Practically it has been found necessary only to remove and encamp the particular body of men from that barrack in which cholera occurs, and this is now the standing order.[2]

[1] On Removal of Troops in Attacks of Epidemic Cholera. 1868.
[2] G.O.G.G. No. 418, 22d April, 1868.

As before mentioned, cholera prevailed at Mecan Meer in 1861, and, also, generally throughout the North-West. This led to the appointment of a commission, with Mr. Strachey as president. After considerable delay, owing to differences of opinion among the members, a report was presented, the third section of which is printed and issued " by authority."[1] Removal, isolation, and the destruction of diseased discharges, are the three great measures of prevention recommended.

In 1866, the report of the Cholera Commission assembled at Constantinople, in which India was represented by Dr. Goodeve, appeared. With one or two exceptions, the members of this committee arrived at the following conclusions. That India is the birthplace of cholera, and its permanent home. That since 1817, that country has been the focus from which the disease has radiated. That cholera is propagated by man, with a swiftness in proportion to the rapidity of his movements. That no fact has been brought forward to prove that cholera is spread by the atmosphere alone. That water and certain *ingesta* may serve as vehicles for the introduction of the cholera germ into the system. That in India the movements of pilgrims are the most powerful of all causes tending to the development and propagation of the malady.

Reasoning on these and some less important conclusions, the Constantinople Commission proposed a huge system of quarantine through Russia, Persia, Arabia, and the Red Sea, in order to prevent the passage of the disease westwards. They also suggested a more systematic supervision over pilgrims and fairs in India. Recollecting that want predisposes to cholera, it was also recommended that each person, before starting on a pilgrimage, should obtain a licence, showing he was in the possession of the necessary means to defray the expenses of his journey. The inferences drawn at Constantinople cannot, however, be adopted *in toto*. The doctrine of a disease being able

[1] Measures for the Prevention of Cholera among European Troops.

to disseminate itself in any climate, while originating only in one, is opposed to the etiology of other maladies.[1] As cholera had once an origin, so its *de novo* birth, under favourable circumstances, can scarcely be doubted. If it be admitted that Asiatic cholera "is never developed spontaneously, has never been observed as an endemic disease in Europe, but that it has always entered from without," a theory very dangerous to public health in European countries will be adopted. Under such a belief, internal sanitary arrangements would soon be regarded as unnecessary. Instead of trusting to home sanitation, an impracticable system of quarantine would be the reed on which public health would lean; and, under such circumstances, cholera, when it did appear, would prove terribly fatal.

In accordance with the suggestions of the Constantinople Commission, the Sanitary Commissioner of Bengal, local administrations, and civil surgeons have been called upon for reports and opinions regarding any practical action which can be taken towards preventing the dissemination of cholera by pilgrims. The difficulties surrounding this subject are, however, great. The prevention of the assembly of multitudes, often insufficiently fed, fatigued by long journeying, and excited or depressed by a pseudo-religious enthusiasm, would strike at the root of the evil. But at the present period such a procedure in India is manifestly impracticable. The most that can be attempted, therefore, is the provision of proper sanitary arrangements at all large fairs and festivals, and the greatest practicable amount of supervision over pilgrims and others proceeding to and from these gatherings. Owing to sanitary measures, epidemics of cholera originating at fairs and festivals during recent years have been less numerous than in former periods. At Punderpoor, for instance, where the disease was generally expected to break out during the

---

[1] The existence of *typhoid* and *typhus* fever in India is now admitted, but no one doubts their *de novo* origin.

last three years, no extraordinary sickness has occurred The experience,[1] however, gained in 1867 at Hurdwar demonstrates that, although no possible amount of sanitary regulation will *secure* immunity, yet comparative safety may be readily ensured.[2]

With regard to pilgrims proceeding to Mecca, it has been proposed that no ship bound for the Red Sea should leave an Indian port without a clean bill of health.[3] The authorities at Jeddah report that pilgrims arrive in a state of nudity and utter destitution, particularly those annually conveyed to the Hedjaz at the expense of his Highness the Nizam of Hyderabad.[4] The consul at Jeddah also points out that the Koran expressly forbids true believers to undertake the pilgrimage, unless provided with adequate means for its performance.

Still more recently, the Ottoman Sanitary Commission of the Hedjaz recommend surveillance and inspection of vessels at Perim.[5] This commission consists of five Mussulman and four Christian members, the majority being medical officers stationed at the various Turkish ports of the Red Sea.

CINCHONA.

If the views at present held by the great majority of the medical profession are correct, the cultivation of the cin-

[1] *Vide* Hurdwar Festival Report of *Gazette of India*, 1867, p. 1027.

[2] From the 3d to the 12th of April, 1867, a mass of people, as numerous as the population of Scotland, converging from the whole Hindoo world, arrived on a bare plain at Hurdwar on the banks of the Ganges. Under the excellent sanitary arrangements enforced, no disease occurred until after the bathing on the 12th. Then cholera appeared, and the people dispersing carried the disease, as Inspector-General Murray shows, from 300 to 700 miles in all directions. (Report on the Hurdwar Cholera of 1867. See above, ch. xii. Vol. I.)

[3] Proceedings, Bombay Government, No. 2083, Dec. 1867.

[4] Proceedings of Sanitary Commissioner, 1868, p. 71.

[5] Proceedings, Bombay Government, General Department, No. 853 7th May, 1868.

chona tree in India must be counted as one of the most important operations now in progress which will in the future affect the public health, and therefore the welfare and progress, of the country. It is now scarcely ten years since cinchona plants were conveyed in Wardian cases from their homes in the Cordilleras to the slopes of the Neilgherries.[1] It was fondly hoped that before this period the cinchona grown on the latter elevated regions would have supplied multitudes in India with the presumed great antidote to malarious fevers, the all-powerful alkaloid, quinine. How this anticipation has been fulfilled I shall now proceed to show.

The reports published at intervals, particularly from the Government plantations on the Neilgherries, undoubtedly demonstrate that several varieties of cinchona will grow in India; but there are many localities, in which it was supposed the plant would flourish, not at all adapted for the purpose. Thus the mountain tracts of Pegu, Tenasserim, and Martaban are described as scarcely possessing sufficient elevation.[2] In a communication of Mr. Markham[3] to the Secretary of State, the Shevaroy and Tinnevelly hills, Mahableshwar and the Himalayas, were mentioned as unfavourable for the cultivation of cinchona. The cinchona being an essentially intertropical plant, requiring a very peculiar atmosphere, the variations of temperature on the Himalayas were found to be too great, while the Mahableshwar range and other hills men-

[1] The practicability of cultivating cinchona in India was first pointed out by the late Dr. Royle. In 1852 a number of plants were despatched from Kew, five only reaching Calcutta alive, and all dying in transport to Darjeeling. In April 1859 Mr. Clements Markham was despatched for cinchona plants to Peru, and in October 1860 reached Ootacamund with a number of plants, all of which eventually perished. About this time, fifteen cases and a large number of seeds were brought by Mr. Cross from Kew, of which a large proportion germinated. In December 1861 Dr. Anderson brought a number of healthy plants from Java.

[2] Brandis, *Calcutta Gazette*, Supplement, Aug. 31, 1861.

[3] *Calcutta Gazette*, Aug. 31, 1861.

tioned were either too dry at certain seasons, or the elevation was not sufficient.

In Netherlands India, similar difficulties induced the Government to put a stop to the cultivation of certain varieties of cinchona, which from the report of scientific chemists in Holland proved to be worthless. The British Government, on learning this failure, decided to discontinue the growth of the same species which had been commenced at Darjeeling.[1] Other varieties are, however, flourishing near the latter place, where three Government cinchona plantations exist.[2]

Mr. McIvor, the superintendent on the Neilgherries, has despatched periodical samples of bark to England. Thus in 1863, specimens of growth in all stages, from one month to fifteen, were thus forwarded.[3] Some of this bark is mentioned by Mr. Howard as " a very promising earnest of much that is to follow ;" while Mr. McIvor enthusiastically states, " The average price of Peruvian bark produced by the best species may be estimated at from five to six shillings per pound, while, judging from the progress our plants have made here, the cost of the production of this quantity of bark cannot possibly exceed threepence."

In 1864, Mr. Howard mentions that *leaves* of Indian-grown cinchona will not supply the material for the extraction of quinine, but that the red *bark* forwarded yielded six per cent. of *quinoidine*. This result was sufficiently encouraging to induce many persons to apply to the Government gardens for cinchona plants ; and accordingly in 1863 no less than sixty-seven persons were supplied with 9,125 plants ;[4] while in 1864, 39,034 were issued. It was,

---

[1] *Calcutta Gazette*, April 8, 1863.

[2] The different varieties of cinchona require a somewhat different climate, and it will probably be found eventually that certain species must be grown in particular localities. The general climate required is excessive moisture of atmosphere and equability of temperature. Good drainage is also a *sine quâ non*.

[3] *Calcutta Gazette*, Supplement, p. 205, 1863.

[4] *Government Gazette*, April 9, 1864.

however, mentioned about this period that the yield from
plantations established in Coorg was inferior to that of the
Neilgherries. In 1865,[1] another favourable report of the
latter gardens was issued; and in this Mr. McIvor, the
superintendent, takes opportunity to argue,[2] that the destruction of forest land on the Neilgherry hills to make
room for cinchona planting is not detrimental to either the
highland or lowland country. In 1866 the plantations had
so increased as to admit of the distribution of 83,676 young
trees.[3] In 1867 the report of an analysis of five remittances
of bark was received from England. These were "more
encouraging" than any former samples, but no good
quinine was produced. The red bark, however, sold in the
English market at 2s. and 1s. 9d. per pound, while some
later samples of the same species yielded as much as three
per cent. of quinine.[4] In 1868 the yield from the sixth
remittance sent was described as "still improved," but
containing a large proportion of quinoidine, cinchonidine,
and other inferior alkaloids. It is, however, stated[5] that
a decoction of the bark has proved efficacious in malarious
fevers ; and if this be indeed the case, the value even of the
present growth can scarcely be over-estimated, in a country
where almost all require an antidote to such disease constantly at hand.

While much credit is due to the energy with which
cinchona cultivation has been pursued, it must be confessed
that the results are as yet small. Sir Gaspard Le Marchant
has pointed out a possible reason why the Neilgherry-
grown cinchonas do not yield more quinine. Reasoning
on what he had observed at the Cape, that the imported
vines growing most luxuriantly were not the best for wine,

---

[1] *Government Gazette*, April 8, 1865.
[2] Referred to in the paragraph on Forests.
[3] *Gazette*, April 1866.
[4] *Gazette of India*, Supplement. 1867, p. 973.
[5] I believe a committee of Madras medical officers investigated and
reported on this subject.

Sir Gaspard opines that Mr. McIvor's moss and straw appliances have forced the growth, and thus rendered the bark of the cinchona plant comparatively valueless. One great fact, however, remains—the plant is naturalized. And although, as with other matters, it is now seen that fortunes will not be made by its cultivation, prospects of an essential supply of Indian quinine are not altogether unsatisfactory.

Recently Mr. Broughton,[1] at the instance of the Madras Government, has been engaged in an investigation into the capabilities of the surrounding country or markets to supply the materials necessary for the chemical process of quinine manufacture, as lime, soda, pearl-ash, acids, alcohol, or their substitutes.

Before leaving this subject, however, it should be mentioned, there appears a growing feeling among the medical profession that quinine is not the certain preventive and cure of malarious fevers which it has been asserted to be.[2]

---

[1] *Gazette of India*, Supplement, May 30, 1868.

[2] Quinine probably owes much of its celebrity to the *vis medicatrix naturæ*. M. de Chambers used to cure his fever patients with water labelled *protoxide of hydrogen*. (*Bulletin Gén. de Thérapeutique*, May 1861.) Mr. Lowe of Madras, speaking of Bangalore fever, remarks, " In many hands quinine has neither proved prophylactic nor antiperiodic." (*Madras Quarterly Journal of Medical Science*, 1866.) Dr. Livingstone states that the men of his party were equally subject to fever, whether they took quinine or not. (Narrative of Expedition to the Zambesi, p. 78.) The American surgeon Woodward also doubts the power of quinine, especially as a prophylactic. (Diseases of United States Army, 1863.) Dr. Rogers, surgeon to the Panama Railways, has not a high opinion of its efficacy. (*American Medical Times*, August 1862.) Dr. Moore remarks, " As with many other febrifuges of reputed efficacy, I believe the celebrity of quinine is as much due to the spontaneous decline of febrile attacks as to any other cause." (*Indian Annals of Medical Science*, No. 21.) Dr. Beattie of Bombay has lost all confidence in quinine. (Paper read at Meeting of Bombay Medical and Physiological Society, April 1868.) Experiments of Dr. Binz, of Bonn, show quinine has a less powerful preventive action on fermentation and putrescence than arsenic. (*Lancet*, 1868.) Dr. Juggo Bando Bose states his faith in quinine is shaken. (*Ind. Med. Gazette*, 1868.) Waring asserts continued use of quinine in certain states is injurious (Tropical Resident at Home).

I have not space for a consideration of this matter; but it appears strange that, as yet, no authoritative trial of the presumed virtues of quinine has been made. Medical men in all countries have acted on their belief in the powers of this remedy. But so it was formerly with regard to mercury, blood-letting, and other pharmacopœial agents, now happily consigned to oblivion.

DELHI SORE.

As mentioned in the remarks below on the cultivation of vegetables, there is reason to suppose the origin of this peculiar sore may exist in a latent scorbutic taint.[1] It has been known to the inhabitants of Delhi for ages under the name of "Aurungzebe," and is therefore by no means confined to Europeans, although the latter suffer severely from the affection. The number of men thus attacked, previous to 1864, led to the appointment of a committee, of which Inspector-General Murray was president, for the purpose of investigating the whole subject. The result of this inquiry tended to prove that the malady, once established, acquires a contagious character, and is capable of being transferred from one person to another. The general opinion, however, still prevails, that the so-called Delhi sore depends altogether on a peculiar degeneration of system, in which the scorbutic diathesis plays the principal part, and that it is simply a variety of the ulcer prevalent at other places, as in Scinde, Aden, Gwalior, and in many localities in Rajpootana.

EMIGRATION.

There are few subjects which have been more carefully legislated for than the requirements of emigrants from India to British, French, and other colonies. The mortality

[1] Chevers, *Ind. Annals Med. Science;* Moore's Health in the Tropics.

which has so frequently prevailed on board vessels crowded with emigrants early attracted attention to the matter, and the rules now in force are pre-eminently distinguished for humanity and sound sanitary principles. Under the persuasions of employed agents, labourers have long been taken from India to other semi-tropical possessions, but it was not until 1860 that emigration to French possessions was authorized by the Government of India. In 1861, an Act[1] was passed securing a proper supply of water in all emigrant ships, and lessening the amount to be stored in tanks, provided the ships were supplied with a distilling apparatus. During the year 1861-2, thirty ships left Calcutta or Madras bound for the West Indies, conveying 19,850 emigrants. From these shipments some valuable statistics were gleaned. In vessels not carrying either a surgeon or a distilling apparatus the mortality was 7.07 per cent.; in vessels with distilling apparatus, only 5.60; in vessels with both a surgeon and apparatus, 3.36.[2] During the year 1863 the good effect of the Emigration Sanitary Regulations was exemplified in the voyage of the *Alnwick Castle* to Trinidad, during which the health of all on board remained excellent. In 1864, however, H.M. Consul at Réunion called attention to the fact that the mortality among coolies, both on the voyage and after arrival, was still very high;[3] and shortly afterwards an Act to consolidate and amend laws in relation to emigration of native labourers was passed. In addition to former general sanitary regulations, this Act provided for the appointment of a Protector of Emigrants at Calcutta, for the establishment of depôts, for the appointment of surgeons, of a colonial emigration agent, and of a medical inspector; for whose guidance rules were afterwards promulgated.[4] In the same year, 1865, regulations for observance in the

---

[1] No. 49 of 1860. See above, ch. xix.
[2] Vide *Calcutta Gazette*, Dec. 17, 1862.
[3] *Government Gazette*, Supplement, April 9, 1864.
[4] *Gazette of India*, April 1, 1868.

operations connected with recruiting and despatch of emigrants to French and British colonies from the port of Madras appeared,[1] while rules with relation to the Emigration Act were applied to Bombay.[2] In 1866-7 additions were made to the dietary scale.[3]

JAILS.

Since the publication of Dr. Ewart's work[4] in 1860, demonstrating the great mortality (58 per 1,000) in Indian jails, much attention has been paid to these institutions. In 1862 the unsatisfactory condition of certain prisons in the Bombay Presidency induced Sir B. Frere to despatch Dr. Wiehe, the Inspector-General, on a tour of inspection to the jails of other Presidencies. From this officer's report it was found that Madras afforded the only example of a prison on the Pentonville model for Europeans, and of a central prison constructed on the cellular system for natives. The European prison at Ootacamund was suited to the climate. The jails of Bengal were only remarkable for successful financial working. In the Punjab Dr. Hathaway's system of dry conservancy was then at work. As a conclusion from his tour, the Inspector-General recommended that session judges should be relieved of all duties in connexion with jails, which should be made over to Civil surgeons, a suggestion which has generally been adopted.

In 1863 a Bill for the better regulation of jails in Bengal was read, providing among other changes for the appointment of an inspector.[5] In June 1863 Mr. Walker,[6] the inspector for the North-West, published some very comprehensive sanitary rules for the prevention of cholera, hospital gangrene, typhoid, and scurvy. In the same year the

---

[1] *Gazette of India*, May 13, 1865.
[2] Ibid. July 8, 1865.　　　　　　[3] Ibid. p. 867, 1867.
[4] Sanitary Condition of Indian Jails.
[5] *Government Gazette*, Nov. 1863.
[6] Circular 84, June 1863.

purchase and storing of food in bulk was proposed, on the
plea of resulting economy and improved quality.[1] A
valuable table, prepared by Dr. Forbes Watson, was also
published, showing the proportions in which the different
Indian grains should be combined in order to secure the
most nutritious dietary.[2] In 1864, in consequence of a
continued high death ratio (being in Bengal 70 per 1,000
for 1863[3]), a committee was appointed, under the presidency of Mr. Roberts, to report on the present state of
jail discipline and management.[4]

Notwithstanding the attention which has been bestowed
on the internal economy of Indian jails, there is great room
for improvement. Since 1860, a peculiar disease resembling
the famine or relapsing fever of temperate zones has prevailed in many of our prisons. In 1860 it invaded Agra,
Meerut, Allahabad, and Lucknow jails. In 1861 it appeared
at Meerut, Umballa, Loodiana, and some other places. In
1862 and 1863 it was still present. In 1864 its deadly
influence was more extended. Four hundred persons died
from this disease in the Lahore Central Prison alone, while
one-third of the whole mortality in Bengal was caused by
this malady. In 1865 it appeared at Jeypore; in 1866 at
Joudpoor; and since that period in other places. Some
of the Bombay jails have also been attacked, but it is
uncertain if this sickness has yet occurred in Madras. The
Bengal Sanitary Commissioner believes this fever to be a
"peculiar contagious malady introduced from without."[5]
In the first Bengal Sanitary report the disease was, however,
mentioned as typhus fever, and it is also admitted that it
"resembles the famine fever of Europe in many important
particulars." In two able articles on the subject, Dr. David
B. Smith[6] has proved that there is at least grave suspicion

---

[1] *Gazette of India*, Supplement, 1863, p. 288.
[2] Ibid.   Sanitary Report, Bengal, 1865.
[4] *Gazette of India*, March 9, 1864.
[5] Annual Sanitary Reports for Bengal, 1865-6.
[6] *Indian Medical Gazette*, February and March 1868.

that the real origin of this disease is due to a defective dietary scale. And the jail reports for 1867 which have recently appeared, evidencing a decreasing ratio of this peculiar fever concomitant with comparative cheapness of food, appear to support Dr. Smith's views.

LEPROSY.

In 1862, at the instance of the Duke of Newcastle, a report on the prevalence of leprosy in British possessions, including India, was called for. The volume containing the result was published in 1867. From this it appears that one or other variety of leprosy is known in most countries, irrespective of climate. It is, however, in the tropics, especially in India, that leprosy is more common and virulent. Most reporters recognise three varieties: the anæsthetic, the tubercular, and the mixed. There is almost unanimity in the statement that this disease is scarcely ever benefited by medical agents. Similarly, nearly all the hundreds of medical men to whom questions were submitted, declare the malady to be intimately connected with defective sanitary arrangements, and insufficient, deficient, or monotonous diet. By a change for the better of such circumstances the disease generally improves, and sufferers have been even known to recover. The report referred to may probably lead to better arrangements than now exist for the welfare of the numbers in India afflicted with the malady. While the eradication of leprosy can only be hoped for with the gradual improvement of the sanitary and general conditions of the masses, the care of those labouring under the disease becomes daily more necessary. In former times it was the custom in many parts of India to bury alive every person affected with leprosy :[1] a father would bury his son, and a son his father. In some of the native states of Rajpootana, as Serohee for instance,[2] the

---

[1] Report on Leprosy, p. 165.
[2] *Gazette of India*, 1868.

inhuman practice is still continued. In British territory it has of course been long since stopped ; hence probably the increased number of lepers now seen, and the impression prevailing that the malady is more common during recent years. A larger number of leper hospitals or asylums than now exist in India are required for the reception of sufferers from this lingering and loathsome complaint.

MALARIOUS FEVERS, INFLUENCE OF THE MOON ON.

The want of reliable evidence in support or refutation of the presumed influence of the moon on malarious fevers having attracted the attention of Sir W. Mansfield, when Commander-in-chief at Bombay, his Excellency directed that, with a view to determine the question, records of paroxysmal fever should be kept in every medical charge in the Presidency. On the termination of a year, the reports were confided to Dr. Geraud for analysis. The conclusions arrived at by this gentleman are altogether opposed to the prevalent idea of the moon influencing the maladies named. It was, however, objected that some of the hospital returns were only records of primary and more severe recurrent attacks. Also, that no allowance had been made for the exhibition of quinine, at that time generally given to men liable to fever, about the spring. Also, that the period mentioned as the spring, viz. five days, was too extended. The whole question must therefore be regarded as an open one. What is yet asserted, and what has not been disproved, is that an impression having once been made on the nervous system by malarious poison, paroxysmal returns of fever are apt to recur, in apparent relation to the phases of the moon. It is not, indeed, supposed that the moon directly influences the fever. But notwithstanding the opinions of certain astronomers (as Arago) to the contrary, there is reason to believe that as the moon influences the tides so it may exert a power over the atmosphere, resulting in changes sufficient to re-excite paroxysmal maladies in the malarious subject. That exposure to cold and wet will often do so we are fully aware; and it appears probable that more subtle atmospheric alterations act in a similar manner. A repetition of experiment is required to decide the question. All disturbing elements should, however, be scrupulously avoided, and secondary attacks of fever or decided malaise only recorded. The statistics of one regiment, carefully kept, would amply suffice.

MEDICAL SCHOOLS.

During the last ten years several of these institutions have been established; one at Lahore, one in the Central Provinces, while another has been proposed for Rajpootana. Vernacular classes have also been instituted during the decade in one at least of the Presidency Medical Colleges.[1] Notwithstanding all endeavours of metropolitan and Mofussil schools, there is employment for a larger number of well-educated native doctors than is yet forthcoming. Besides the Government service, there is a wide field for this class of men in native states, on railways, and on tea plantations. Doubtless in the course of time they will also be in requisition as private Mofussil practitioners.

MEDICAL SERVICE.

The most important matters connected with the Medical Service especially affecting State medicine and public hygiene, occurring during the decade, are three in number. First, the failure of the attempt to amalgamate the Indian and British services; secondly, the regulation rendering it incumbent on all young medical officers to attend a course of instruction at Netley, previous to entering on an Indian

---

[1] Vernacular classes existed in the other Presidency colleges before the commencement of the decade.

career; thirdly, the order under which medical officers pass an examination before promotion to the rank of surgeon.

After the assumption of the government of India by the Crown, the amalgamation of the two medical services was confidently expected. But it appears Earl de Grey, the then Secretary of State for War, differed from Sir Charles Wood regarding the advisability of the measure. Accordingly we find the latter, in a despatch dated November 1864,[1] offering Earl de Grey's reasons for the decision then promulgated, that there were still to be two medical departments in India. It was argued that the employment of medical officers in civil capacities would interfere with the continuous training required for military duties; that officers so occupied would have no experience in the treatment of the diseases of Europeans, and that in civil employ they would acquire habits of independence unfitting them for the subordination required from regimental officers of inferior rank. Accordingly all European charges were taken from Indian medical officers and given over to surgeons belonging to the British service, a larger number of whom were ordered out to India for that purpose. As an inevitable result, an increase to the administrative staff of the latter department, and a decrease in the same grades of Indian service, also took place.

The regulation now existing, by which all medical officers, after obtaining their commissions, pass through a six months' course at Netley, is one which secures an amount of special information on sanitary subjects to every surgeon entering the public service, which could not be obtained in any other manner. During his term at the Army Medical School at Netley, the young medical officer receives additional instruction to that which he obtains at the Civil schools, where he is fitted to enter the portal of his profession by examination for a diploma. At Netley young army surgeons, whether destined for the British or Indian services, may learn *all that is known* respecting

[1] G.O.G.G. No. 1060, 23d December, 1864.

hygiene generally, and particularly regarding the preservation of the soldiers' health. Diet, clothing, education, habits, peculiar duties in times of peace, situation and circumstances in time of war, principles of ventilation, warming, draining, conservancy, architectural arrangements, influence of geological formations, epidemics and their causes, camp diseases, form only a small portion of the special knowledge now conveyed to the young medical officer. In short, he is fortified, at his entrance into the service, with that special information which others before him only acquired after years of experience and research, and is thus rendered capable, at the outset of his career, of advising on all sanitary subjects. The peculiar knowledge thus imparted, and actually necessary for the application of sanitary principles to communities, pertains, as Lord Herbert so truly observed, "to the special qualifications of the physician, physiologist, geologist, meteorologist, topographist, chemist, engineer, and mechanic."

The examination to be passed, previous to promotion to the rank of surgeon,[1] is security that the acquirements of earlier periods will be increased rather than diminished by the progress of time. As demonstrating the truth of certain observations prefacing this review of the progress of sanitation in India ; also as showing both the increased estimation in which the special acquirements of medical officers are held, and the desire of military officials to benefit by such peculiar attainments, the following occurrences may be compared.

Sir Ranald Martin[2] states, that when serving in one of the most pestilential countries known in India, he made certain recommendations tending to prevent epidemic disease, which was apprehended, the answer from the commanding officer being, " I'll be d—— if I do." Again, when landed at Rangoon during the first Burmese war,

[1] G.O.G.G. No. 1060, 23d Dec. 1864, par. 41.
[2] Influence of Tropical Climates on the European Constitution. p. 109.

the chief medical authority warned the general that certain precautions against scurvy would be necessary, in return for which he was snubbed by the reply, "Medical opinions are very good, sir, when they are called for." "Now here," says Sir Ranald, "were no blundering subalterns, but in the one case a field-officer (whose neglect cost him his own life), and in the other a grey-headed general of reputation (who received much honour and profit, after his army had perished miserably)."

During the present year, Dr. Murray, Inspector-General of Hospitals, published a report, "On the Removal of Troops in Attacks of Epidemic Cholera." It is here stated that, when this malady attacked the troops in Agra, General Showers thus replied to the recommendations made, "It is a medical question which you understand better than I do. Point out what ought to be done, and it shall be carried out; but bear in mind, the responsibility rests with you." Again in 1867 at Umballa, as Dr. Murray mentions, the recommendations of the medical staff were most efficiently carried out by the military authorities. And this, it is believed, is now the rule, and not, as in former times, the exception, throughout India.

METEOROLOGY.

In former days meteorological observations, as far as regards the direction of the wind and the amount of rainfall, were made at most regimental and civil hospitals. But the duty, being entrusted to native subordinates, was frequently inefficiently performed, and the results were characterised as worthless by the Royal Sanitary Commission appointed under the presidency of Lord Herbert. Since the commission in 1863 issued the result of their labours, observatories provided with paid officials have been established in various parts; those in the North-West being presided over by an accomplished meteorologist, Dr. Murray Thompson of Roorkee. Too much gratis and ar

officio work still, however, appears to be expected. If performed faithfully, such duty will demand constant, almost
hourly attention ; yet the application soliciting extra pay
for extra work has not always been successful. Under
these circumstances it can scarcely be expected that
many of the present meteorological observations will be
more reliable than those formerly submitted. Almost the
only meteorological observations of interest published
during the last ten years are Dr. Cook's reports of the
registration of ozone in 15 stations of the Bombay Presidency during 1863-4, and a report of the rainfall of mountainous regions in the same Presidency, referred to under a
different heading. By the former papers it appears that
ozone is more fully developed in August, September, and
October than at other periods. Dr. Cook endeavours,
fruitlessly as I think, to establish a connexion between
ozone and cholera. In the Bombay Presidency during the
periods in question the two were certainly concomitant in
some localities, but in others not so. Schultze, Voltotine,
Lamont, the Society of Medicine at Königsburg, and many
others, deny any such connexion. Enough, however, has
been demonstrated to establish a practical deduction, that,
when the question of moving troops on account of cholera
is on the *tapis*, the absence of ozone in the atmosphere would
justify a greater amount of caution.

MOUNTAIN REGIONS, RAINFALL ON.

In 1864, the Bombay Government published a report
on this subject. The fall on the mountain ranges varies
greatly in different parts of the same hills. On the
Paunchgunny range, at one station, 190 inches generally
fall ; at another, 21. On the *Mahableshwar* range, the
variation is from 252 to 51 inches ; on the *Mulla* hills, from
337 to 76. The fall rapidly decreases from the parallel
of the Western Ghauts eastwards. The influence of local
position is exemplified thus : at Mulla, latitude 17° 16',

337 inches fell; and at Malcolm Perth, 17° 57', 252 inches. From the Mahableshwar returns, extending over 30 years, it appears there is a periodical excess and deficit every five years, a fact which might be taken advantage of by cultivators, into whose tanks and fields the waters flow. The rainfall on the Himalayas is generally less than on the intertropical ranges; but in some localities, as at Nynee Tal, 100 inches have been measured.[1] On the Neilgherries, the average fall differs very materially in localities. On Mount Aboo the average during the last eight years is 70 inches.

MOUNTAIN-RANGES, DISAFFORESTMENT OF.

The alleged diminution of the rainfall from the destruction of the forests and jungle of mountainous regions has received considerable attention. In 1864 Dr. Anderson[2] was requested to report as to the past and present condition of forests about Darjeeling, with a view to determine if recent clearances had affected the climate and water. In 1865 Mr. McIvor[3] combats the opinion that Cinchona clearances on the Neilgherries had disturbed the climate. He remarks that it is the height and cold which condenses moisture, but admits that trees increase the rainfall by offering a large evaporating surface. In dry weather, however, a different agency is at work. Trees then draw the moisture they evaporate from the soil, and it is calculated that in 150 dry days one million and a half gallons of water are dissipated by an acre of forest. Mr. McIvor asserts, that streams rising in and flowing through valleys destitute of trees maintain their flow much better than when passing through wooded valleys. "If the Neilgherries were destitute of trees, twice as much water would flow

---

[1] Report on the Extent and Nature of the Sanitary Establishments for European Troops.

[2] *Gazette of India*, June 25, 1864.   [3] Op. cit., April 1865.

into the low country during the dry season." These arguments, however, contain fallacies, as Mr. Bowring, Commissioner of Coorg,[1] points out. Although the height of mountains will always attract and condense moisture, the rain, without the innumerable impediments offered by root-fibres, would run off to the low country immediately, leaving the hills dry, and *becoming soon absorbed* or evaporated by the earth and heat of the plains. Again, although trees dissipate the amount of moisture mentioned above, not one-tenth part is absorbed by the roots. During the greater part of the year, the atmosphere of mountain ranges is moist at night, and at such periods trees absorb and do not exhale. Moreover, in the absence of trees, the waters would not convey to the lowlands that fertilizing material composed of decaying rock and the *débris* of vegetation, which, when deposited, becomes an alluvial stratum. Baker[2] points out that the difference of colour between the Blue and White Nile depends upon the alluvial material which the tributaries of the former bring from the highlands of Abyssinia. This, partially deposited in Egypt, is the source of wealth to the Pashalic. Were the Abyssinian woods all destroyed, Egypt would become altogether desert. In other countries, the connexion between disafforestment and sterility is unfortunately practically manifest, as in some parts of America, in Greece,[3] in Tartary,[4] in the Mauritius,[5] in Barbadoes and Jamaica.[6]

Similarly, the influence and value of forest trees on the lowlands is unquestionable. Kirk attributed the dryness, and consequent sterility, of the country west of the Aravellis to the absence of trees; while Balfour long since demon-

---

[1] *Gazette of India,* June 13, 1868.
[2] The principal streams joining the Lower Nile are *Bahr el Arek* or Blue Nile and the Atbara, both rising in the Abyssinian mountains. (The Nile Tributaries of Abyssinia, by Sir Samuel Baker.)
[3] *Builder,* 1864.   [4] Huc's Travels in Tartary, vol. i. p. 11.
[5] *Delhi Gazette,* June 1868.
[6] Chevers, *Ind. Ann. Med. Science,* vol. xii.

strated how a country might be ruined or enriched by the presence or absence of horticulture.[1] As Colonel Sleeman observes,[2] hot and dry countries, denuded of their trees, and by that means deprived of a great portion of the moisture to which they have been accustomed, soon become dreary, arid wastes. The lighter particles of soil blow away, leaving only the heavy arenaceous portions ; thence those sandy deserts in which are often to be found signs of a population once dense. Whatever may have been former shortcomings, there is sufficient evidence that existing forests will be preserved and tree-planting encouraged. Thus, during recent periods, Government has issued rules for the preservation of the Namba,[3] the Darjeeling,[4] the Barmil,[5] the Central Provinces,[6] the Coorg,[7] Sikkim,[8] and other forests. In 1865 an Act was also passed[9] to give effect to the rules for the management and preservation of forests. Tree-planting has been encouraged on the west coast of Madras,[10] on Chettesgurh,[11] and other localities. The mahogany-tree has also been introduced into Bengal.[12]

MOFUSSIL SANITATION.

During the decade under review, several parts of India have been ravaged by a peculiar fever, evidently of a *typhoid* character, aggravated by the malarious, and probably scorbutic taints, so common in India. The districts in which this disease has appeared are Baraset, Hooghly, Nuddea, in 1863 ;[13] some parts of Rajpootana in 1862-3 ;

[1] Balfour, On the Influence of Trees on Climate: *Madras Journal of Science*, No. 36.
[2] Rambles in India, vol. ii. p. 198.
[3] *Calcutta Gazette*, 1862, p. 2070.
[4] *Gazette of India*, Sup. June 25, 1864.
[5] Ibid. August 2, 1865.;   [6] Ibid. Supplement, 1865, p. 26.
Ibid. 1865, p. 16.   [8] Ibid. 1865, p. 17.
[9] No. VII. of 1865.   [10] *Gaz. of India*, Sup. 1867, p 630.
[11] *Gaz. of India*, 1866, p. 637.   [12] Ibid. 1867.
[13] Vide *Calcutta Gazette*, Supplement, 1863, p. 157.

North Canara in 1863,[1] and Guzerat in 1865. Dr. Elliot,
who reported on the malady in the first-mentioned provinces, states that the fever chiefly showed itself on the
banks of the Hooghly, where dense jungle, decaying vegetation, no drains, dirty tanks, and total want of conservancy, are the characteristics. Some villages were totally
depopulated, and it is calculated that during the six years
ending 1863, some 12,000 persons must have died. Great
difficulty was experienced in inducing the natives to adopt
even ordinary sanitary measures. The most wealthy were
the least willing to aid. The commissioner, Mr. Schalch,
reported, " I have spoken to the inhabitants, and urged
the necessity of their immediately undertaking sanitary
measures, but my appeal has met with no response." And
it has recently been stated that a similar disease prevails
near the Hooghly to this day.

In some of the native states of Rajpootana, notably in
Scrohee and Marwar, after the heavy rains of 1862, a
somewhat similar malady presented itself. This declined
spontaneously during the next hot season.

The epidemic in Canara was reported on by Dr. Leith
of Bombay, who found a want of ordinary sanitation prevailing scarcely less melancholy than the condition of the
Hooghly villages. The prevailing disease was essentially
the same typhoid remitting fever, with its sequelæ of spleen
disease and dropsical effusions.

In 1865 a rumour originated that a malady similar to
the Palee Plague (which in 1856 and succeeding years
spread from Kutch to the Himalayas) had broken out in
Palanphoor and the north of Guzerat. Dr. Martin, of the
Bombay service, who investigated the subject, reported the
malady to be simply the typhoid bilious type of malarious
fever.

Notwithstanding the issue of various appeals to the
people, and the promulgation of sanitary regulations,[2] the

[1] Vide Calcutta Gazette, Supplement, 1863, p. 294.
[2] Bengal Sanitary Report, 1865, p. 102.

Sanitary Commissioner for Bengal states, in one of his recent reports,[1] that, "although in the chief towns some progress has been effected, on the villages and people little impression has been made." And the same statements apply to other Presidencies. But outbreaks of epidemic fever in the Mofussil fully prove that there is a certain limit of sanitary neglect incompatible with human existence, and it would therefore appear desirable that simple ordinary sanitary precautions should be rendered compulsory in every village throughout the land.

OFFICERS, SANITARY MEASURES FOR.

Although so much has been accomplished to secure the health and welfare of the rank and file, but little has been directly attempted for the benefit of the officers. The advisability of establishing hospitals for the officers at the Presidency towns and sanitaria has been often mooted ; also the provision of good nurses.[2] In 1861[3] something of the kind was attempted in Calcutta. At a later period, in 1863,[4] an old Peninsular and Oriental Company's ship, the *Bentinck*, was converted into a floating invalid depôt, with some small accommodation for officers. Both these establishments have, however, it is believed, been discontinued. Shortly after Sir William Mansfield became Commander-in-chief in India, he proposed a plan to secure better house accommodation for military officers in cantonments. This had been already rejected by the Government of Bombay, and unfortunately appears to have met with almost similar treatment from the Government of India. The proposal was, briefly, that land in cantonments should be sold, the proceeds forming a fund by which houses now occupied might be purchased and new quarters

---

[1] Bengal Sanitary Report, 1866, p. 61.
[2] Moore, Health in the Tropics, p. 147.
[3] G.O.G.G., No. 252 of 1861.
[4] *Government Gazette*, 1863, p. 80.

built, Government thus becoming eventually the landlord
of all officers.

The fact that some plan is really necessary in order to
afford officers better accommodation than the miserable
bungalows so frequently inhabited, has been partially
acknowledged. G.O.G.G. 984 of 1867 allows officers to
borrow from Government, according to a certain scale,
money for the erection of houses in cantonments where
suitable accommodation is not available. In India, so
much of the time of Europeans is passed indoors, and
effectual shelter from vicissitudes of weather is so necessary,
that the sanitary value of better residences for military
officers can scarcely be over-estimated.

PUBLIC BUILDINGS, SPACE IN.

Formerly, in most public buildings a degree of over-
crowding was the rule rather than the exception. When,
some fifteen years ago, attention became more particularly
directed to this subject, a certain amount of cubic space
was regarded as the great requisite. Hence various narrow
high barracks were constructed without any respect to
superficial space. Such edifices are, however, now confessed to be a mistake.

The most recent regulations of the Public Works Department lay down the following as the minimum amount
of cubic and superficial feet :—

Barracks for Europeans on the plains:—90 superficial
feet per man ; 1,800 cubic feet per man.

Barracks for Europeans on hill-stations:—77 superficial
feet per man ; 1,232 to 1,408 cubic feet per man ; according to altitude.

Hospitals for Europeans on the plains:—120 superficial
feet per inmate ; 2,400 cubic feet per inmate.

Hospitals for Europeans on hill-stations:—102 superficial
feet per inmate ; 1,632 to 1,836 cubic feet per inmate ;
according to altitude.

European married quarters :—Sitting-room, 16 ft. by 14 ft.; bed-room, 14 ft. by 10 ft.; and bath-room, 7½ ft. by 6 ft. Verandah in front, 12 feet broad; ditto in rear, 10 feet broad.

Native hospitals :—99 superficial feet per inmate ; 1,584 cubic feet per inmate.

Native jails :—40 superficial feet per inmate ; 648 cubic feet per inmate.

RAILWAY STATIONS.

The want of sanitation in connexion with railways, and at the stations, although not altogether supplied, has not been lost sight of. Rules exist, limiting the number of persons to be conveyed in each compartment. A resolution of the Bombay Government, as early as 1862,[1] directed that waiting-rooms, especially for ladies, should be provided at all stations ; also a "dhurmsala," or resting-place, for natives, and a good supply of drinking water. At a later period the condition of the stations attracted the attention of the Government of India, and the Bengal Sanitary Commission reported that "the allegations of inadequate provision for the health, comfort, and decency of both travellers and railway *employés* were well-founded." The remedies proposed were proper accommodation at stations and improvement of the dwellings of the company's servants. These requirements, it was thought, the railway authorities were bound to supply. Upon this, the Secretary of State communicated with each of the latter at home, from whom answers were received expressing more or less readiness to meet the wishes of Government.[2]

SALT.

Closely connected with public health and State medicine in India is a due supply of salt at a cheap rate to the

[1] October 16, 1862.
[2] Vide *Gazette of India,* April 1866.

masses. I have not space to prove the assertion, but it
will be readily admitted that in India, among a people
many of whom exist on vegetable diet, salt is a necessary
of life. The policy, therefore, of the increased duty on
salt imported by sea and land into the Bombay Presidency,
imposed in 1861,[1] is questionable. Without entering into
the great subject of the salt-tax, it may be remarked that
the above and other regulations of British provinces and
adjacent native states deprive the inhabitants of large
tracts in India of the full advantage of salt at the cheapest
possible rate. There are salt-producing districts in Rajpootana, the great Sambhur Salt Lake, situate between Jey-
poor and Marwar, and the salt springs of Putchbudra, also
in Marwar, from which the supply of salt is practically un-
limited. But owing to vexatious imposts, to oppressions
of the Brinjarriee carriers, to the want of roads, and to
the injustice of durbar officials, salt, which at the great
Sambhur lake[2] costs $1\frac{1}{2}d$. per maund (80 lbs.), costs at Agra
half a guinea.[3] It is evident, therefore, that the resources
we have at hand for the supply of salt are not yet fully
available.

Having referred to salt as a sanitary want, it must be
mentioned that in 1863 this substance was brought forward
as a preventive of cholera.[4] Scouting the idea of any
special prophylactic agency, I should not have mentioned
this subject, had not the names in connexion with the
suggestion arrested attention. Dr. Beaman, a London
physician of repute, has long advocated the use of salt as a
cholera prophylactic. Dr. Beaman, jun., of the Bengal
service, when civil surgeon at Hoshungabad, pursued the
plan in the jail at that place. Captain Wood, deputy-commissioner, reported the method to Colonel Meade, who

[1] Act VII. of 1861.
[2] For a description of the Sambhur Salt Lake *vide* "Marwar, the
Land of Death," by Dr. Moore: *Ind. Ann. Med. Science*, vol. xx.
[3] *Friend of India*, April 1867.
[4] *Calcutta Gazette*, May 20, 1863.

communicated it for the information of Government. A pice weight of salt is to be given with each meal. Salt cooked with the food loses, it is stated, the peculiar virtue.

SANITARIA, HILL.

"A Report on the Extent and Nature of the Sanitary Establishments for European Troops in India"[1] was published by authority in 1862. In this volume may be found accounts of upwards of sixty localities, only six, however, of which were then occupied by Europeans. In the Bombay Presidency, the principal military sanitaria, then as now, were Poorundhur and Mount Aboo; and in Madras, Ootacamund, or rather Wellington, on the Neilgherries. In both Presidencies small sanitary stations have been more recently established; as, for instance, the one on the mountain known as "Salabut Khan's tomb," in the Deccan, and "Taraghur," near Nusseerabad in Rajpootana. These latter, however, can scarcely be regarded as more than affording refuge from intense heats in the summer seasons. During the decade, no hill-station has been added to the number of those permanently occupied by European troops as a military cantonment, in which healthy men might reside. The fact is scarcely yet sufficiently acknowledged that the climates of elevated regions in India are more adapted for the prevention than the cure of disease. The Royal Sanitary Commissioners recommended that at least one-third of the Anglo-Indian army should be located on the hill-ranges. And this number, it is thought, might certainly leave the plains without denuding those stations of troops where, from political or strategic reasons, the presence of Europeans is required. But it is the expressed opinion of those better qualified to judge, that corps fresh from Europe should be sent to the hills, taking their tour of duty on the plains

[1] The title of this volume should be "Sanitary Establishments in Bengal," those of Madras and Bombay not being included.

afterwards. Both theory and experience teach that change to the hills, after a prolonged sojourn on the lowlands, is frequently followed by increase of sickness and mortality.

SANITARIA, MARINE.

The acknowledged fact that numerous diseases are not removed, or even ameliorated, by the climates of the hills has led to the establishment of various sea-side sanitaria, as Ghizree near Kurrachee, and Bulsar in Guzerat. Other places have also been proposed, as Callagouk or Curlew Island. It was thought, and rightly too, that the peculiarities of climate of the sea-coast, arising from the physical properties of land and water ; the slightly lowered temperature—the consequence of air in daily motion from the land and sea breeze; the peculiar atmosphere, impregnated with saline particles, iodine, and moisture; the opportunity of a fish diet ; even the sight and smell of the ocean, would prove beneficial to invalids from the arid burning districts of the interior. Hence also the establishment of the *Bentinck* as a floating sanitarium, referred to under a different heading.

SERAIS.

Sanitary rules regarding these places for the accommodation of native travellers were published in 1867.[1]

SNAKE-BITES.

Of the 219 varieties of snakes described by Professor Gmelin, forty-three are said to inhabit India, of which about one-fourth are poisonous to man and large animals. For years past, under directions from Government, destructive war has been waged on these reptiles. In Scinde, for instance, some years ago, 10,000 snakes were killed in

[1] *Gazette of India*, 1867, p. 26.

three months. But with regard to the discovery of the nature of the serpent-poison and the antidote, nothing has been authoritatively attempted. This, as with most matters pertaining to medical science, has been left to private and individual research.

Some years back, in 1861, by order of the Bombay Government, rules for the treatment of snake-bite, recommended by Drs. Beattie and Wyllie, both of the Bombay service, were published. The former gentleman advised the immediate application of a ligature above the bitten part, scarifications, suction, and stimulants internally. The latter officer recommended thirty or forty drops of liquor ammoniæ every ten or fifteen minutes. The chief of the medical department wisely combined these two methods of treatment. There is nothing, however, very novel in them : all had been previously suggested.[1]

Although little encouragement has been afforded by Government, recent independent investigations have not been wanting. Thus, the impression that the mungoose is proof against the poison of snakes has been proved erroneous by Dr. Francis.[2] Hence the non-existence of the mysterious antidotal herb the mungoose was supposed to eat may be presumed. The same author has also shown that one cobra cannot hurt another, and the question immediately suggests itself, may not the body of the snake contain an antidote to the poison ? Dr. Fayrer[3] has called attention to the fact that carbolic acid is repulsive and poisonous to snakes. Dr. Shortt,[4] of Madras, has investigated the serpent-venom chemically and microscopically. Dr. Cookson[5] remarks, that both cats and sharp terrier dogs are

[1] Vide *Lancet; Mirror*, 1852 ; and writings of Dr. Boaz, Malte Brun. Pennant, Russell, and Forbes.

[2] Experiments with the Poison of the Cobra : *Medical Times*, May 16, 1868.

[3] Experiments on the Cobra Poison : *Ind. Med. Gazette*, June 1868.

[4] Experiments on the Poison of the Cobra : *Medical Times*, May 1868.

[5] *Ind. Med. Gazette*, May 1867.

useful in preventing the entrance of snakes into houses, and discovering them when there. Waring [1] has investigated the claims of certain herbs, and pronounced all useless. Interesting experiments have also been made in Melbourne by Professor Halford.[2]

The grant of a few thousand rupees, and the appointment of a practical and scientific committee to investigate the whole subject, is much to be desired. Such an inquiry would probably terminate in the laying down of more certain methods of treatment than those now practised; possibly even in the discovery of an antidote.

Those who are aware of the useless nostrums used by the natives in cases of snake-bite, and the great loss of life resulting therefrom, will confess the magnitude of such a boon.

SOLDIERS, EMPLOYMENT OF.

In 1860 Sir Hugh Rose, as Commander-in-chief, called for a report on the means of instruction, recreation, and employment for soldiers, with a view to place such means on a permanent footing. By various succeeding regulations this was accomplished, and at the present period the workshops, reading-rooms, and other methods of employing spare hours, at the command of every soldier, amply testify that in this respect little is wanting which could fairly be desired.

The employment of soldiers on public works, such as road-making and building, has frequently been recommended. It was, however, too much the custom to regard soldiers as mere machines for military duty, and to supply them by native agency with everything they require. French soldiers in Algeria, in a climate assimilating to that of our

---

[1] *Madras Quart. Journ. Med. Science*, Jan. 1862.

[2] *Medical Times*, August 3, 1867. This author (Professor Halford) described peculiar appearances in the bodies of animals bitten, but other writers fail in finding similar conditions : *Ind. Med. Gazette*, August 1868.

hill-stations, build their own residences, and do not necessarily deteriorate either in *physique* or discipline. And
experience has now amply demonstrated that soldiers may
be similarly employed in India. The head-quarter wing,
56th Foot, at Sinchal, effected extensive repairs to their
barracks when workmen were not procurable. Men of
H.M. 33d Regiment, at Asseerghur, were utilized on public
works; also, more recently, the soldiers of the 56th, on
Aboo.

A standing order now exists in the Public Works Department, dated 13th April, 1864, that at all stations where
there are European troops, the executive engineer, on
receiving sanction for a work, shall invite a tender from
such troops, which, if favourable, is to be accepted.

It was not, however, until 1866 that soldiers were utilized
in the construction of roads. In April of that year, men
from the 3d battalion Rifle Brigade, and 79th Highlanders,
to the number of 648, commenced operations on the Murree
and Abbotabad road, in the Himalayas : thirty-seven miles
of road were completed at a cost of 62,644 rupees. This,
on account of hutting and commissariat expenses, was
estimated to exceed the value of the work done by
18,165 rupees. But, as Colonel Maclagan remarks, the
gain in health and welfare of the men has a money value
much higher than the expenditure. They were contented,
enjoyed the work, were peculiarly benefited, and acquired
renewed physical health and vigour. Politically, also, the
effect of so many Europeans, and a wide road in the
mountains, must be good. There is yet work for many
more seasons. Hutting soldiers on the mountains cost
30 rupees, barracks on the plains 900 rupees, per man.
The question therefore is worth consideration, if a large
number of men might not be constantly located in the
Himalayas and engaged in road-making. During the
summer of 1868, working-parties of the 38th Regiment were
employed on the same road, but, instead of receiving a
daily payment, were remunerated by contract—a method

more profitable to Government, and, it is also stated, more pleasing to the men.

SOLDIERS, VITAL STATISTICS OF.

Those conversant with military statistics are well aware of the difficulties of obtaining results at once brief and exact. Even the Annual Blue Books recently published, examples of labour and research as they are, have scarcely, excepting perhaps the latest reports issued, reached statistical perfection. Hence, it must be confessed, the materials on which conclusions are now drawn may not be all that could be desired. It is imposssible to collect and tabulate the annual statistics of the British army—the safeguard of an empire on which the sun never sets—until *years* have elapsed. But a reference to the Report of the Royal Sanitary Commissioners appointed in 1858 to inquire into the sanitary state of the Anglo-Indian army, abundantly demonstrates that the mortality among soldiers, from our first occupation of the country to the year 1856, oscillated round the high figures of 69 per 1,000 annually. And in thus quoting the death-ratio among Europeans in India, the Royal Commissioners simply reiterated the statistical conclusions of Sir A. Tulloch, Colonel Sykes, Drs. Chevers and Ewart.[1] There is, however, ample evidence in the

---

[1] When the report of the Royal Sanitary Commission was published in 1862, the statements made were received at home with astonishment and indignation. The *Times* commented on the "appalling mortality now brought to light," and the cue was followed by most of the other journals. Sir Charles Wood in the House of Commons, on the 14th July, 1863, stated that the report of the Commission "had brought to light a rate of mortality which, before its publication, no one believed to exist." Yet the sanitary condition of the British troops in India had been previously thoroughly investigated by several Indian officers, from whose published works the amount of disease prevailing should have been well known ; of these latter may be mentioned, Tulloch's "Statistical Tables ;" Sykes, *Statistical Society's Journal*, vol. x. ; Chevers, "On the Means of preserving the Health of European Soldiers in India:" *Indian Annals of Medical Science,*

Commissioners' own tables, that the rate of mortality steadily diminished throughout the period from 1800 to 1856. The following table, compiled from Statement No. 10 of the Report of the Royal Sanitary Commissioners, shows the gradual decrease of mortality during the first half of the present century.

Years.	Ratio of Mortality per 1,000 in			
	India.	Bengal.	Madras.	Bombay.
1800—1810. . . .	73.70	91.50	54.80	84.50
1810—1820. . . .	84.80	68.70	97.00	99.60
1820—1830. . . .	90.70	84.50	95.20	97.90
1830—1840. . . .	55.70	60.10	55.50	46.30
1840—1850. . . .	65.40	79.50	43.50	68.30
1850—1856. . . .	50.70	67.80	44.30	31.10

We thus find the mortality among British troops in India had sunk, for the quinquennial period ending 1856, to less than 51 per 1,000 of strength. There is also evidence that in after years the death-ratio, particularly in the Bombay and Madras Presidencies, had still further diminished. Even including the Mutiny years, the mortality among Bombay troops, up to 1860, averaged only 27 per 1,000. But owing to the greater disturbing causes during the last half of the decennial period from 1850 to 1860, the mortality from the first half, or from 1850 to 1856 may be most fairly taken for purposes of comparison. And this mortality we have already seen, by the Royal Sanitary Commissioners' own showing, to have been something over 50 per 1,000.

This gradual diminution of mortality occurring during the first half of the century may be attributed to several causes. First, as facilities for doing so became available, a

No. xi. et seq.; Ewart, "Vital Statistics of the Anglo-Indian Armies;" Sir Ranald Martin, "Influence of Tropical Climates;" Waring, Indian Annals of Medical Science, vol. vi.: Moore, "Health in the Tropics, or Sanitary Art applied to European Soldiers in India," &c. &c.

greater number of men were invalided towards the termination of that period. Secondly, better habits of life gradually prevailed. There was more attention paid to personal hygiene. With the introduction of malt liquor, less spirits were consumed; and intemperance, as at home, became less common. Thirdly, the system of medical treatment underwent a radical change. Instead of the bleedings *ad deliquium*, the purgatives, and the salivations of former days—a practice well designated by Ewart[1] *spoliative*—a comparatively stimulating, or rather supporting treatment, with the use of quinine, was generally adopted. With regard to fevers, the author just mentioned demonstrates by statistical evidence that the mortality from this class of diseases alone is not one-fourth of what it reached in former years.

Now it was not until after the mutinies that what may be denominated the sanitary era was inaugurated in India. Previous to that period, although attention had been drawn to the subject by various medical officers, the sanitary regulations in force were comparatively few in number, and certainly not based on scientific principles. In comparison with the magnificent barracks of the present day, troops were ill lodged; the diet rolls were less cared for; a minimum of attention was bestowed on the dress of the army as regards sanitary requirements; less care was paid to the enlistment of recruits for Indian service; the length of service in the country was greater; and from the day of their landing men were exposed to various sources of disease, from which immunity has been attempted, if not secured, by recent sanitary regulations. Yet, notwithstanding this, we see the mortality, under the influence of the causes previously mentioned, declining to 50 per 1,000 of strength annually.

But to find the *total loss* to the service occasioned by disease, the amount of invaliding must be added to the above figures. This, during the second quarter of the

---

[1] Review of the Treatment of Tropical Diseases: *Ind. Ann. Med. Scienc.* vol. xiv.

century, appears from the best authority—viz. Colonel Sykes' tables—to have averaged 29 per 1,000. The latter figures, added to 50.70, give 79.70 per 1,000 as the *total loss* to the service from disease during the period in question.

Leaving the Mutiny years out of the account, as seasons of extraordinary trials and sickness, and dating the commencement of army sanitation in India from 1860, the year for which Indian Army Vital Statistics first appeared in the statistical, sanitary, and medical reports, we turn to the latter blue-books for information regarding the great diminution of mortality which might reasonably be expected from sanitary regulations. And the results are contained in the following table :—

India.				Bengal.			
Years.	Average Strength.	Ratio per 1,000 of Strength.		Years.	Average Strength.	Ratio per 1,000 of Strength.	
		Sick.	Died.			Sick.	Died.
1860 . .	64,455*	2,279	35.21	1860 . .	42,371	2,023	39.37
1861 . .	57,082*	1,768	36.74	1861 . .	37,483	1,954	45.57
1862 . .	63,713	1,736	25.68	1862 . .	39,312	1,851	27.55
1863 . .	67,525	1,634	23.64	1863 . .	42,575	1,759	22.26
1864 . .	65,002	1,530	21.93	1864 . .	39,936	1,557	22.56
1865 . .	62,589	1,476	28.14	1865 . .	37,631	1,548	26.65
			28.55				30.66

* Exclusive of Hon. Company's troops.

Now, although these figures undoubtedly show the mortality during more recent years, they do not by any means give the *total loss* to the service caused by disease in India. *Invaliding*, which has very properly been carried to a much greater extent during recent years, renders the total loss to the service in India more nearly approaching that of the period previous to the sanitary era. Since 1859 the number of European soldiers annually invalided, either for discharge from the service or for change of climate, has gradually increased, and of late has amounted in Bengal to the high figure of 40.04 per 1,000[1] of strength, and in Bombay to 60.6 per mille.[2]

Therefore, to arrive at the total loss to the service from disease during the period taken for comparison, the average amount of invaliding, as shown in the following table, must be added to the 28.20 per 1,000 deaths.

	INDIA.			BENGAL.	
Years.	Strength.	Ratio per 1,000 invalided.	Years.	Strength.	Ratio per 1,000 invalided.
1860 . .	64,455*	†	1860 . .	42,371	†
1861 . .	57,082*	31.68	1861 . .	37,483	28.09
1862 . .	63,713	28.17	1862 . .	39,312	31.50
1863 . .	67,527	35.00	1863 . .	42,575	34.97
1864 . .	65,002	44.10	1864 . .	39,936	36.75
1865 . .	62,589	38.27	1865 . .	37,631	46.87
1866 . .		‡	1866 . .	35,013	49.04‡
		35.44			37.87

* Exclusive of Hon. Company's troops.
† The total amount of invaliding for 1860 is not available from the Blue Books.
‡ Not yet published 1868).   § Vide Third Bengal Sanitary Report.

The total loss, therefore, during the periods in question, 1860—1865, is for the Bengal Presidency 68.53, and for India 63.64. The latter numbers, deducted from the total loss during the period ending 1856, give the *apparent gain* from recent sanitary regulations; which for the whole of India amounts to 16.06.[3]

[1] Third Annual Sanitary Report for Bengal, p. 25.
Report of the Sanitary Commissioner for Bombay for 1867.
[3] If the statistics of the Bengal army for the last two years for which they are available, namely 1865-6 only, are compared, the gain, in consequence of the great amount of invaliding during those years, will be seen to be much less, thus:

Total loss to the service from invaliding and mortality from 1850 to 1856 . . . . . . } 79.70 per 1,000.
Ditto in Bengal army during 1865-6 . . . . 72.55 „ „
Gain . . . . 6.15.

[Since

Of course the whole of those invalided home do not die ; but in the absence of statistics showing the mortality among this class, and knowing that soldiers are not sent home for any trifling ailments, it may be assumed that few, if any, ever again return to duty. The great majority are invalided for discharge from the service ; the minority for change of climate. The former class are as much lost to the service as though dead, while the progress of tropical disease must eventually kill many of the latter. Moreover, before the true value of local sanitary arrangements can be estimated, other conditions, tending to reduce mortality, must be considered. There are the Ten Years' Enlistment Act, and the number of Queen's troops now in the country. It is a well-authenticated fact, supported by physiological arguments and experience,[1] and demonstrated by numerous statistical tables,[2] that the mortality of Europeans in the tropics increases with length of service. Acclimatization of the inhabitants of temperate zones to the widely different circumstances of the tropics has never yet been accomplished. As the negro[3] and Esquimaux[4] sicken and die when removed to temperate regions, so the European degenerates, and ultimately succumbs, when transported near the equator. Could the Anglo-Saxon race be introduced into India in successive waves and through centuries of time, as were the Aryan Hindoos during their gradual passage from the Hindoo Koosh, it is certainly probable that acclimatization—involving, however, certain physical and mental changes—would take place. But all experience

Since the above was written, the Report of the Sanitary Commission for Bombay for 1867 has been issued. During that year the loss in the Bombay Presidency amounted to 60.6 per *mille* invalided, and 15.6 died : total 76.2. This, deducted from the total loss in former years, as above, gives only 3.5 as the gain.

[1] Moorhead, Clinical Researches, p. 13 ; and Moore, Health in the Tropics, p. 274.

[2] Report of Royal Sanitary Commission, p. 528.

[3] Davies, Statistics of *New York Medical Times*, 1865.

[4] Hall, Life among the Esquimaux.

forbids any hope of sudden acclimatization. As a rule, Europeans enjoy the best health during their first years of residence in India. Now, as so many soldiers go home under the Ten Years' Enlistment Act, after having served but a comparatively short period in India, and as others whose ten years are not expired often leave with their regiments in the usual course of reliefs, it follows that some reduction of mortality must occur from these causes alone. And we have the means of estimating the increase of mortality consequent on age and prolonged residence. Table 10 of the Royal Sanitary Commissioners' Report gives the average annual mortality at certain periods of service. From this statement it is found that, whereas the death-rate was 47 per 1,000 among men of from 5 to 10 years' service, it increased gradually until it amounted to 62.5 per 1,000 among men of 20 years' service and upwards. The difference between the figures named is 15; only 1 below the 16.06 per 1,000 mentioned as the *apparent gain* from sanitary regulations.

The actual amount of sickness, as shown by the number of admissions into hospital, has been considerably lessened. The returns compiled by Sir Alexander Tulloch show that the attacks of illness among soldiers formerly ranged from 988 to 3,225 per 1,000 annually. A battalion of 1,000 men sent yearly, on an average, 2,045 cases to the hospital, each soldier thus being exposed to two attacks of illness in the year. This is stated to have been the proportion during the ten years ending 1854, before the introduction of the sanitary rules now in force.[1] For the six years ending 1865, the number of admissions into hospital per 1,000 of strength averaged 1,767.[2] Here, then, is indisputable evidence of a diminution of sickness, to the extent of 278 per 1,000. Local sanitation cannot, however, be altogether credited with this improvement. Short periods of service and increase of invaliding, the latter relieving the hospitals

---

[1] Royal Sanitary Commissioners' Report, p. xvi.
[2] *Vide* former tables ; also Royal Sanitary Commissioners' Report.

of the classes most frequenting them, must be taken into
consideration. With such facts before us, it is evident that
too much importance may be attached to local sanitation
as the means by which the total loss to the service has been
reduced. It is demonstrable that other causes have aided
in inducing beneficial results. Could we be furnished with
separate statistics, showing the number of attacks of *primary* disease, we should be better able to estimate the
advantages of sanitation, as now practised in India. If the
number of primary attacks, making due allowance for length
of service and age, approached the ratio of former years,
the effects of climate and the meagre results achieved by
our system of sanitation would be more evident. When the
statistics for the current quinquennial period are published,
it is feared that the continued increase of invaliding, while
perhaps diminishing the death-ratio, will give an average
of total loss greater than for the five years for which figures
are now available.

SOLDIERS' WIVES AND CHILDREN, VITAL STATISTICS OF.

Notwithstanding the reduction of sickness and mortality
among the men, the death-ratio among European women,
as soldiers' wives, remains pretty much as it was twenty
years ago. According to the best authority,[1] European
females died in barracks, in former years, at the rate of
44.4 per 1,000 in Bengal, and at a reduced rate in the
other Presidencies ; but giving a mean for the whole of
India of 35.47 per 1,000. Up to the year 1866, the
mortality in Bengal never fell below 42.[2] Among children
in 1865 the death-rate in Bengal is stated to have been
83 per 1,000,[3] and in 1866, 75.11 per 1,000.[4] Ten or

---

[1] Chevers, *Ind. Ann. Med. Science*, vol. xii.

[2] Second Bengal Sanitary Report, p. 26. In 1866, in Bengal, the
mortality of the women fell to 26 per 1,000 ; but however favourable
this appears, it cannot yet be accepted as the average rate.

[3] Op. cit. p. 26.

[4] Third Bengal Sanitary Report, p. 100.

twelve years back, the ratio was almost the same, viz. 84 per 1,000 in the Presidency[1] last named, and 70.7 in Bombay. Now it is certain that if sanitary regulations, as adopted in our military cantonments, had been altogether instrumental in reducing the mortality of the men, so would the chances of life of the women and children be increased by such measures. But this is shown not to have been the case. The mortality among females and children has not diminished from the ratio it attained in former years; and the explanation of this would appear to be, that women and children are seldom invalided. Even in the usual course of reliefs, comparatively few women and children return to England. It is the married man who generally prefers remaining in India. Hence, length of residence, notwithstanding all sanitary arrangements, tells on the European female. No less authority than Mr. Simon has observed that "a high local mortality among children must always necessarily denote a high local prevalence of those causes which determine degeneration of race." That such influence has not yet been eradicated from India by sanitary reform, must be painfully apparent.

It is well to face the facts bravely, and admit that some penalty, in the shape of sickness and mortality, must be paid as the price of tropical possessions. The Army Statistical Blue Books incontrovertibly demonstrate that loss of service from sickness and death increases as the military stations stand south-east of Great Britain, until the acme is reached in India or China. We therefore do not entertain the Utopian idea that Europeans on the plains of India, under any system of sanitation, will ever enjoy the robust health characteristic of similar classes in Great Britain; either a heavy mortality or a long invaliding list must be accepted. We have now to a great extent removed the money loss consequent on a soldier's death, to the expenditure under the head of

[1] Chevers, *Ind. Ann. Med. Science.*

invaliding; *plus* the expense of maintaining as ineffective, for an indefinite period, either from military or civil sources, all those who ultimately die, or who are discharged with broken health from the service. It has been shown that the mortality among the men during the first period of the sanitary era, or to 1865, was 28.55 per 1,000, being a reduction of 22.15 from the 50.70 for the period ending 1856. This, however satisfactory, falls far short of the mortality, 8 per 1,000, among the rank and file at home. In order still more to assimilate home and Indian sickness and death-rates, greater advantage must be taken of the climates of elevated regions. Hill stations are indeed, more than ever, State necessities.

SOLDIERS' WIVES AND CHILDREN, CONDITION OF.

Although the mortality of these classes is not, as previously demonstrated, materially reduced, their position has been considerably improved. European families do not now, as was formerly too often the case, lodge in one room, "with no other separation than the curtains drawn round the bed."[1] At present twelve per cent. of strength are permitted to marry, and it is remarked, that in the majority of corps this number is scarcely attained. Formerly, the State allowed each European wife five rupees, and each woman of country birth two and a half rupees per mensem. For each child, half the subsistence-money of the mother was passed. These rates, as regards the women, have recently been increased to eight rupees per month.

By G.O. No. 509 of 1860,[2] preserved milk was allowed to nursing women and children on board ship. More recently, half and quarter rations for women and children were sanctioned, in addition to ordinary subsistence allowance, when the exigencies of the service require the

[1] *Vide* Evidence before Royal Sanitary Commissioners.
[2] *Calcutta Gazette*, 1860, p. 1070.

separation of the men from their families.[1] Subsistence
was also granted to the families of soldiers, volunteering
from regiments going home, and who might be in excess
of the prescribed twelve per cent.,[2]—an order which one
may well wonder had never been issued before.

Subsistence money and barrack accommodation have
also been allowed, for a period of six months, to all
soldiers' families who, from any cause, find, on their arrival
in India, they have no claim to the ordinary provision ;[3]
while in case of death of the husband on foreign service,
the period for which the family claims subsistence dates
to the time of intimation of the event to the party concerned.[4] Before leaving this subject, I may remark, that
there is scarcely any more difficult subject to deal with
than marriage in the army. Both morally and medically,
there can be little doubt of the desirability of a large
number of married men among the rank and file. There
can be no question that marriage opposes a barrier to
immorality of a certain nature, and consequently to
disease. Sir John Lawrence himself stated: "I believe
a great deal of the unhealthiness (among soldiers) arises
from their being unmarried. I have always observed
myself, among Europeans, that those who were married
were better and more steady fellows, more manageable,
and less likely to get into scrapes and mischiefs than the
unmarried men."[5] Some, urging that the public service,
or rather the Government, has no right to debar its servants from matrimony, propose that the percentage shall,
at least, be increased from twelve to twenty-five. Few,
however, of the experienced officers who were examined
before the Royal Sanitary Commission were disposed to
add to the former number. Colonel Durand remarked,
"However much one's feelings might go in favour of

[1] *Gazette of India*, 1864, p. 49.   [2] Ibid. 1864, p. 538.
[3] *Calcutta Gazette*, 1860, p. 2,302.   [4] Ibid.
[5] Evidence before the Royal Sanitary Commissioners, Blue Book,
vol. i.

extending the permission to marry in India, I must say I
am not at all clear that it would be an advisable thing."
Colonel Campbell, when asked if it would be well to increase the proportion to twenty-five per cent., replied,
"Certainly not." Brigadier-General Russell would have no
objection to a slight increase under " certain restrictions."
Colonel Greathead, while admitting that an increase
would in many respects be advantageous, discerns almost
" fatal objections." The whole matter is, however, simply
a question of finance. As with many other desirable
objects, the condition of the public revenue will long,
probably ever, forbid the spectacle of a standing army
of married men, either in England or India. So long
as sufficient means are not available, the mere affording
greater facilities for the contraction of matrimony would
be an evil rather than an advantage. It has been
proposed to limit the term of military service to
very short periods, as six years, under the idea that
men would then leave the service, get married, and
become the better citizens from their previous military training. The policy of such a step is, however,
questionable.

TRANSPORTS.

In 1864, under instructions from the Secretary of State,
the Admiralty scale of provisions was ordered to be
adopted in all troop-ships leaving India.[1] At a later
period, some modifications were made ; the chief being an
addition to the amount of limejuice issued, and the replace-
ment of the weight lost by salt meat during cooking.[2] But
the most important change connected with the subject is
the establishment of the Government Overland Transport
Service, through the medium of the magnificent vessels
recently built for the purpose. The long-cherished idea,

---

[1] G.O.G.G., No. 772 of 1864.
[2] G.O.G.G., No. 1011 of 1867.

that the voyage round the Cape acts as a kind of preparation or acclimatization on men proceeding from one zone to another, is now confessed to be erroneous. Neither does rapid change to a temperate climate from the tropics prove injurious, provided ordinary precautions are taken, excepting in the case of certain maladies which any medical officer is able to define.

The magnitude and importance of the Transport service in a sanitary sense are obvious. Invalids may be transported to a different climate within the space of a few days; and the very knowledge of being on the homeward route is to many a more powerful stimulus than any medicine. The physiological effects of the rapid changes of climate will probably prove a powerful therapeutic agent; and when the hospital at Suez is complete, the necessity for conveying all sick from the heat of the tropics to the cold of England will not exist. Healthy men, again, will be landed fresh from Europe on the shores of India, and therefore in the possession of the maximum of vital and physical energy.

VACCINATION.

There are, I believe, no British provinces without a staff of paid vaccinators, presided over by a European superintendent. But although tens of thousands are thus vaccinated annually, existing establishments are scarcely adequate to the duties which should be performed; yet the State can scarcely be expected to vaccinate all gratuitously. In European countries, it is only the poorer classes who are thus favoured; those able to pay for the performance of the operation would, as a rule, decline even this eleemosynary aid from the hands of the parish or dispensary doctor. In India, however, it is different; not one native in a thousand will willingly pay for prevention of disease, although the majority are ready to promise liberally for cure. Moreover, in many parts of India there

is an objection based on religious grounds, against interfering with the course of smallpox; vaccination, in fact,
is considered as little short of sacrilege. "Seetla" and
"Mata" are regarded as goddesses, to whom old and
young, rich and poor, are bound to pay homage. An
attack of smallpox is actually in some districts esteemed a
favour; particularly when the disease passes off lightly.[1]
Festivals in the honour of these deities are held all over
India; near many villages is a holy spot called "Mata Ka
Than" (the place of Mata). It was but a year or two
ago that H.H. the Maharaja Scindiah, G.C.S.I., on the
seizure of a member of his family by smallpox, spent
several lacs of rupees in feeding Brahmans, in paying for
the beating of gongs and the blowing of shells, in order to
propitiate the mythical deity who is supposed to reign over
this disease.

The practice of *inoculation* is, however, the great means
by which smallpox is disseminated in India. Every fresh
case produced by inoculation becomes a centre of infection.
When a person afflicted with smallpox either naturally,
or artificially by inoculation, comes in contact with the
unprotected and uninfected, the latter are almost certain
to contract the disease; and this goes on daily, from Cape
Comorin to the Himalayas. In Great Britain and most
European countries, vaccination is now *compulsory;* if there
are objections to such a law for India, there should certainly be none to the prohibition of the spread of a
loathsome disease by *inoculation*, and by the exposure of
infected persons in public places.

As regards vaccine operations, until comparatively recent
periods, a too general mistake has been committed. Blame
and praise have been too often meted out according as
vaccination showed a large or small number submitted to
the operation; hence, probably, many of the false returns
so frequently complained of as submitted by native assis-

[1] Moore, Marwar, the Land of Death : *Ind. Ann. Med. Science*,
vol. xx.

tants. It would be better thoroughly to vaccinate a village community or district, and thereby to let the people see the true value of the prophylactic. Sir J. Y. Simpson[1] of Edinburgh has latterly stated his deliberate opinion that it is quite possible to "stamp out" smallpox altogether by vaccination and isolation of the sick. If the experiment were thoroughly tried in localities where Hindoo prejudices in favour of "Mata" and "Seetla" least abound, the result would demonstrate (as it has often previously done) that careful vaccination is the certain preventive of smallpox. Did space permit, the relative liability of vaccinated and unvaccinated to smallpox might be shown to be highly in favour of the former;[2] while the rapid decline of the malady in Great Britain since vaccination was adopted, and especially since compulsory vaccination became the law, might also be adduced. But to secure the full value of vaccination, the operation must be carefully performed by competent persons, the lymph must be chosen, taken, and preserved as skill and experience dictate, and above all, both the subject selected from which lymph is secured, and those to which it is conveyed, should possess at least ordinarily robust constitutions and health. Vaccination cannot be regarded a sa purely mechanical duty; and the better educated the men employed as vaccinators may be, the more likely is their practice to prove successful.

The only alterations of importance which have been instituted in the Vaccination Department during recent periods are the revision of certain establishments, the appointment of European medical officers as superintendents-general for various provinces, and the introduction of the system of vaccinating from lymph preserved in glass tubes instead of from the crust, where circumstances do not admit of the actual conveyance of the lymph from person to person.

---

[1] *Medical Times*, Feb. 1, 1868.
[2] *Vide* Ballard on Vaccination, its Value and alleged Dangers : 1868.

VEGETABLES, CULTIVATION OF.

A very important point connected with the diet of Europeans in India, and especially of soldiers, is a due supply of fresh vegetable food. The Scorbutic diathesis is a very prevalent condition among both Europeans and natives, and there are extensive tracts, particularly in Western India, where scurvy may be said to be endemic. It cannot be too frequently insisted upon, that there is in most Anglo-Indian constitutions an underlying scorbutic taint, to which the term " latent scurvy "[1] has been applied. This condition may scarcely afford even obscure evidence of its presence until the individual becomes affected with one or other of the maladies of the tropics, or until some other exciting cause is applied. For instance, the diathesis exists among the men of a regiment, European or native, but the death-ratio and sickness is small. The regiment moves, perhaps on active service, when the attendant fatigue and privations induce the development of scurvy. From precisely similar causes, the malady frequently develops among pilgrims travelling long distances to the famous Indian shrines. In this manner, the latter are debilitated, and therefore incur a further predisposition to the cholera, from which they so frequently suffer. Latent scurvy, moreover, predisposes the system to malarious diseases and dysentery, aggravating them when present. The union of scorbutic, malarious, and syphilitic cachexia, so often seen among both Europeans and natives in India, is one of the most intractable maladies the physician can be called upon to treat. There is reason to suppose the Delhi boil, Aden ulcer, Scinde boil, and other local maladies of similar nature, are but manifestations of a hidden scorbutic taint.[2] Dr. Parkes[3] truly observes, "If scurvy were prevented, every other war-

---

[1] Moore, Health in the Tropics, p. 227.
[2] Chevers, *Ind. Ann. Med. Science*, vol. xii.
[3] Practical Hygiene. p. 595.

disease would be comparatively trifling." Happily, attacks
of scurvy afflicting whole regiments and ships' companies
are now rare. During recent years, however, scurvy in an
epidemic form has appeared among Europeans in India,
evidencing that, as regards vegetable antiscorbutic diet,
very little neglect will cause the development of disease.
As a rule, people in India insensibly acquire a habit of
consuming less antiscorbutic vegetable material than is
actually necessary, and than Europeans habitually use in
Europe. This partly arises from scarcity of fresh vegetables of the desired species, and partly from the loss of
appetite experienced during the hot weather. The diet of
natives, also, even when vegetable, does not comprise a
just proportion of fresh antiscorbutic material.

During the last ten years, various attempts have been
made to secure a better supply of vegetables for the troops.
In 1860, with the view of encouraging soldiers' gardens,
station-committees were appointed to fix the price to be
paid to the men for vegetables.[1] But, notwithstanding
different orders on the subject, and much encouragement,
soldiers' gardens do not (and cannot be expected to) supply
sufficient vegetables for the consumption of the army.
Every regiment, indeed, will not become a gardening
regiment. Hence the barrack-tables are yet dependent on
contractors, who in many places find difficulty in producing
the requisite amount and quality. And so it must be
until the natives take to cultivating European vegetables,
especially the potato, for their own consumption. And to
this, on sanitary grounds, they should be encouraged by
civil officers.

Among all edible vegetables, the potato is that possessing the nutritive and antiscorbutic properties to the greatest
extent. In Ireland, the labouring classes have for upwards
of a century been constantly fed on potatoes, and all must
admit the general *physique* of the "finest peasantry in the
world." Buckle[2] traces the proverbial debasement and

---

[1] *Calcutta Gaz.*, 1860, p. 1925.   [2] Hist. of Civilization, vol. i. p. 108.

want of physical energy of the Hindoo principally to the
food he eats. Rice, although one of the most nutritious
of cereals, is deficient in nitrogenous elements. To render
this grain equal in nutritive properties to bread, ninety-two
per cent. of grain, or chunna, is required.[1] The reproductive
power of the potato is also enormous. One acre of average
land planted with this tuber will support twice as many
persons as the same space sown with wheat. No skill,
and little irrigation, is required for its cultivation. The root
can be carried about without the edible portion coming in
contact with anything unclean, can be easily cooked, and
therefore appears in every respect peculiarly fitted for the
food either of Mahommedans or Brahmans. By the cultivation of the potato, the natives would gain an article of diet
possessing great nutritive and acknowledged antiscorbutic
properties, while Europeans would be able to purchase in
the markets, where at the present time, in many districts,
the potato is never seen for sale. In 1864[2] some attempts
were made to raise potatoes from New Zealand and
English seed, but the yield, at most of the places where
the experiment was tried, was not satisfactory. There
are, however, innumerable localities where the soil and
climate are well fitted for the cultivation of this and other
European vegetables.

The great scarcity of such necessaries in many stations
(particularly in Western India) occupied by European
troops has resulted in a proposal to supply, in lieu, a proportion of European compressed preserved vegetables.[c]

VENEREAL DISEASE, PREVENTION OF.

As we are unable to apply the means of preventing
prostitution, viz. universal morality and marriage, it is now
pretty generally admitted that endeavours to lessen or

---

[1] *Vide* table composed by Dr. Forbes Watson.
[2] *Gazette of India*, May 14, 1864.
[c] No. 318 Circular, P. I. G. Med. Depart. Bombay, 1867.

mitigate resulting disease are justifiable. Until the character of our soldiery and populace generally may be elevated above the instinctive frailty of humanity, there can be no doubt of the propriety of instituting a well-regulated prophylaxis to syphilis. The following table, showing the prevalence of the disease during recent years (from 1861 to 1865) as compared with a former period (the ten years ending 1856), abundantly demonstrates that not only has there been no very decided diminution of syphilis among European soldiers in India, but also the necessity of lessening, by any lawful means, the loss to the service entailed by this malady.

PERIODS.	BENGAL.		MADRAS.		BOMBAY.		INDIA.	
	Ratio per 1,000.		Ratio per 1,000.		Ratio per 1,000.		Ratio per 1,000.	
	Admitd.	Died.	Admitd.	Died.	Admitd.	Died.	Admitd.	Died.
Ten years ending 1856 . .	209.2	0.44	329.0	0.49	267.2	0.22	268.4	0.38
1861	361.4	0.37	259.6	0.37	342.6	0.57	321.2	0.49
1862	307.7	0.30	294.2	0.24	302.1	0.42	301.3	0.32
1863	272.8	0.28	253.6	0.40	262.4	0.16	266.6	0.28
1864	241.5	0.33	271.9	0.62	243.7	0.41	249.0	0.45
1865	216.9	0.27	223.4	0.23	191.8	0.25	210.0	0.25

From the figures given in the Army Blue Books it may also be ascertained that the proportion during the quinquennium ending 1855, invalided on account of venereal disease, amounts to nearly 80 per 1,000 of the whole number invalided. And although the actual death-ratio attributed to syphilitic affections bears but a small ratio to the total mortality, it must be recollected that many cases of so-called debility and rheumatism are in fact cases of *syphilitic cachexia*, or syphilitic rheumatism, aggravated by malarial degeneration. The condition of system resulting from the union of two or all of the undermentioned blood deteriorations—syphilitic, malarial, scorbutic—constitutes one of the most intractable forms of disease afflicting the human race. Each one present aggravates the other; the syphilitic cachexia rendering the frame more susceptible to both malaria and scurvy.

The desirability of measures for the prevention of venereal disease early attracted attention, and in 1795 Lock Hospitals were established in certain stations in Bengal. But an outcry was raised against them on account of their supposed demoralizing tendency, and, although statistical evidence proved their beneficial effect, they were abolished in 1830 by order of Lord William Bentinck.

Still, however, in most military cantonments some little supervision was exercised over public prostitutes by the bazaar authorities. But it was not until 1864 that, by the new Cantonment Magistrates Act,[1] the prevention of all matters affecting public health, safety, and convenience was legalized. According to the provisions of this Statute, measures for the prevention of venereal disease having been framed and approved by local governments,[2] are now acted on in most cantonments. These consist, with local modifications, in the registration of public prostitutes, the prohibition of public prostitution by unregistered women, the adoption of means for the detection of venereal disease among registered women, the establishment of Lock Hospitals for the treatment and detention of women suffering from such malady.

In 1867, the surgeon of H.M. ship *Octavia* brought to notice the great prevalence of syphilis among sailors, and suggested that the Act known as the "Contagious Diseases Act" should be enforced at Bombay, Madras, and Calcutta, as at Malta and other British possessions, where its introduction has been followed by very beneficial results. The commodore commanding Indian stations also urged the matter on the attention of Government. Accordingly the Contagious Diseases Act was brought before the Supreme

---

[1] Act XXII. of 1864.
[2] Bengal Second Annual Sanitary Report.

Council and passed during 1868 [1]—from which much good
may be expected.

WATER.

The Royal Sanitary Commissioners, in their report
several times referred to, state the unsatisfactory condition
of the water supply to be one of the cardinal defects at
Indian stations, and they recommend a comprehensive
system of analysis, and measures for the constant supply
of pure filtered water to all public buildings.   As there is
no doubt certain diseases, as cholera, typhoid or intestinal fever, dracunculus, malarious fever, &c., may be conveyed into the system through the medium of water,[2] any

[1] *Gazette of India*, Supplement, 1868, p. 479.

[2] That diseases of various kinds are conveyed into the system by
water we have convincing evidence.   As regards *Cholera:* In 1849
Dr. Snow first pointed out the probability of cholera germs being conveyed into the Metropolitan, Horselydown, and Wandsworth districts
through the medium of the water supply.   In 1854 occurred the
celebrated instance of the Broad Street pump.   The spread of cholera
in Russia has also been traced to the use of melted snow, on which
cholera evacuations had been thrown.   *Diarrhœa.*—Organic or in-
organic matter suspended in water will alike induce diarrhœa.   Most
people who have drunk the water of Aden, Nusseerabad, or Marwar,
will admit this.   Mr. Cox (*Sanitary Review*, No. 1) gives some striking
instances of diarrhœa from impure water; also *vide* "Report on
the West Coast of Africa:" *Army Stat. San. Med. Report*, 1863 :
also "Evidence before the Royal Sanitary Commissions," vol. i.
p. 475.   *Dysentery.*—Vide *Madras Med. Journal*, No. x. p. 354;
"Practical Hygiene" by Dr. Parkes, p. 63.   *Guinea-worm.*—Vide
Carter, *Bomb. Med. Phys. Soc.*, 1853; Moore, "Manual of Diseases
of India," p. 192.   *Tapeworms and other Entozoa.* — Vide Dr.
Knocks, *Lancet*, January 25, 1862 ; Parkes, "Practical Hygiene;"
Aikin, "Practice of Medicine," vol. ii. p. 125.   *Leeches.*—Parkes,
"Practical Hygiene," p. 44; *Army Stat. San. Med. Report*, 1863.
Yellow fever.—Vide "Papers respecting the Origin of Yellow Fever
in Bermuda." *Malarious fever.*—Hippocrates and Rhazes held the
opinion that malarious fevers and spleen affections arise from bad
water.   So do the Singhalese (Marshall, "Medical Topography of
Ceylon," p. 52); also the inhabitants of Hungary and Holland,
when obliged to drink marsh water, always mix spirits (Parkes,
"Practical Hygiene," p. 52).   The inhabitants of the Eusufzye attribute

one recollecting the condition of the sources of supply in former years, or even in some localities at the present time, must admit that the Royal Commissioners could scarcely be too severe in their remarks. The open wells, the too frequent fæcal contamination of surrounding localities, the mode (still practised) of conveying the water for house use, the dirty tanks, from which so many draw their supply, and the total absence of analysis, were among the chief subjects of complaint; the majority of which, in British cantonments at least, have been wholly or partially removed.

Shortly after the organization of the Indian Sanitary Commissions, the Bengal Board proposed, in accordance with the previous recommendation of the British Commission, a comprehensive analysis of all waters used in the cantonments of the Bengal Presidency. Medical officers were detached for the purpose of receiving practical instructions in the art of analysing water, and a report on the subject has been recently published.

In order to render tank water, used by the inhabitants of so many villages, drinkable, Mr. Campbell,[1] Inspector of Police in North Canara, recommended double baskets with charcoal between to be placed in the water, which filtering through appears clear and limpid inside. Of course

fever to impure water (Lyell, *Ind. Ann. Med. Science*, vol. iii.). In Albania it is the same (Marsden, *Edin. Med. Journal*, Feb. 1862). The inhabitants of the Shevaroy Hills believe the water of the plains produces fever (Cornish, *Madras Med. Journal*, October 1861). The waters of nullahs have been supposed to cause fevers (Bombay Gov. Records, No. 20). Instances of malarious fever following the use of impure water are also on record; *vide* Moore, " Health in the Tropics," pp. 164, 165. Parkes, " Practical Hygiene," p. 53, mentions several places in India and Europe where *ague* ceased after good wells were constructed. Nothing can be stronger than both the positive and negative evidence of the connexion between malarious fevers and impure water. Other maladies conveyed by the medium of this fluid are stone in the bladder, goitre, paralysis (from lead impregnation), dyspepsia, gout.

[1] Papers relating to the North Canara Epidemic: *Calcutta Gazette*, 1863.

such structures might be made of more durable material than basket-work. It does not appear that this plan, although so simple and efficacious, was adopted, but the suggestion deserves to be generally known and acted upon.

Another proposal is that of digging holes in the immediate neighbourhood of tanks, into which comparatively clear water filters.[1]

The question also of the purification or deterioration of water by the presence and action of aquatic plants and animal life has received much attention.[2] By direction of Government in 1865-6 upwards of 100 officers, 27 of whom were medical men, were consulted on this subject; the result being a decision that both animal and vegetable life are requisite for the due oxygenation and purification of water.[3]

In 1867, opinions were called for regarding the best means of purifying or filtering water for drinking purposes. The result of this inquiry has not, however, at the period of writing, been made public.

The preceding review, although confessedly imperfect, of the progress of sanitation in India, while showing that very much has been effected or attempted, also proves the absence of certain requirements, without which further improvement cannot be confidently expected. The aim of all State medicine and hygiene is the welfare and conse-

---

[1] Memorandum by Dr. Arnott, Inspector-General of Hospitals, Bombay, Nov. 1865.

[2] If vegetable and animal life exist together in certain proportions, stagnant water need not necessarily be bad, as carbonic acid and oxygen are given off in compensatory ratio. If the equilibrium is destroyed, the water becomes bad or putrid.

[3] When Sir Charles Napier was Commander-in-chief, he observed native soldiers drawing water from a foul cooking tank, covered with a slimy greenish weed. This was ordered to be cleared away, the result being, that the water soon turned putrid; not becoming wholesome until a fresh crop of the weed had been produced.

quent happiness, the longevity and resulting increase in the productive power, of the people. It may, indeed, be asserted that the country in which the most careful attention is paid to such matters will, *cæteris paribus*, become the greatest and most powerful. In India, indeed, there is an additional incentive to sanitation in the broadest sense of the term. The manner in which we must consent to hold this country is now clearly apparent. The economical possession of Hindostan by the British rests mainly on sanitary art; for without the strong arm the sword is as nothing. The expectation of brilliant and rapid fortunes, formerly so alluring to Anglo-Indian adventurers, does not now exist: hence the greater necessity of rendering the country more tolerable and habitable that it even now is for Europeans. It cannot be too frequently repeated that, with certain allowance for climatic peculiarities, health in India is to be promoted by similar means, and by the same considerations, as regulate sanitary matters in other countries. As, however, was the case in Europe, so in India, time is required to improve, consolidate, conciliate, and teach.

The more urgent necessities at present existing, are perhaps as follows :—For the benefit of those few officials, civil or military, juvenile or senile, mentioned in the introduction to these remarks, who still passively or actively ignore sanitation, an authoritative intimation of the imperative necessity of acting according to the spirit of the orders of Government; for the health, and comfort, and increased value of life of the European soldier, a more extended occupation of the mountain ranges and elevated regions of India; for the public benefit, an Act rendering the exposure of persons affected with contagious diseases punishable. This should include the conveyance of persons suffering from cholera, or smallpox, in railway carriages; to prevent which no laws at present exist. Inoculation with smallpox matter should also be made penal, and the spread of vaccination encouraged by some more certain

means than are now employed. The passage of persons
infected with any contagious disease into British territory
should be authoritatively interdicted, and the native
princes should be requested to institute efficient sanitary
measures within their own dominions. For, situated as
the independent states now are—in many instances altogether surrounded by British territory—we can scarcely
expect to maintain the latter free from epidemic malady,
while disease may be imported daily from the former.
Mofussil (or rural) sanitation is also a *sine quâ non.* As
already remarked, experience proves that there is a limit
beyond which neglect of sanitation is incompatible with
human existence. Villagers should be compelled by law
to institute and carry out ordinary sanitary regulations in
their localities. And in this nothing impracticable is
involved. Ordinary sanitation and common cleanliness
are almost synonymous in meaning ; and it does not
appear too much to expect this proportion of duty towards
his neighbour from every member of a community. No
man should be permitted to endanger the health and life
of his fellows by measures, or by neglect, tending to disseminate epidemic disease, any more than by the discharge
of fire-arms, or by the infliction of grievous injury or
bodily hurt in other ways. Lastly, there are the questions
of a better vegetable supply, of an improved method of
conveying water for household use, of the disafforestment
of mountains and lowlands* now going on, of the requirements of cinchona planting, of the measures for prevention
of contagious diseases, with many other matters urgently
requiring prolonged attention from the sanitarian.

APPENDIX.

Despatch from the Secretary of State to the Governor-General of India, dated March 11, 1869, relative to the proposal to provide inducements, in the shape of increased Pension and Bonus, for Officers of the Indian Army to retire.

INDIA OFFICE, LONDON, March 11, 1869.

My LORD,—

Par. 1. I have very carefully considered in Council your Despatch, No. 443, dated November 7, 1868, forwarding certain papers relating to the present condition and future prospects of the several Staff corps, and proposing a scheme for inducing a limited number of the senior officers to retire at once, and for the prevention of an undue growth of the class of field-officers in future by certain modifications in the present retiring rules.

2. After reviewing the several opinions expressed on this subject by Sir W. Mansfield, Sir R. Temple, and Colonel Norman, and referring to the statements and calculations given in a memorandum by the Controller-General of Military Expenditure, your Government state that, having given this important question due consideration, and carefully weighed the several suggestions contained in the Minutes above referred to, you feel bound to record your opinion that some remedial measures are indispensably necessary, especially to meet the present exceptional increasing excess of field-officers, and generally to counteract the permanent tendency to an undue proportion of the higher grades, and to an extravagant number of recipients of the colonel's allowance.

3. With reference also to the existence of a considerable number of unemployed officers, many of them of the higher grades, who are either unfitted for or unwilling to accept employment, your Government recommend the following measures:—

1st. That, within a limit of 200, any substantive lieutenant-colonels in the Indian Staff corps or Indian army, who are entitled to a retiring pension, may be allowed to retire with an addition of 150*l.* per annum to whatever pension they may be entitled to, together with a bonus of 1,000*l.*, provided they do so within a given date from the issue of the order sanctioning the measure, such date not to be less than six or more than twelve months distant; the senior applicants to have the first claims. 2d. That, as regards those officers who may retire subsequent to that date, the period entitling them to the lieutenant-colonel's pension of 365*l.* per annum may be twenty-five instead of twenty-eight years as heretofore, including three years' furlough; and the period entitling to the colonel's pension thirty instead of thirty-two years, including four years' furlough. Further, that the colonel's pension may be increased from 456*l.* 5*s.* to 500*l.* per annum. 3d. That it may be notified that, from the date fixed as the limit for retirement with the additional pension and bonus, the system of appointing field-officers to perform general or station duty will cease, and all those who may be holding no appointment, civil or military, permanent or officiating, will be placed on an unemployed list. 4th. That such as remain continuously unemployed for a period of three years, will, after that period, be restricted to the English pay of their rank without any Indian allowances, but will be allowed to reside wherever they may elect, either in India or in Europe; and that, when they may have been continuously out of employ for a total period of five years, they will be placed on the retired list, with the pension to which they may then be entitled. Lastly. That all officers who may be considered by Government and the Commander-in-chief as unfit for either civil or military employment suitable to their rank, will be transferred to the retired list, if entitled to pension, or to the half-pay list, if not so entitled.

4. I have perused these papers, and considered your proposals with much care and attention, and have now to inform your Excellency of the reasons which have led her Majesty's Government to dissent from the conclusions at which you have arrived, and to withhold their sanction from the several measures submitted by your Government with a view to facilitating retirement among the senior officers of the Indian service.

5. The grounds upon which your proposals are based on the present occasion are mainly financial.

6. You apprehend an alarming increase of expenditure on account of officers in receipt of the colonel's allowance, as a result of the strong inducement to remain in the service held out to them at the present time, in the certainty of attaining that great prize within a given period ; and you hope, by the measures now proposed, to prevent the evil which you thus anticipate, and further to remove, in a great degree, the present burden of unemployed officers. You seem to entertain some apprehension, also, of administrative difficulties arising from an undue proportion of field-officers in the several Staff corps.

7. The apprehension expressed in these papers of future embarrassment arising from the organization and present condition of the several Staff corps appears to me excessive, and in a great measure unfounded.

8. In the allusion so frequently made to the large number of field-officers in these corps, there is a too great tendency to measure their organization by the conventional standard of a British regiment, to which they bear no analogy.

9. On the creation of these corps as substitutes for the bodies of British officers in the Indian service previously borne on regimental lists, an entirely new system of promotion was introduced, after much deliberation ; a system under which the maintenance of a fixed proportion between the several grades was given up as unnecessary in a body formed for staff employment only.

10. The object aimed at was to render service in these corps attractive by the certainty of regular promotion in the army ; and it cannot be affirmed that under this system the promotion of officers destined to pass the best years of their lives in India is unreasonably rapid.

11. The effect of it, however, will of necessity be to increase the proportion of officers of the higher grades ; an effect which will be the more marked, inasmuch as, of the twelve years' service in the grade of subaltern required for promotion to the rank of captain, at the least two, and in practice more than two, will be passed in a line regiment ; and thus very few officers will be borne on the rolls of the Staff corps in the grade of subaltern for more than eight or nine years.

12. And I must remind your Excellency that the employment of the officers of an Indian Staff corps is practically, and has been authoritatively declared to be, independent of their military rank. I need hardly point out, indeed, that an officer's fitness for a staff situation, whether in a civil or military department, does not depend on his army rank, but upon his moral, physical, and intellectual qualities; and no better evidence can be required in support of this view of the case than the fact that officers of the Staff corps promoted from time to time under the present system from one grade to another, are not necessarily disturbed in the appointments they hold, or disqualified by such promotion for the duties they have to perform. In fact, the men are the same in age and qualification, though it may be in a different and higher grade from that which they would have held under the former system. Thus, many officers who would have been subalterns, and perhaps brevet captains, under the old rules, are now substantive captains; but not, therefore, the less qualified for the performance of similar duties.

13. Admitting, however, the propriety of conforming to usage and tradition in regard to regimental service, and of providing officers of the subaltern grade for the subordinate positions with native regiments, as well as a certain proportion of young officers for departmental employment, there is no reason to doubt but that the several Staff corps, in their normal condition, will at all times provide sufficient numbers for this purpose.

14. The number of native regiments, even were it considered necessary that the regimental staff should be of the subaltern grade, which is certainly not the case, would, at four subalterns per regiment, require about 700 subalterns, whereas a very simple calculation will show that in the normal state of the Staff corps the number of subalterns, assuming Colonel Norman's estimate of their aggregate strength to be correct, will be generally between 1,000 and 1,100.

15. At the present time, it appears from the statement of the Controller of Military Finance, in paragraph 31, that there are in the service, including officers on the local list, not less than 1,069 officers of the subaltern grade; and yet frequent allusion is made to the want of subalterns, many of them moreover being placed in departmental employment in positions not unsuited to officers

of higher grade, while others are unemployed from not having passed.

16. The introduction of the Staff corps, with new and more favourable rules of promotion, and the transfer of nearly the whole of the remaining officers of the Indian army to those corps with the immediate benefit of those rules, has of course tended to swell temporarily the numbers in the higher grades; while the contemplated future reduction in the aggregate number of officers required for employment in India, and the actual reduction of the number serving with regiments, places a certain number of officers out of employment until absorbed.

17. As an administrative question, the necessity of maintaining for any time a considerable number of officers out of employment is to be regretted; but considered under its financial aspect, as contrasted with the former state of things, the evil is more apparent than real, inasmuch as the officers who would formerly have been all posted to and employed with regiments are now classed as unemployed in consequence of the introduction of a new regimental organization, involving a great reduction in the number of regimental officers. Indeed, they are only now unemployed in the sense of holding no staff appointment, and are doing duty either in garrisons or with regiments.

18. Upon this subject I shall only further observe that the present lists show very few officers of such length of service as to lead to the supposition that they have become inefficient from that cause. In fact, by far the greater number of the older officers are employed, and many in positions of great responsibility, requiring more than usual experience, energy, and capacity.

19. I cannot, therefore, admit that there are, in this increase in the number of officers of the higher ranks, sufficient grounds for introducing this exceptional measure for inducing some of them to give up the service.

20. I have now to notice your proposal with reference to the present number of unemployed officers.

21. I find, from the latest reports, that the number of officers of the several grades unemployed in India, below the rank of colonel with colonel's allowance, was nearly as follows, viz.:—

	Lieut.-Colonels.	Majors.	Captains.	Lieuts.	Total.
Bengal—Staff Corps .	28	27	18	9	82
,, Local Service .	27	5	14	26	72
Madras—Staff Corps .	23	20	25	19	87
,, Local Service .	17	2	14	17	50
Bombay—Staff Corps .	1	5	7	2	15
,, Local Service	4	—	3	7	14
Total	100	59	81	80	320

And it appears from an analysis of the reports noted in the margin,[1] that the reasons for the non-employment of these officers, as far as they are given, though the reports are incomplete in this respect, are as follow :—

	Lieut.-Colonels.	Majors.	Captains.	Lieuts.	Total.
Not passed, or otherwise unfit. . . . . . }	58	28	48	60	194
Removed for incapacity or misconduct. . . }	1	2	—	3	6
Resigned appointment at their own request . }	7	8	2	2	19
Various causes . . .	32	17	22	5	76
No cause assigned . .	2	4	9	10	25
Total	100	59	81	80	320

22. It appears, therefore, that a large number of these officers are considered ineligible for employment in consequence of their not having qualified in the languages; not a few have been

---

[1] Statements have been prepared from Enclosures to—
    Military Letter from India, No. 487, dated December 22, 1868.
      Ditto   ditto   No. 374, dated September 26, 1868.
      Ditto   from Madras, No. 427, dated November 26, 1868.
      Ditto   from Bombay, No. 136, dated November 25, 1868, par. 15.
The statement of the unemployed local officers in Madras has been prepared from the Army List of October 1, 1868.

allowed to resign employment, and thus by their own act to swell the unemployed list; others have been thrown temporarily out of employment from causes that must always operate to some extent in such a service as that of India, whether in the civil or military departments, since—with a varying number of absentees occasionally vacating appointments during absence—there must inevitably remain at all times a margin of unemployed officers.

23. I understand from your Despatch that you look to the present scheme to reduce this list of unemployed officers.

24. With some misgivings as to the voluntary acceptance of your offers on the part of any very large number of the senior officers, misgivings shared in and expressed by Sir R. Temple in his minute of October 20 last, you say that if the inducement in the shape of either increased pension or bonus were coupled with a notification that this special offer was final, and that after a given date all field-officers continuously unemployed would, like general officers in the Staff corps, be placed on English pay after three years; and that all those who might be considered clearly unfit for military or civil employment suitable to their rank would be removed to the retired list, you are of opinion that a very extensive reduction in the senior grades might be effected.

25. Upon this I must observe, that there are no grounds whatever for anticipating that the officers now unemployed would be more ready to accept the terms offered than other and more efficient men; that, in many cases, to purchase the retirement of officers of the latter class would be to inflict an injury on the State, and to cause considerable embarrassment to the public service; while, with regard to the former, it would be simply, in many instances, to offer a premium upon indolence or incapacity; and I must remind your Excellency, with reference to the coercive measures proposed in this paragraph of the despatch, that your Government would, strictly speaking, be in no better position to enforce these measures after the promulgation of this notice than at present.

26. The officers of the late Indian service who joined the Staff corps, under Lord Cranborne's despatch of August 8, 1866, have been informed that they have not rendered themselves, by so doing, liable to be placed on half-pay, under G.O., No. 826, of September 17, 1861, upon any grounds other than such as would

have justified their removal from the effective strength of the army, had they not joined the Staff corps.

27. Under the spirit of this notification, the removal of an officer who entered the service before 1858, on the ground of his having failed to pass in the native languages, will not be justifiable. Other measures, to which I shall presently allude, must be resorted to, with a view to the speedy reduction of the unemployed list.

28. In the meantime, your General Order No. 1,168, dated December 10, 1868, passed in accordance with the instructions of her Majesty's Government, communicated in Sir Stafford Northcote's Despatch, No. 259, of July 23 last, will, it is hoped, effectually put a stop to the practice of allowing officers on the effective list either to decline or to resign employment, and remain unemployed to suit their own convenience; and it is not without some surprise that I am led to conclude, from the remarks contained in the 37th paragraph of your despatch, that the power of an officer thus to make a convenience of the public service is still practically admitted. So long, however, as this is the case, there can be no limit to the list of unemployed officers, and no want of excuse for expecting some special measures, with a view to getting rid of the burden. Under the present constitution of the Indian military service, it is imperatively necessary that the service at large should understand that no officer can escape active employment but by resigning the service.

29. I have now to consider your proposals in their probable bearing upon the finances of the State.

30. The statements and calculations submitted by the Controller-General of Military Expenditure in his memorandum dated May 23, 1868, lead to such startling results, that I considered it desirable to subject them to the test of investigation by some person thoroughly conversant with questions of this nature; and with this view I caused the whole of the papers to be placed in the hands of Major-General Hannyngton, formerly Military Auditor-General in Bengal, an officer whose ability and experience in the conduct of inquiries of this nature must be well known to your Government.

31. I now forward for your information a copy of his Report, by which you will perceive that the results obtained by the

Controller-General, and upon which the apprehensions of your Government have been raised, are greatly exaggerated; that, instead of the Government saving expense by the adoption of your proposals, it would, if the full number of 200 officers retired, involve an absolute loss to the State of upwards of 467,000*l.*, including an immediate payment of 200,000*l.* (assuming that none of the unemployed officers are absorbed), to say nothing of the inconvenience that might be caused by the simultaneous retirement of many of the most valuable members of the public service.

32. It may, however, be reasonably expected that some of the unemployed officers would accept the offer, and, to the extent of their unemployed pay, the above capital sum would require reduction, but no assurance can be felt that many of this class would do so, not to speak of the impolicy of purchasing the retirement of such as are unemployed by reason of incapacity; while no reliance can be placed on their fitness to succeed to the offices vacated by others, a fact illustrated by the circumstance pointed out in Sir Stafford Northcote's despatch of July 23 last, No. 259, that, while the unemployed list in Bengal had been reduced during the year 1867 by five only, there had been, during the same period, 28 fresh admissions to the Staff corps.

33. It seems, also, from General Hannyngton's Report, that, instead of the number of officers of the several Staff corps receiving the colonel's allowance being likely to amount in 1892 to 981, they will not exceed 487, according to the Controller-General's tables, or 629 according to tables more favourable to life; and that, instead of the total number of such officers both in the Staff corps and local service being 1,154, and the aggregate annual cost on that account 1,227,835*l.*, the entire number will not exceed 573 in the one case, or 740 in the other, and the total cost 644,551*l.* or 832,405*l.*, according to the tables used; and this calculation is made irrespectively of any intermediate retirements on ordinary pension.

34. I must further observe, that, while referring to the inducements now held out to officers to remain in the service, with the view of attaining the colonel's allowance, and calculating the ultimate charge on that account, no allusion seems to be made to the consequent reduced charge for pensions, the fact being

that, in the extreme case supposed, of all surviving officers remaining for the colonel's allowances, those allowances would,
with the pay proper of the officers, represent very nearly the
whole of the cost on account of retired officers, showing an
amount of 832,405*l.* in 1892, against 687,957*l.* as it stood
(shortly after the formation of the Staff corps) in 1863. Meanwhile, a considerable saving is taking place. During the last
five years the charge (excluding that for the medical and clerical
services) has decreased by 13,100*l.* a year.[1] This reduction
will go on for some years to come, and may be fairly regarded
as a not unimportant set-off to a future temporary increase
brought on by the Staff corps, before those corps reach their
normal condition.

35. It would appear, therefore, not only that the alarm which
your Government expressed at the prospect of future expenditure
on this account is unfounded, but that the remedy proposed on
financial considerations would probably result in an absolute and
considerable loss to the State.

36. The above observations relate to a proposal made with a
view to the removal of a temporary embarrassment by the adoption of a special measure. I have now to consider your further
proposals respecting a modification in the present pension rules,
with a view to keeping down in future the number of field-officers
of the several Staff corps.

37. I cannot concur with your Government in the necessity or
expediency of thus holding out special inducements to officers of
the Staff corps to retire before the Government have had the
full benefit of their services. It appears scarcely consistent with
sound policy to create a body of officers, and to hold out inducements to them to enter and qualify for a special service, and
then to frame subsidiary regulations, with the avowed object of
inducing them to retire at a time when their services are most
valuable.

38. There appears to be, in the minds of many, an entire mis-
apprehension of the object with which a scale of pensions is laid
down for any department of the public service ; and this or that
rate of pension is not unfrequently alluded to as insufficient to
meet the requirements of an officer, and the support of his family.

1 See General Hannyngton's Second Report, dated February 15, 1869.

39. The fact is, that pensions are intended, not as inducements to officers to retire while still capable of work, but as a recognition of former services, in the event of their retiring to suit their own convenience, or from failure of health before they have reached a disqualifying age.

40. To tempt men to retire at ages between forty and fifty, by the offer of enhanced pensions, framed with a view of rendering them independent of further employment, would be extremely impolitic; men are then usually in the vigour of life, and have reaped something of that experience which is of special value in India : knowledge of the languages, right understanding of native character, softened prejudices, all the fruits of matured intellect and experience, have then been attained. To encourage early retirement is not only to sacrifice wantonly the interests of the service by depriving it of the best men, but tends also to bring up a class of officers whose thoughts are bent from the first upon early retirement, an object incompatible with an earnest and contented public spirit. The pension is intended generally for the worn-out servant, not offered for the purpose of inducing an efficient public servant to retire.

41. The pensions now granted to the officers retiring from Indian service are framed on a scale more liberal than in any other military service in the world; while the remuneration to those officers, when actually employed, is amply sufficient to enable them in most cases to provide for the present and prospective necessities of their families.

42. The one retiring allowance which is given at the close, or assumed close, of an officer's career, is the colonel's allowance ; and no question has been raised as to the sufficiency and liberality of that allowance.

43. It may be necessary to notice, with regard to this allowance, and to the remark made by your Government as to the inducement held out to officers to remain in the service by the certainty of attaining thereto, that the present rule, which gives the allowance after twelve years' service in the grade of lieutenant-colonel, was introduced, as a purely temporary expedient, to meet the difficulties which arose from the conflicting claims of the officers of the Staff corps prior and subsequent to Lord Cranborne's Despatch of August 8, 1866, and applies only to officers

who joined the Staff corps before or under that despatch; and that, even allowing the aggregate length of service required to qualify for the position under present regulations to be less than the average period within which it was attained under the former system—and, according to the conclusions of the Royal Commission of 1863, it is not much less—the increased inducement to remain must be measured by the difference between those two periods, and cannot be considered independent under the present system, of those contingencies which, from various causes, induced or compelled officers formerly to retire from the service before the attainment of that position. When the time shall have arrived for carrying out the instructions contained in Sir S. Northcote's Despatch of July 9, 1867, No. 184, and placing a limit to the establishment of colonels with colonel's allowance, all apprehension of an undue charge on this account will of necessity come to an end.

It would appear, indeed, from a calculation made by General Hannyngton, that, when the Staff corps shall have attained to its normal condition, the whole of the retiring allowance, including 100 colonels' allowances, will probably not exceed 500,000l. annually.

44. Your proposals have yet to be considered from another point of view, and that is, as affecting the efficiency and contentment of the officers at large.

45. There can be no doubt that the effect of measures of this nature, disturbing the faith of a body of officers in the stability of the ordinary rules of the service, is to excite a general feeling of restlessness and discontent, which even a declaration like that proposed in the 21st paragraph of your despatch would be insufficient to allay for many years.

46. Your Government will remember that a similar declaration was made on the occasion of special annuities being offered to a number of officers in 1861, in the 25th paragraph of Sir C. Wood's Despatch, No. 320, of August 10 of that year, in which the Government of India were instructed to intimate that it was a final arrangement, and that no further proposals connected with schemes for the retirement of Indian officers would be entertained. Notwithstanding this notification, the precedent then established has been made use of to keep alive the expectation

of a similar proceeding in the minds of officers of the army in India. an expectation that has received continual stimulus from the public press, has doubtless tended to arrest the course of ordinary retirements, and has now been, in some measure, justified by the action taken by your Government.

47. The explicit declaration above quoted from Sir C. Wood's despatch may have escaped the attention of your Government ; and, at all events, it will not be irrelevant to notice in this place the claim that officers who have since retired might put forward to participate in any scheme such as that now proposed.

48. The determination of her Majesty's Government not to offer any further inducement to retire will, no doubt, create a feeling of disappointment in the minds of all who were looking forward to the promulgation of some such scheme as that now proposed by your Government ; but, on the other hand, its adoption, especially after the above-quoted announcement by her Majesty's Government in 1861, could hardly fail to create in the service at large a chronic state of dissatisfaction with the retiring rules, and an expectation that each officer in his turn might reasonably expect to derive benefit from some similarly special measure.

49. Another objection to the introduction of measures of this nature, if not absolutely inevitable. deserves notice, while the extensive changes made in the late Indian service are still recent ; and that is, their effect on the minds of that large body of officers who have been transferred from the local to the British army. It is not unreasonable to expect that the contemplation of measures of this nature, from the benefits of which they are excluded by their recent transfer to the British service, would give rise to feelings of irritation and disappointment. greatly to the prejudice of those branches of the service to which these officers belong. and in which they now form a very valuable and important element.

50. It is upon the above considerations that her Majesty's Government have arrived at the conclusion that the adoption of the several proposals contained in your letter under acknowledgment is neither necessary nor expedient.

51. I desire, in conclusion. to communicate to your Excellency the wishes of her Majesty's Government regarding the disposal of

the unemployed officers. These may be divided into two classes:—1. Those qualified in all respects for employment. 2. Those from various causes not qualified.

52. With regard to the former, I need only observe that admission to the Staff corps from the line should be restricted to some extent until this class of unemployed officers has been provided for.

53. With regard to the latter, it must be assumed that their disqualification is due to causes that may be divided into two classes :—1st. Such as would, under the system in force before the amalgamation, have led to their removal from the effective list ; such as moral delinquency or intellectual incapacity. 2d. Not having passed the language test, a disqualification for active employment under present, but not under former rules, according to which an officer of this class might have served with his regiment.

54. Among the latter class it is generally understood that there are many officers otherwise well qualified for active employment, and who in many cases possess a colloquial knowledge of the language. Her Majesty's Government consider it advisable, under present circumstances, that all of this class of officers, whose names were borne on any regimental cadre prior to the re-organization of the army, should be employed on the staff, whether passed or not, in such departments and positions as your Government may consider them individually best fitted for. Such a course of procedure will doubtless involve a departure from an established and very important rule, but can form no embarrassing precedent, inasmuch as all officers, before entering the Staff corps hereafter, must qualify in the native language.

55. In the case of the young officers who entered the service since 1858, and under special conditions, your Government will cause all of them who may not have passed to be addressed individually, and informed that, in the event of their not passing the higher standard within a given period, which it will be for your Government to determine, they will be removed from the service, as her Majesty's Government cannot permit an officer voluntarily to disqualify himself for useful employment, and at the same time to enjoy the benefit of pay and promotion in the public service.

56. With regard to those officers whom it may be considered not desirable to continue in active employment, by reason either of questionable conduct or intellectual incapacity, you will cause

a special report to be made in each case, with a view to their removal from the effective list, upon such conditions as their several cases may render just and expedient.

57. By the adoption of these several measures, it may be confidently expected that the ordinary casualties of the service, and the effect of the new furlough rules upon the number of absentees, will lead to the absorption of the present unemployed officers at no very distant date.

58. I cannot close this despatch without pointing out to your Excellency the evils resulting from the discussion of projects of this nature in India before the views of her Majesty's Government have been sought and ascertained. In the present case, it would appear, from the frequent notices in the public papers, to have been well known for many months past that a scheme of this nature was under consideration; and that, while the date of the Memorandum by the Controller-General of Military Expenditure is May 23, showing that the information therein given must have been for some time under preparation, the Secretary of State, in utter ignorance of what was taking place, replied, on April 3, 1868, to a question put to him in the House of Commons, that no such scheme was contemplated.

59. Not only has the fact of its being under consideration been generally known, but in one case, in the *Calcutta Review* for August 1868, a paper has been published relating to the subject, bearing the clearest marks of having been written by one who had access to at least a portion of the papers now for the first time submitted to her Majesty's Government. Still later, an abstract of your proposed scheme has been published in several Indian newspapers of a recent date.

60. Her Majesty's Government consider it very desirable that, in the consideration of questions of this nature, affecting the interests of a large body of public servants, publicity should be avoided as much as possible, so long as the intentions of the Government are undetermined; and, moreover, that in all possible cases, the views of her Majesty's Government should be ascertained before a proposal of this nature is made the subject of formal and departmental investigation.

I have, &c.,

(Signed)   ARGYLL.

INDEX.

THE END.

www.ingramcontent.com/pod-product-compliance
Lightning Source LLC
Chambersburg PA
CBHW030912270326
41929CB00008B/670